# 11 WEEKS

## The Real-Time Chronicling Of A Breakup

By

Roo Phelps

ISBN: 9781791550363

# Dedications

To

Jason,

Who shows me time and time again that I can become whomever I want.

Who tells me "it's tough out there kid,"

but whose friendship makes the world seem easier.

**For**

*Little Sir and Madame,*

*I never fell so in love with anyone, as I did with you two.*

*Muppet, loving you three, has been the joy of my life time.*

*Thank you for letting me be part of your world,*

*If only long enough to learn what truly matters.*

*You have all brought me one step closer to the person I want to be.*

## September 23

He pulls a chair up beside me on the deck.

"So . . . I read some of the book."

My heart can't keep rhythm, my throat tightens in on itself.

"And?" I ask him.

He doesn't speak.

"I figured you must not like it much, or that we weren't going to talk about it. I knew you'd either read it all right away, or it was going to be an absolute grind for you."

I sense his unease with this whole conversation. I'm astounded he's even broached it. He takes a long drag off of his colt.

"Grind." He agrees with me.

"Why?" I don't want to push but I have to. I've been waiting desperately for his response.

"Just reading it was really . . ."

"Surreal," we say at the same time. He nods.

"How far did you get?" I can't stop questioning him. I need to know everything.

"Right before the first time I was going to see you."

"So, was it upsetting? Because that wasn't my intention . . ."

"No, no . . ." he protests. "It was just, I can't explain it, it was difficult because . . . everything you write about . . . I did that to you." He says this slowly as if realizing it for the first time.

"Well, yeah . . ." I say. It's such an obvious statement and yet he's said it as though it's new information. "We did this to each other. I have a few people I'm not super stoked on reading it, but it's . . . the truth, my truth anyways. Not jacked for my folks to read about me almost throwing myself off a pier . . . but its reality. And I think I'm pretty clear the whole thing is my perception of you versus claiming to know your actual feelings. I certainly had no intention of painting you in a bad light, and I don't think it comes off that way. I think anyone who reads it will be able to tell I think the world of you. If anything I'm the one who comes off as a lunatic." He nods, and it's silent.

It's pitch black save for one solar patio light and the moon, which is huge and full above the trees.

"The moon is beautiful." I try and change the subject. I turn my head toward it so he can't see the tears I'm dabbing. It's obvious what I'm doing and only serves to make the moment more uncomfortable.

"You write well, it was just difficult."

"Why?" Like it's the only word I know now.

"Because . . . that was a difficult time for me too, and it just brought a lot of the way I felt then back up . . . I don't know what I was expecting, but it wasn't this."

"It starts slow, because obviously it was worse at the beginning. But it does get lighter as I get better," I assure him. "But I don't want you to do anything that causes you discomfort, so if it's not something you can read or if it's making you sad, I'll just take it back."

"I can keep trying if you want."

"Nah, it's OK. Just ask Greyson when he's done reading, make sure there's nothing in there that he as your best friend thinks is unfair or that you should be concerned about."

We sit on the couch watching an episode "The Purge." I'm normally totally engrossed, I normally can't take my eyes off the screen. Now I stare and I watch, mimicking the face of someone engulfed in the action. What would it be like to be loved by someone so much that they'd write an entire book about having lost me? How on earth could you not want to read a book about yourself? About the impact you've had? Months and months of work by someone you care about, devoted to you, inspired by you, written . . . *fuck, WRITTEN FOR YOU. . .*

We stand awkwardly near the door as I'm leaving.

"The book?" I ask

"Oh, right." He runs up the stairs and returns, handing me the heavy black binder.

"When someone else is done with it I could try again," he tells me nicely.

"S'alright," I say. "Thanks for having me."

At home I grab a bottle of Crown Royal from the liquor cabinet. I don't pour any but instead carry it, and the book, out onto the front porch. For a full hour I stare at the bottle, and the binder. I see now I did it all for him, and true to form it had no effect. Every word, every sentence, every feeling, was just a wish, a hope, a desperate attempt that one day he might understand. Perhaps it was unfair of me to ask him to weather the pain it would take to understand? If the words are painful and difficult, then so too am I. If he dislikes the book, how could he not dislike me?

I don't move, I don't crack the bottle or the book. Any motion at all will result in only one possible outcome. I am going to take every last copy out to the fire pit in the backyard, down that bottle, and burn the fucking book to ashes. I am destructive tonight. I wish I was someone else. I wish I never wrote this book.

## Ninety-three days earlier

## Week One

## June 22

I can barely make my eyes meet his, dreading and knowing the answer.

"So are you done with me then—like done done?"

He sighs and turns back to place his cup in the kitchen sink. Slowly, he turns to face me, expressionless.

"I don't know what that means."

"Are you breaking up with me?"

"That's where we're headed, yeah." He walks away.

I've already offered to drive him into town to retrieve his truck, where we left it the night before to catch a cab, both of us too drunk to get behind the wheel. I'm now awkwardly lingering, not sure what to do.

"I understand if you don't want to drive me now," he calls from the other room.

"No, it's fine," I lie.

We don't talk on the ride, which is longer than normal due to traffic. The silence is killing me.

"Listen," I say, "you've done and said a lot of stupid things while you were drunk . . . so just keep that in mind when you're thinking of how I acted last night."

He doesn't say anything in reply, and so I'm silent for several more minutes. I look right at him. "You must really fucking hate me."

"I don't hate you." He rubs his eyes under his sunglasses and then his hands through his beard and eventually over his whole face, exasperated. "I just need to get to work."

I drop him off at his truck, and he hops down from our shared one, looking up at me. "I'll call you tonight." And then Wes is gone.

I pull over at a corner store to buy cigarettes. I light one inside the cab, something I've promised Wes I wouldn't do. We bought this truck together back in March and we call it "The Beast" because it's a monster of a beat-up badass machine. The small act of defiance and betrayal instantly makes me feel guilty, so I hop down and stub it out. I text my friend Jeremy.

"Can I come over?" It's 8 a.m., for chrissakes—who does that? I just need someone. "Sure. You okay?"

"Nope. Be there in five."

I met Jer seven years ago at my work, where both he and his then wife were working. I formed a fast friendship with him. Being so far away from my family, my ex-husband James and I had been lucky enough to spend many holidays with them over the years. I walk in his front door and wordlessly slip into the kitchen, where he's making me a cup of coffee. He barely looks at me before extending his arms and wrapping me in a huge hug.

"What's wrong, lady—what happened?"

I erupt. I sob. I shake. I get tears all over his shirt, and he just holds me for what seems like the longest time, not saying anything and not pressing it further. I haven't been hugged like this in so long; I hug back even tighter, clinging to him. I choke the words out.

"Wes dumped me." Saying it out loud solicits another round of heavy sobbing.

"Breathe," he tells me. "Take a deep breath, there ya go."

He leans his head on top of mine.

"Breathe—deep breaths," he repeats over and over.

When my breathing stops hitching and hiccupping, he asks, without letting me go or even looking at me, still leaning his head atop mine, "Were you drinking last night?"

I can tell I smell like booze and my breath tastes awful; I'm not even sure I brushed my teeth.

“Yeah,” I tell him. “I tried to smash the microwave with my hand.” I pull back and present him with my very swollen, very bruised wrist, which is now hurting like hell.

“You know those things are one of the strongest appliances, right, literally made to keep rays inside, lined with lead.”

I sniff and laugh.

“I know.”

“Couldn’t you have dented the dishwasher?”

“He didn’t buy me the dishwasher.”

“Ah, I see. Coffee?”

He hands me a cup, and I walk past him to his sliding glass door.

“Yeah, and I wanna smoke.”

He follows me outside. I cry it all out to him. My extremely drunken behaviour, my shame, my embarrassment, my attacking of the microwave with my fist. The awful things I said to Wes that I didn’t mean. I worry Jer’s opinion of me will change, but his eyes dance with the same affability and sense of play they always do.

“We’ve all been there,” he reassures me. I can’t picture it with Jer: he’s such a gentle giant. At six feet two inches, he looms over me, but there’s not a single thing about him that’s imposing in my mind. He’s one of the most positive people I know; he truly has an outlook on life that’s contagious, and because of his genuine ability to talk to and be interested in anyone, it’s not surprising that he excels in sales. He always wears a grin, and it must be genetic because his tiny little son sports a matching one at all times. Jer recounts to me several tales of times in his past when he himself was less than proud of his actions. He is inside the first year of a separation, and no one has more empathy for heartache than he does at the moment. I find comfort in knowing my incredibly sane and calm friend has had his metaphorical microwave attack moments too. He passes no judgment—he doesn’t speak ill of Wes, whom I know he had genuinely come to like. He simply listens and assures me I will be OK. He has to go to work, and so I head home.

I call my ex-husband, James. Oddly enough, he lives in the basement suite of one of my best friends, Lucy, but he's away a lot. We were supposed to have coffee later that day, after he gets a haircut. I ramble to him selfishly and without even asking him how he's doing.

"Shit, I'm sorry, Roo. It's gonna get better, I swear." His words are accurate, I know, but they fall nowhere inside of me, instead landing with a thud like a newspaper at my feet. They're just noises. Just words.

"Hey, when you come, what would it take for me to convince you to bring me spare keys so I can crash at your place while you're gone? I can't stay in my house; it's just too hard right now. There's the kids' stuff and I just can't. . . . actually *cannot* be there."

"For sure—I'll call you later and bring keys. I'm going to rip home to tidy up first."

I tuck myself into bed and I cry. I stare at the ceiling, I stare at the dogs. James will be here in only an hour, but it seems to be taking forever for the time to pass. I check the time on my phone obsessively. Eventually, he arrives. He is classically handsome, like old-time movie star handsome. Very tall, dark eyes, lean now, as he's taken up working out and running, with dark hair streaked with flecks of grey he's had since his early twenties. His resting expression is that of a male Greta Garbo. He is such a welcome sight walking up the driveway, carrying me a coffee and a yogurt.

We sit on the back deck and I tell him about what I've done to myself.

He finds the microwave-smash attempt hilarious in the way that only an ex-husband can, considering he hasn't seen that side of me in nearly a decade.

"Still got that temper, hey?"

"Apparently."

James is quick to remind me of my strength, tenacity, and kindness, and my ability to overcome anything. We talk about other girls he's dated since our divorce and each relationship's fiery demise. We talk about time healing things. We talk about the loss of our life together and how surviving that made us stronger.

"You'll bounce back from this better than you think," he assures me.

"Don't think I will this time . . ." I disagree.

"It always feels like that at the time, but trust me, you will."

He's headed out of town for work and to go visit his girlfriend. I follow him out to his car to get the keys to his suite.

"There's probably no toilet paper and there's definitely no food," he cautions me.

"Doesn't matter . . . I just need to get out."

"Cool. I'll be back Sunday around 8 p.m."

"So be gone by then, is what you're saying."

"Yup," he smiles.

"Thanks." I start to walk away but turn back around to hug him. We hug rarely these days but when we do, he always pulls back and only uses one arm. Today, though, he wraps me up in the most familiar, amazing, full-force hug. I can feel his heart hurting for me; his empathy is palpable.

"I'm always here for you," he tells me and then starts to get in his vehicle. I walk back to the house. Suddenly I turn on my heels.

"Hey, James!" I call to him. He stands up half-in half-out of the door of his SUV.

"Any rules for the dogs, can they go on the couches?"

"Yeah, no problem."

"OK . . . and . . . Can I sleep in your bed?"

"Yup."

"Thanks." I start to walk away and then, turning one more time, I sing back to him, "Not weeeeeeeird at all."

He laughs, we wave goodbye, and I'm alone again.

I pack a bag for my change of scenery. What does one need to be alone? Nothing, really. What does one need to be comfortable alone? I don't remember at this point. I just know I can't stay in this house staring at those tiny little kids' shoes knowing soon they'll be gone. Knowing everything I never thought I was capable of having is going to go away forever.

I video-chat my dad and let him know what's happened and that I'm going to stay at Lucy's house in James's suite for a bit. He is endlessly supportive, as always, and agrees with my immediate assertion that my drinking has gotten out of hand. He gave up drinking almost a decade ago for medical reasons and then just never picked it back up again. Smart man.

"Yeah, probably wise to slow down with that a bit," he agrees.

"A lot," I say, embarrassed.

"Yup," he agrees again.

He's the kind of father who has never in my life made me feel judged. He's always seemed to understand I learn things in my own time in my own way, often at my own expense. When I admit my faults or flaws, they're clearly things he's seen coming a mile away, but he gives no indication of that, simply supporting whatever I'm doing however he can.

I throw some things in a bag: a book, my tablet, some sweats and workout clothes. I grab my blanket and pillow and load up everything my two dogs will need and drive to Lucy's.

When I arrive, I unload my stuff and the dogs, then plop down on the couch. I am immediately hit by a wave of tears and the overwhelming sense that I have no clue how to make the time pass.

I cry for quite some time. Once I get my breathing back to normal, I leash up the dogs and wander around the neighborhood.

When they're sufficiently tired, I head back to the suite. I toss all my blankets on top of James's bed and fetal-position it hard, sobbing. I hope Lucy and her husband and kids can't hear me, but they probably can, as I can hear their voices through the walls. I cry all afternoon, well into the evening. Around 5 Lucy texts me to check in and invites me up for dinner. I met Lucy seven years ago when I first moved here, through a charitable organization she runs that I wanted to become involved with. It was winter, and I had worn Ugg boots to the meeting. The next day I got a message from her asking if I had accidentally worn her boots home, because the pair that was left looked similar to hers but were not. We exchanged boots and phone numbers, and formed a friendship. I watch her now, flitting about the kitchen. She has a natural beauty that she seems unaware she possesses. Over the years many of my male friends have commented something to the effect of how beautiful she is, invariably followed up by how she doesn't even have to wear makeup to be stunning. I don't think I've even seen her wear makeup. She looks far younger than she is, although she has only just turned thirty so it's not like she's old; there's just something very youthful about her. You'd peg her more at twenty-two and wouldn't guess she's the mother of two children. Her skin is clear and radiant, and she has beautiful blonde hair and blue eyes. We're an interesting combo because she speaks very softly, while I'm deaf in one ear. For dinner she makes deep fried yams, chicken, and zucchini. I scarf down way too many helpings, having only eaten the yogurt earlier today. I rudely excuse myself back to the basement after we eat, but I know she understands. Looking at her daughter, who had become pals with Wes's daughter, is too much. The kids . . .I can't even. Will I ever get to see them again?

When I can't cry anymore, I turn on my tablet and find a stupid show to binge-watch, my brain totally not active in what's going on. I toss and turn. Sleep eludes me. The dogs are unsettled in this unfamiliar place, and Ducky keeps whining to go outside. I'm up every hour or so to walk them around the block. At home I'd just open up the sliding glass door and let them out, but here they have to be leashed and it's a whole process with two hyper rescue dogs. It accentuates our chosen displacement and constantly reminds me why we're not at home. Sometime after 4 a.m. I finally fall asleep.

## June 23

It's 7 a.m., and there's no food in this house, although I'm really not actually hungry. Coffee is a must. I'm running on three hours' sleep and feel like absolute shit. I throw on some clothes and leash up the dogs with the intention of taking them on a hike, but I don't even know anywhere to go in this neighborhood. I hit a drive-through for coffee and then just start aimlessly driving around. I have literally no destination. I pull over several times to smoke in various parking lots. I Google dumb shit like, "How long does it take a broken heart to heal?" I am surprised to see there's some sort of consensus amongst psychologists that says roughly eleven weeks. 77 days. I gravitate to this for some reason. Eleven weeks, and I won't be all healed, but apparently that's the approximate time it will take for me to no longer feel awful every day. Eleven weeks until your average person is able to see the relationship in a positive light after it has ended. This makes me start to cry again. Will everything we've done really not matter come eleven weeks from now? I don't want to forget a single second of our amazing time together. I don't want space and distance to "heal" me into believing it wasn't the most amazing time of my life. I don't want to not want Wes. I search frantically for what the date will be eleven weeks from now. September ninth. What will life be like by then? I can't even picture my future without him and the kids, but I have to start trying.

I could not for the life of me tell you what I did in the first eleven weeks after my ex-husband, James, moved out. My life was on autopilot. I know I had a breast reduction surgery sometime in that first several months, which put me out of commission for a week or two. I threw myself into my work, which isn't an option I have these days. I think of when my high school boyfriend and I split in my early twenties. What did I do? Same. Work. I honestly cannot remember. The timing of a breakup is never good, but now seems especially bad for both Wes and me. He has been seeking stability for himself and the children for as long as I've known him; this will further shake up his life in a way he really doesn't need or deserve. I'm a fourth generation broadcaster, I started working in radio for my family as a kid back in 1999. This is how, at 33 years old, I have almost twenty years experience in the industry. I left my employment recently to focus on other endeavours. Wes gave me the strength to know I would be able to live without that part of my life. He and the kids gave me new priorities and new focus. We had started a podcast that I loved doing. I had started writing a novel. Now I have no job to throw myself into. Financially I will be fine, as I've always been good with money and I have a rental suite that can help cover my living expenses, but the distraction of work is one I could really use right now. I know his plan is to throw himself into his career.

I have lost Wes. The kids are gone. I have ruined everything and lost the three most important people in my life. What am I going to do for eleven weeks? And that's when the idea to write came to me. What if someone actually chronicled every single day for eleven weeks post-breakup?

My phone dings, and I pray it's him . . . it is. He's stopped by our house, I guess soon it'll just be my house again, to grab some stuff and saw I wasn't there. He wants to know if I've gone away for the weekend. I tell him where I am, and he says he's going to bring the kids to stay there tonight. I say OK and wait for a response, which doesn't come. Nothing more to be said. I stare at the phone every few minutes obsessively checking. It finally dings again, but it's not him; it's his best friend, Greyson. We were all at the same party the night everything went sideways. He kindly asks how I'm doing and offers to bring me a hot beverage or take the dogs for a walk. I'm thrilled to have company, so I agree and he sends me a map of where to meet him.

How I met Greyson is actually a really weird story. Several months before my first date with Wes, I went on a date with Greyson.

We met at a coffee shop down the street from my house, and I thought we had really hit it off. I had called Lucy and told her all about it, how he seemed similar to me with his love of dogs and hiking and his avoidance of material things. He was divorced like me and came across as intelligent and kind. I was really surprised and bummed out when he had sent me a follow up message to say he didn't want to see me again for reasons he didn't want to get into. It sucked because he felt like I was a cool person but it just wasn't right. I wrote back and said, "Thanks for letting me know I appreciate your honesty and wish you all the best." Then the son of a bitch blocked me on the dating website! I could understand if I'd reacted horribly or kept reaching out to him, but what the hell did I do to warrant that? I called Lucy, dismayed because I had no clue what I had done wrong and it had actually really hurt my feelings. What was so bad about me that he wouldn't want to at least be friends? We speculated that maybe he was married or something and once he found out all about the public nature of my job he knew that would be problematic. We wrote all kinds of stories in our heads about what Greyson's deal could be, and eventually he faded away and we forgot about it. Fast forward several months later. I'm going on my first date with Wes after we've been texting for a while, but I haven't told him what I do for a living yet. I figured "I'm a nationally syndicated radio host" is a conversation better had in person, and my interaction with Greyson had made me gun-shy about telling people. I met Wes at that exact same coffee shop. It was the dead of winter, and he told me he would be wearing an embarrassingly large jacket. Right from the second I saw him he killed me, he had this way of twisting me up in all the best kinds of knots. Butterflies like absolute crazy. Shoulder-y, muscular, slightly below six feet. A closely trimmed beard and a movie star smile. He carried himself with all the confidence of a rock star and truly had a charm about him that I've never encountered before and I'm certain I will not again. His eyes were a steely captivating combo of greens and greys with flecks of brown. His voice was syrup smooth and his laugh genuine and enticing.

Here's where it got weird though: he tells me he's super sorry, but he found out what I do for a living without even meaning to. He had mentioned our upcoming date to his best friend Greyson, who had said, "Oh, the chick from radio, yeah, you two will hit it off." I was floored—I mean this town is small, but his best friend? I remember thinking I was done, because Greyson obviously had something against me. I had told Wes as much and he dismissed it right away,

"Oh no no, he just hates mainstream stuff and you're in the public eye, and that's just not his thing. But he said really nice stuff about you." And thus, slowly, Wes and I came into each other's lives and, weirdly, Greyson came back into mine. It took me a long time to get over the idea that he secretly hated me, but the more he was around our place the more we became friends. Life is so weird.

We meet up on a beautiful nature trail along a creek. I tell him all my sad, and I feel bad because I know I'm being verbally selfish. He walks at a quick pace along the trail, which I like since I'm used to slowpokes harshing my walking or hiking vibe. His dog and my dogs have a great time. He reminds me to keep moving, get outside, and be a tourist in this town. An hour and a half later, when we circle back to my vehicle, "the Jammer" as we call it, I linger weirdly. We aren't close enough for me to ask for more company than what he's already provided, plus I shouldn't be coveting Wes's main support system. I dread going back to the basement. I thank him and hug him, and he leaves.

I need my Fox. Fox is my other best girlfriend, and yes, that actually is what everyone calls her. When I first moved here I was running a radio contest that required listeners to find me and put their name in a ballot box for a once-in-a-lifetime concert experience . . . stupid fucking concept, really, but irrelevant to the story. Fox was a huge fan of the artist and kept showing up at all the entry points. It used to totally freak me out; like, why is this girl always where I am? Until I realized she worked in sales and drove and travelled for work. The flexibility of her schedule allowed her to keep hitting the entry points. I always liked her, but it took a really long time for me to let her all the way in. When we met I was still reeling from the death of my best friend, and I wasn't sure I was ready for a new one. I didn't want to replace Tese. Slowly but surely, and with a few bumps along the way, we forged an inseparable bond.

She's short; I'm only five feet four inches, and I'm tall next to her. Italian and boisterous, she has naturally dark hair and a stunning tan complexion. The tiniest feet I have ever seen—her shoes are like that of a child. Her eyes are wild. They're brown, but I swear to God if you look closely you see specks of orange and gold. Her voice is raspy and loud like mine, and she gestures excessively when she talks. For a tiny woman, she's a force. I decide to go over to her house. She'd made some dumb moves the night Wes and I broke up too . . . fuck, we were all just way too drunk, and I want to see how she's doing. We sit in the courtyard of her house drinking coffee while our dogs play together. We're mostly wordless, both absorbing the consequences of our actions.

Finally she looks and me and says, "Just think, that was a Thursday and look how out of hand it got. Today is Saturday, what else can we fuck up?"

We both laugh sadly.

"Just gotta keep our shit complicated, don't we?" I shake my head.

There isn't a ton to say, so we don't. I decide to leave somewhat abruptly when my one nervous dog Atticus is barking too much at Fox's husband, Clive, who's trying to get yard work done. Back to the basement I go. I alternate crying and watching TV for several hours. I take pictures of the dogs, whom I adopted with James, and send them to him. He doesn't write back. A text rings in, and I suspect it will be him finally replying to my onslaught of dog photos but it's Wes wondering if I want to chat tonight. *Oh my god, yes*. I say yes but carefully ask him to clarify if he means in person or on the phone. My heart soars when he tells me in person but them immediately sinks again when I realize I'm not sure I'm going to be able to keep it together in front of him. I have about two hours until I need to leave to meet him, so I attempt to let it all out now. I sob and choke into my pillow. I cry because of how much I miss him already. I cry because I already miss the kids so much and it's only been a few days since I've seen them. I cry because for the first time in my life I was part of something that filled a void I didn't even know I had, and now it's gone. Deciding I didn't want children had been the fuse light that led to my divorce, so falling in love with those kids? I never in a million years saw it coming. When my timer goes off signaling that I should leave, I switch out of my crying outfit (oversize sweatpants and a hoodie) and throw on jeans and a tank.

When I reach the house I don't go through the front door because I don't want to wake the kids. I sneak around the gate into the backyard and up on the deck, texting him to let him know I'm here. When the sliding glass door opens and he comes out, my heart skips all the beats. I don't know if I'm going to throw up or cry. Before he says anything, ashamed of my behaviour and knowing we're already done, I ask him if we can just focus on wrapping things up as kindly and lovingly as possible. He does me one better and says the kindest, most gentle, and loving things to me. He expresses gratitude for all I've done for him, and he's very clear that he is not mad at me and doesn't hate me. He does explain it's about more than just the microwave-smashing attempt, though, which we both know is true. There'd been challenges for a while. He feels he can never give me what I need. It had all just become too much for him. I am too much for him. He can't keep disappointing me. I sense the firmness in his resolve that now is not our time, but he does mention more than once that maybe the timing will be right later, and he doesn't know what the future holds. The term "fresh start" gets used. I don't know if it's a platitude or a hope. I wish I had his certainty that ending this is the right thing; I'm both envious and enraged by it. He's so extremely gentle. He asks what I'll do with the suite downstairs and I'm not sure, but I'm surprised when he suggests maybe Greyson could move in. I bought this house several years ago when I was still married. When James left I had paid him out so I could stay. I had lived alone in the top half of my house for two years. I'd had great tenants downstairs who I had served notice to so that Wes and the kids and I could have the full run of the house when they moved in. Now that he's broken up with me he will obviously be moving all of them out. I guess I'll have to rent the suite again. I don't even care about that right now, I can't fully process the idea. There are tears on my part, a few laughs, and then I sob again and rip through almost an entire box of Kleenex. My eyes turn racoony with mascara and black eyeliner streaking down my cheeks. He wisely suggests we reconvene and let cooler heads prevail later.

The whole way home all I can think is, "Maybe some space will be good and he will want me back." This is called a coping mechanism. I know it's not healthy, I know he certainly won't ever want me back, but it's the light I need to cling to until I don't need to cling to it anymore. I go home and curl back up into bed. I cry until 5 a.m., when I finally fall asleep.

## June 24

I've slept for two hours, maybe, but I can't lie in this bed anymore. Hardly awake, I text Fox and see if she will hike with me. I'm annoyed with myself; I used to hike and do things alone all the time. Being by myself never made me lonely before, but I just can't bear it at the moment. Thankfully she agrees. We meet at the same trail that Greyson and I took yesterday, although we do it twice as slow and one of her bulldogs nearly dies on route. He throws up every few minutes. *I feel your pain, little buddy*. We talk about the idea of Greyson moving into the suite to help cover costs. Is that a great idea or a horrible one? I honestly don't know. My judgement has seen better days as of late. I know Wes would feel better having someone he trusts nearby. I'd feel good not having a stranger in my home. Greyson would save money, but it feels like some desperate attempt to keep Wes nearby and, ultimately, I'm not sure if that's best. Would it mean he would still come to the house sometimes? Is that good news or bad news? Fox laughs when I'm done explaining.

"Oh, why not make complex even more complicated," she tells me. "But really, though, you don't even have to make any decisions about that right now. Just get through the next little bit and see how you're feeling." It's solid advice. There's no reason to make decisions.

I do the same thing to her that I did to Greyson and linger weirdly in the parking lot at the end of the hike. I'm realizing it wasn't not being super close with him that made it awkward; it's just me, right now. All awkward. Uncomfortable in my own skin. My sadness permeates my being, and I'm not even moving or standing like myself. It's just uncomfortable to be me at the moment. I give her a hug and head back to the basement. I curl up in a little bundle, now feeling less guilty because I hiked, and just cry and cry and cry.

I wake up to my phone dinging. It's Lucy: "Get your shit and be ready to go in five. I'll be right home."

*What?* I'm about to text her and ask if I did something wrong and why she wants me to go, when a flurry of texts come in explaining some devastating information she has uncovered regarding her marriage and betrayal by people she loves and had trusted. *Holy actual fuck.* My brain springs into a mode I didn't know it had and I pack three days' worth of stuff in minutes. When she pulls up, the dogs and I are loaded and ready to go. She hops in the passenger seat, doesn't even look at me, and just says, "Drive." I have no clue where to go, but we ride silently south out of town and hit the highway. We just keep cruising. I hear a noise from her and look over; I can't tell if she's laughing or crying or both. The intricacies of her story and the details we discuss are not mine to share, but I will tell you this: when my marriage ended she fought for me, truly fought to keep me OK. There were days when she would just show up at my house with a six-pack and a meal after I hadn't answered my phone, baiting me into the kitchen with both, like I was a stray dog who needed coaxing to come out from a hole. Seeing her there in the passenger seat, living a nightmare, I know I will do whatever it takes to see her through what comes next. I am going to fight this with her and live this with her, any way that I can. The old me, who isn't heart-shattered and unsure of everything, approached the world with an incomparable sense that things were unfolding as they should be, even in the face of total destruction. For the first time in a long time, I feel the old Roo whispering, "This is why you're here. You are exactly where you're supposed to be." My mind runs through images of what Lucy would have done had I not been there to leave with her. A mother of two, angry, distraught, distracted, getting behind the wheel. In seven years I have never once slept over at her house. What were the odds I would be there, right there, when she needed me? If this entire life I've lived and lost served no other purpose than leading me to be here for her in this moment, that gives me comfort. I have a purpose beyond my own sadness now, and it is 100 percent commitment to making sure I can be the warrior for her, that she was for me.

When I get home that night I'm exhausted both physically and emotionally. The house is silent. Wes has gone to stay with Greyson and the kids are at their moms. My heart has all the hurt inside of it. For Lucy and her marriage, for Jer and the ending of his, for Wes and for the kids. For Fox and her relationship challenges. Is anyone's love not broken? Can it ever last? I take two 10-mg melatonin capsules and pass out.

## June 25

Waking up in my own bed should feel nice, but there are so many reasons it isn't:

1) This is technically Wes's bed.
2) I can't stop thinking about the kids.
3) I hugged his pillow all night
4) I didn't really "wake up" so much as the melatonin's effects wore off, and I've decided that it was time to try and "day" again. I walk out of the bedroom and through the kitchen to the sliding glass door to let the dogs out to pee. Before I even make it, I notice something is very wrong. Through the giant kitchen window I can see the lid on Wes's hot tub is absolutely fucked. It's opened the wrong way, half off, and there are large branches protruding from the tub itself. I open the door to the deck and see the hot-tub lid is just a fraction of the damage. There are willow branches and maple branches all over the yard, and the deck chairs have been blown out onto the acreage. *Fuck my life*. I decide this is a later-me problem. I have plans to hike with my girlfriend Meesh this morning, and I don't want to get behind.

Before I owned a home, James and I rented out an entire house just up the street from where I currently live. We used to sublet the basement so that we could choose our own tenants. Meesh and her then boyfriend were the first couple we rented to; she was brand new in town as well, and we spent so much time together in those first few years. I dress for the hike and take the dogs out front to load them into the truck. I'm stunned to see work crews all over my front lawn, which is also covered in downed willow branches from the backside of the property. *Holy fuck, I missed one hell of a storm. Thanks, melatonin.* The work crews are from the septic company I'd been calling for weeks regarding some pooling near one of the tank lids. Of course they would finally show up today. *Ughhhh*. Meesh arrives and we pile into the "The Beast" with the dogs. She hops in the front seat and staring straight ahead says, "What happened to the fence?"

I hadn't even noticed it. To the side of my house was a beautiful lattice fence Wes had just finished building me so that when the kids were with us the dogs would still have access to the yard. He'd blown my heart up when he'd written our initials inside a heart in the cement he used to set the post. Fucked. The whole thing is fucked. The storm ripped the cement post right out of the ground, the lattice is cracked where it adhered to the post, and the entire nineteen feet of fence lie in a decimated pile. Oh, the fucking irony. I burst into tears and pull away.

Meesh is nothing but blunt with her advice, and while it's hard to hear, I know she's giving it from the highest place of love and respect.

"Let's be serious, you knew he was going to dump you and you'd been assuming the crash position for a while."

She is a positive person, the kind who believes all things happen for a reason. She reassures me this will make me stronger and better when in the end I've made my peace with it. I gave her this same speech when her heart was shattered four years before. I know she is right, but it's hard to hear. Today I don't want input; I just want to be held. We have coffee on the deck at the end of the hike, and when she goes to leave, I sob on her shoulder. She breaks the hug before me, which seems odd but I realize she's just removing her backpack. Once it's down she re-hugs me, tighter and with all her heart. I cry and cry, and she hugs and hugs, and the intention of her embrace gives me so much comfort. After she leaves I look around again at all the damage. I'm not sure if I should tell Wes about the storm. I don't want to add more to his plate, but I am worried about his hot tub getting destroyed or messed up. The fence is a moot point. I'm hoping I'll hear from him so I can let him know at that time, rather than bothering him at work and stressing him out further. I check my phone to see if I have any other plans or commitments today. Stress always turns my brain to shit, and the first thing to go seems to be my memory. *Ahhhh Hendrik, yes! I knew there was something*. I grab my gym bag and jet out the door.

Hendrik is, where do I even begin. First and foremost, he's Jer's cousin; that's how I know him. I used to be really overweight. After some time cutting the weight down on my own with at-home videos, I hit a plateau and was frustrated and sad. When I told Jer about this he introduced me to his cousin Hendrik and his wife Roxy, who are both personal trainers. Not only are they trainers, they're truly the best at what they do; they've spent decades in the fitness industry and seen every fad and trend come and go. He is tall, six feet one inch, has long dark hair that often falls down into his eyes, and a face that could be misread as serious or possibly even unfriendly if you didn't know him. He's an observer, and I love the way he sees the world, like he has special glasses that allow him to notice bits of it that the rest of us cannot. His and Roxy's gorgeous personalities are matched by their fabulous physiques. She is stunning, thick long hair, a beauty of a smile, a radiant energetic bubbly personality, and obviously a rocking body. They have helped me change my life in ways that could be a whole book on its own. They have been godsend friends for me the last five years or so. The fact that he's related to Jer just makes it extra cool because they make me feel like I'm part of something, they often joke they have deemed me an honorary member of their family. Jer and Hendrik. So the same but so insanely different. I grapple with the notion that I could ever find truer, more loyal friends than these guys. I had told Hendrik and Roxy last week that I felt Wes was going to break up with me soon, so they won't be surprised at all. Roxy had even bought me flowers. I'm embarrassed to tell them I knew it was coming and still couldn't stop it. I felt him pulling away. I felt him leaving before he ever left. How in the actual fuck did it come so hard off the rails?

I walk into the training facility and Hendrik isn't here yet. I pace back and forth. When his muscular frame finally appears from around the corner, he takes one look at me and knows.

"Well . . . I called it," I say, dissolving into tears.

"Ah, kid . . . I'm sorry." He hugs me, all his height bending down to meet me. Roxy is there and ready with hugs as well. He starts me off on the rower and while trying to keep the pace and hit the distance he's set, I tell him the story of my attempted microwave-smashing meltdown.

"Did not see that coming . . . I mean we knew something was coming but the microwave, I'll hand it to ya, that . . . was a plot twist. Did not see that one coming." He doesn't judge, he isn't cruel, in fact he most often just repeats, "I'm sorry for the hurt you're going through. But you knew, you knew it was risky, right? That was the whole concept."

"Sure did."

Understand that months ago, when things were ramping up with Wes, I came in ranting and raving to Hendrik about how in love I was and how this time I'd do it differently and throw caution to the wind. I believe my exact phrase was "make a glorious fucking mess of things." He wisely told me to slow down, move carefully, be excited, but hold off on moving in together as long as possible. A week later I told him Wes was moving in.

"Well, alright then."

This is a person who has watched me make some insane messes. Not only has he never spoken a judgmental word about the inevitable problems I'm creating that he can see a mile away, but he's always been there with a hug and empathy when it falls apart. There is no judgment here. There's no "sorrys" in the gym, a rule he taught me.

I deadlift and kettlebell swing my life away for the next hour, and while my usual oomph isn't there, I think my body holds up OK.

"Maybe we should do a project, the transformation of Roo. We could talk about it so much on social media people will either love it or they'll say I never wanna hear those two motherfuckers say another word again. We could chronicle the whole thing. I could do you a meal plan and we could talk about your progress so far. We could getcha into the best shape of your whole life."

I explain about my upcoming away dates for a wedding and for a holiday to Palm Springs I'd already had planned, but I tell him I'd love that for when I'm back. I know it's the slightly wrong thing to say because his offer is hugely generous and the reality is, in fitness, if you're waiting for a good time it'll never come. But I also know he knows me well enough to trust my gut about when I'll be able to commit. He hugs me again, this time to say goodbye.

On my way home Wes sends me a detailed text of all the plans he's made. He has arranged for a Sea-Can shipping container to be dropped off at the house in a few days. He will come and load his stuff Friday and Saturday, and they will take it away on Tuesday. He knows this is hard for me but figures that's the fastest and best solution to get his stuff out of there. He says he would have called to talk but he's at work and it would be too emotional. That last part means a lot to me, although I'm not sure why. I hate that he's sad. I guess it's just comforting to know that I'm not the only sad one. I thank him for letting me know, and then I tell him about the fence and his hot tub. He says he'll come over after he's done at work to get them both sorted.

When Wes arrives, I can't stand it. I can't stand the intense feeling of longing inside my chest, it hurts so badly. "Ohhhhh my god," my brain keeps saying. Every time he speaks, his voice sends chills through my body. He surveys the damage; we clean up and set the fence parts aside. He fixes the hot-tub lid and gets it covered properly. For a while we sit at the kitchen table—the table he bought me—and we talk. Tears get shed, and, pathetically, I fish to see if there's any chance of reconciliation, or at least my being able to still see the kids down the line. He tells me, "Nothing is off the table at this point." I try not to cling to false hope, but it's there, and it's a buoy I can hold onto in the middle of this harsh sea.

"Can I ask a favour of you, though?"

"What's that?" he asks.

"If stuff starts coming off the table—like, I know occasionally you've said down the line maybe there could be a fresh start, but you don't know or whatever—if that changes and things are coming off the table or like, you decide you want to date or sleep with someone else, and you do know that I'm not what you want ever, can you just tell me so I'm not waiting around like an idiot?"

"Of course."

This gives me huge comfort because the last thing I want is to be blindsided. Wes and I were not bad together, as far as I'm concerned, although maybe he sees it another way. We ended poorly, that's for sure, but to me it's not indicative of the nature of our relationship or the deep bond we share on the whole. Sure, we brought out the worst in each other in the end, but I also feel we had the ability to bring out the best in each other through so many other trying times.

We just met at such a weird time in both our lives. He was healing from the end of his marriage, and he wasn't as healed as he thought, or I had thought. I was in a transition phase, moving away from previous employment and considering other options. Secretly, I was very close to moving and had a job offer lined up in a major market for another morning show. I declined the job solely on the basis that I felt meeting Wes was the sign I was supposed to stay. He was so certain back then of how he felt about me, so forthcoming with feelings and dreams. I remember once he woke up excited to tell me about a dream he'd had of us and the kids living together and me teaching his daughter to ride a horse.

"I never remember my dreams, but this was so clear! I'll draw you the house one day," he'd told me. He made me feel like the world was ours for the taking, and I wanted nothing more than to stick around to take it with him. Declining that job was still the right decision.

Somewhere in the middle of two people who loved each other exceptional amounts, came a whole bunch of miscommunication and unchecked grief. A chasm opened. A seed of doubt got planted, resentment started to fester, and it all blew up one night. But you can't convince me that's actually us. When I sit across this table from him I am certain, 100 percent positive, this could have been fixed, but, and that's one epic, monumental, insane but, he simply doesn't want me, and that cannot be fixed. Once someone has come to a point where they can picture their life being better and happier without you in it—nuked—it's over. There's no coming back from that thought.

It's so hard because here I am, certain my life will be worse without him and the kids. I'm over here like, "Hey, I'm losing three people and it feels like the world is ending." For him this is all beginnings. He's a good person, and if a fresh start will see him through to a happy end, that is all I could ever want or hope for, for him and the children. He hugs me when he goes to leave, and I start to cry. I hold him too tightly and pathetically say, "I wish you could stay." He tells me its best he continues to stay at Greyson's right now. I feel foolish for having said it, but I don't care.

After he leaves, Jer texts.

"How we doin', lady?"

"Not great . . . can I come over?"

"Course."

I drive to his place, where we sit on patio chairs and watch the gas fireplace burn, swapping heartbreak stories until it becomes undeniably time for bed.

## June 26

*What the fuck is that sound?* The dogs are barking. I hear the beeping of some sort of large equipment being operated and a cacophony of problems on my front lawn. I part the curtain, and there they are. Crews, men, strangers, dressed in little yellow safety vests flitting about my yard like bumble bees. Clearly the problem with my septic tank has not been resolved. This is bad news. I sigh and throw sweatpants on. I take the dogs into the backyard and then head out front to see what's up.

"What's the latest?" I ask. The foreman of the crew is assessing the pooling again and I see now the beeping was them unloading an excavator onto my front lawn. *Fuck.*

"Well, it's not the septic, most likely a broken water line. We're going to have dig to see if we can repair it."

"Well, is it at least good news it's not my septic?"

He shakes his head laughing.

"When you run an excavator company you're rarely digging for good news." He goes back to work.

This is my regular coffee date day with Fox; her driving route for work has her going past my house, so she always stops in. When she arrives she looks baffled by the work.

"What's all this about?"

"Wish I knew."

"Great timing."

"Just perfect."

We have coffee on my front deck and I lament how sad I am. I've never known sadness like this before, and that's saying something. We talk about my life, my losses, the death of my best friend, in 2010, and my bizarre elevator accident that same year. My divorce just a few years before. This one is so different somehow. This one seems insurmountable. Maybe it's the weight of all the other losses? Maybe it's the kids? Maybe it's the fact that for the first time in years I truly was happy, and while there were struggles and challenges, I had foolishly convinced myself that Wes and I were the kind of people who could make it through anything. I was so sure of us that I felt safe to be honest when things were bad, not knowing that honesty meant he would no longer want to find the good. I expected that this, or any relationship, would include downturns and struggles and efforts and work. You power through it. You fight for one another. I was positive he was the person I would do life with. My best friend, always. I'm too tired now to face the world alone.

The excavator starts up while we sip our coffee and by the time she leaves, the hole in my lawn is concerningly large and deep and getting bigger every minute. The tears start again. *God, how much can one person cry?* I leash up the dogs and head into the woods, hoping the problem will be solved when I get back.

On the trail I think of Wes. I think of his face, I think of his laugh. I think of the insane amount of adventures we had in such a short period of time. I think of how safe he made me feel. I wander through the woods weeping like an idiot. Each time the kids' faces come to mind I forcibly shove them out. I'm locking that grief up in a box; it's just too much, too much for me to address having lost. My heart aches to feel his son's little hand take mine the way he so often would ask to. *Get out!* I tell the thoughts. *Please just go. He doesn't want you and they will forget you. They were never yours to love.* When I return from hiking several hours later, the guys are still working. The foreman informs me I'm looking at potentially a potentially five- to eight-thousand dollar bill. Fuck it, I'm going to get a massage. It's not a good use of money, it's probably the last thing I should be doing right now, but I need to get away from this crew of strangers accentuating how fucked and alone I am.

I cry the whole massage, silently. It's not enjoyable at all. I'm too trapped in my own mind.

When I get home that evening, the hole has been filled so I'm assuming things are fixed. I step inside and go to fill up the dog's water dish; no water. I call the foreman and he sends crews back out to try and see if they can get it going. *You've got to be kidding me*. The Wi-Fi in the house has been down on and off throughout the day while they do their work and it's fucking with my phone. A message comes through from my dad checking in, but I can see it's time-stamped from several hours earlier. A message comes through from Wes asking if the hot-tub cover stayed on OK. I'm so happy to hear from him and furious about the text delay. I don't want him to think I was doing that thing where you intentionally take a long time to write back.

I text back apologizing for the delay and say I've had the day from hell, including a picture of the diggers in my yard for good measure.

We exchange a few texts and he tells me he's sorry that's happening, and asks if I need anything.

I tell him, "I'm just really overwhelmed, kinda a meltdown day for me." Then I do a stupid thing and send a text that says, "I don't want any of this to be happening."

Half an hour later he sends me one that says just, "I'm sorry."

I'm sobbing so hard I can't breathe. How is it possible that just a few days ago this would have been our problem, we would have tackled this together. Now I'm alone and I have no running water and he's not even coming over. I've embarrassed myself by dumping this on him. It's so clearly—correction—I am so clearly not his problem anymore. I text him back.

"No, I'm sorry. I shouldn't be coming to you about this stuff anymore. I didn't mean to overstep."

"You didn't overstep." Then nothing else comes. I call James and just sob, I'm crying so hard he can hardly understand me and keeps having to ask me to repeat myself to be able to piece it together.

"You're good with money, you'll get the bill all sorted. I'm sorry you have to do this alone."

Shortly after I hang up with him, Jer calls to check on me and I nonsensically weep to him too. "I'm getting no sleep," I cry.

"Here's what you do: throw on a podcast, the most boring one you can find, like fucking basket weaving, take some Nyquil and just crash."

"Will that work?" I ask.

"It's how I got through all of January," he confides.

## June 27

I wake up to the sound of diggers for the second day in a row, although this time the noises hardly solicit a reaction. I'm nothing. I have no feelings about anything. I am blank . . . or at least I want to be. I'm trying to check out so I don't have to feel what I'm feeling. I let the dogs out, make coffee, and sit at the table staring into the abyss. Greyson texts me to check in and see if I want company, a coffee from Starbucks, or a hike. I want all three. He arrives and I attempt to give him the rundown on the water situation, although explaining it out loud makes me realize I really don't know what's happening. More and more workers arrive, and Greyson runs interference with them, trying to get a good understanding of what exactly the problem is. They decide they need to re-excavate the front lawn to repair whatever is wrong still. The bill is mounting.

Greyson and I take his dog and mine and we wind ourselves up through the hills in my neighborhood. It's a pretty day, at least, and moving keeps my mind focused on being in my body, which may or may not be a good thing. Greyson has to go to the office and eventually he heads out. The day feels tedious; my house is full of strangers. I don't want to leave, because there isn't really anywhere to go and I want to know what's happening, but locking myself in my bedroom with the dogs watching endless TV depresses me. I head to the gym.

Wes is really fit, and working out together was one of the things I really enjoyed about our relationship. He has just switched to a membership at my gym last week, since it's closer to the house. I feel bad that he's spent all that money and now probably won't want to come here, or it won't make sense depending on where he lands. I wonder if he will avoid it because he knows I come here. *Does he miss me? Is he thinking about me?* He's extremely good at shoving down emotion, and though it drove me insane when we were together, I find some shitty part of me that's envious of that right now. I would give anything to not have to feel what I'm feeling. My workout is painfully pathetic. I can't seem to lift or press any of my normal weights, and my whole body feels sluggish. I head back home and hide in my room. I tidy while I'm in there and gather up all my "Wes" stuff into a beautiful box. Pictures the kids have drawn me, papers, souvenirs, receipts, and tickets; they all get placed carefully in the box. Around 3 my phone dings. It's Wes, and my heart soars.

"How is the septic thing going today?"

I explain they are still working away on it, nothing resolved yet. He tells me what town he's in for work today. He asks if the delivery of the Sea-Can for his stuff needs to be changed, if it will be problematic or in the way of the work. I tell him it's OK. This is all so business-like. By 10 p.m., when I still don't have running water and I am audibly crying in my bedroom, one of the workers, Al, knocks on my bedroom door.

"Roo? Sorry, you around?"

I'm mortified to step out, as I know I look like shit, but he needs me to tell him if the pressure in the bathtub is how it always was. It is. Finally done.

Al asks me sheepishly, "You ok?"

"Oh yeah . . ." I mumble. "Just living my best life. Just bad timing. Boyfriend broke up with me and all this water stuff, just a little overwhelmed."

"Ahh, but I thought he was here earlier?"

"Who?"

"Your boyfriend?"

"Oh no, that's Greyson, just a buddy. I think he's gonna move into the basement suite, actually, so I guess kinda a roommate." I'm over explaining. He doesn't care.

What will it be like down the line to tell people I'm single? I dread the thought of having these types of awkward interactions. Yes,

I'm single, but no, I'm not on the market. Yes, I'm lonely, but no, I don't want anyone. I inherently know that my heart is going to take a long time to heal from this one, and I hate it. I hate knowing the only thing that can help is time. I want it not to be now. I finally let my mind wander to where I had been trying so hard to keep it from going. Wes's birthday is tomorrow. I had so much planned and had been working on it for months. It was going to be a several-days-long celebration, and the sorrow I feel at failing to see it through to completion is immense and overwhelming. Thursday we would do a proper birthday dinner with the kids, and then I'd worked it out with their mom for them to spend two nights with her. I had paid for his brother, who I really like, to show up and surprise him that night. Friday we were going to kidnap him at the end of his workday and take him for dinner and drinks at his favourite pub. Saturday I'd purchased a foursome of golf for him, his brother, Greyson, and another friend. While he was out golfing I'd set up the house for a barbecue that was, ridiculously, going to be douchebag-themed. Dress like a complete asshole; just come as the worst person you can be. It would have been hilarious, and all his friends were invited. I was also going to have the camper I was purchasing ready for him when he got back from golf. I'd been secretly shopping for one for weeks in my spare time to surprise him. *Thank God I didn't buy one*. Sunday afternoon we'd get the kids back and then, because of the long weekend, we would still get them that night and all day Monday. Happenings aside, I'm just so sad that I won't get to see him for his birthday at all. I'm heartbroken I won't get to watch the kids excitedly give him their cards and gifts.

On my birthday we had an amazing time, he celebrated me over the course of a few days. Wes made me an amazing dinner, partied with my friends at Lucy's, hung out together at home, had a fire in the backyard, spoiled me, and treated me. He bought me a beautiful necklace of a symbol that meant "protection," and it had brought me to tears. We made love next to the fire place on the living room floor. It was perfect.

Now I won't even get to see him for his birthday. I'm not even sure I should call tomorrow or that he'll want to hear from me. I lie in bed and just cry and cry and cry. I am such a fool for believing I wasn't going to be alone. I am so fucking sick of crying . . . why can't I just shake this? Why does it hurt so much? I would take any kind of physical pain over this deep ache in my chest that won't subside. I'm scared, actually scared, that this one may have broken me for good. Eleven weeks? I don't believe I'll ever be better from this, let alone better eleven weeks from now. September ninth feels like a lifetime when, these days, I think I'm just holding on by a thread.

## June 28

I didn't know it was possible to wake up crying, but I have. *Thanks, body.* My eyes feel disgusting, my nose is stuffed, and my sinuses hurt. It's Wes's birthday. My whole chest is ripping open. I keep thinking of medical dramas when they show the metal device used to crack open someone's rib cage. A great visual for how I feel. Should I call him? Should I text him? The only thing in the world I want is for him to be able to have a good day, and if hearing from me makes it worse, then that's the last thing I want. I also don't want him to think I don't care. I care so so much. I decided maybe a Facebook message is best, that way it's not super intrusive but he still also knows I'm thinking of him. I spend about ten minutes trying to get the message right. I want him to know that he, and this day, are important to me, but I also don't want to make him sad. Finally I send: "Hi...just wanted to say happy birthday. Hope you can sneak some laughs and celebration into this day. I know this year ahead will bring amaaaaazing things for you." I want him to know that I want him to be OK, and to be happy. I nervously hit send.

A reply comes fifteen minutes later.

"Thanks, not sure what the day holds for me, or the year but I appreciate your message a lot."

I can't help but reply: "I was gonna call but I didn't wanna accidentally harsh your vibe or be intrusive, just know my thoughts are with you and I'm celebrating you today!"

I can see him typing.

"Can I call ya after gym?"

*Yesssssss.*

I type back: "Sure."

When the phone rings, I'm weirdly nervous to answer. He sounds sad, and it hurts me more than I even thought I could be hurting. He's having a tough day. His pain and his sadness kill me. This is hard for him too. I hate myself that this has all happened. I hate that this is real. We talk briefly, I try and be as upbeat as possible, I don't want him to worry about me or have any added stress today. The second we hang up it comes spilling out. Big messy snotty sobs. I actually say over and over again out loud: "You're OK, it's OK, just breathe, you're OK."

My phone dings: another text from Wes.

He has written me a beautiful message about how much he appreciates everything I had planned for his birthday, and how sorry he is to be hurting me. He apologizes for sending it but says he just needed me to know and couldn't say it on the phone.

I write back: "You're so welcome...it was really fun for me to plan it. It was 100% my pleasure...I'm just sorry I fucked everything up before it could come into fruition. I'm envious of those who will get to be with you today, but I know you know I'm with ya even if I'm not with ya. Today is gonna be challenging but this is the turning of an awesome new page and everything is gonna get better for ya from here on out. Just know it! I'm here if you need me. Keep your head up. You've got this."

I don't think things are going to be better for me. I'm not excited for the turning of this page. I have no clue how to keep my head up, and I certainly don't "have" this. I want better for him than I believe or expect for myself, though, and so I cling to the hope that if he winds up happy I can at least be OK.

I spend all morning crying. I force myself to go the gym, and I cry while I deadlift. I cry while I drive. I call my parents and just sob. They are now getting worried. I'm the first to admit I've had my struggles, but July has traditionally been an exceptionally bad time of year for me. July is when epilepsy took my best friend's life. July is when the elevator accident happened. July is the month I was married in and the month my marriage ended, and it's the month when things so bad that I can't ever even talk about them, happened to me. It has become the month when all my built-up, unprocessed trauma seems to rear its ugly head.

I had thought this year would be different. For the first time ever, not only was I going to be happy in July, but I was so looking forward to spending five days celebrating someone I love so much. And now here I am. A giant Sea-Can has been delivered to the driveway so that Wes can move. This huge looming metal canister is mocking me, a giant reminder to me and the entire neighborhood that I have failed again. LOOK, WORLD! SHE STILL CAN'T DO IT!! SHE'S ALONE AGAIN! NO ONE WANTS TO STAY WITH HER.

I open the cupboard looking for Tylenol, and there they are. Pills. Doctor-prescribed sleeping pills that I never took. Pain medication from my breast reduction I never used. Two kinds of human-grade antidepressants prescribed to each one of my neurotic rescue dogs. Thoughts are taking hold that scare me. *I don't want to live. I'm not intended for this world. I can't keep letting the failures add up*. I never even wanted children, but those two, oh my god those two, I never, ever, ever knew! I never knew love until I knew what I'd be capable of for a child. I never knew fear until I knew them, either: the amount of all-consuming focus or worry or concern you can have for someone's safety. To them, six months will be nothing in the grand scheme of things. But what I learned about love in its truest form has left me with 100 percent certainty that I will never ever ever have another love like I had for those kids, and now they are gone. And not only that but they potentially have been hurt or will be hurt by having known me. *I have left those kids and Wes worse than I found them.*

I shut the medicine cabinet and send a text to my mom

"I really would like you guys to come here, please." She must see this for the out-of-character SOS it is, because they begin making arrangements right away. I start cleaning the house hoping they hurry. I don't know how long I can fight downing every random pill in the house, and just stopping the pain.

## Week Two
## June 29

When my best friend died, I found there was this sweet moment of peace in each day that I came to live for. It was the two seconds when I first woke up, before I remembered, and then this awful sense of panic would set in right afterward. A panic like you've been charged with watching someone's child and realize you've gotten distracted and taken your eyes off them. A panic like the plane hits a huge bump and you get that ominous drop in your stomach and the certainty that the plane is going down. Right before that moment, though, would be these beautiful two seconds of peace, where I would wake up not having remembered how the world had fallen apart; there was this teeny tiny window of time in which my mind managed to forget what had happened. So how, how on earth, after having retained those two seconds in the face of death, can I not find them now? It hurts every second. I don't even get peace in my sleep these days, because I dream of him and the kids. Waking up is just a continuation of the pain. Maybe my body and mind truly don't know how to be at peace anymore? I must be too full of sadness for the mind or the body to escape, even for a split second.

Today is Friday, meaning it's day one of Wes moving his stuff out. He's going to get it done over the course of today and tomorrow. I'm not sure what time he's coming, and while I desperately want to see him, I can't be here while it's happening. I don't want to go back and basement-dwell in my ex-husband's suite at Lucy's. The thought further depresses me, but I want even less to see all the traces of my life with Wes carted into a Sea-Can parked in the driveway of the home that I still feel is ours.

I get a text from Wes telling me he will be here around 9 a.m., so I let him know I'll get gone, I pack my things and head to the basement suite. En route I pass the trail that Greyson and I have hiked several times, and I decide to take the dogs for a walk along the creek. I want nothing more than to think of anything but him, but his and the kids' faces are the only things I can think of. I put on a podcast and walk eight kilometers like a zombie.

When I'm finished I text James to let him know I'm headed to his place. I'm really happy when he tells me he's forgotten his work laptop and asks if I would be able to bring it to him and then maybe meet for lunch. I drop the dogs off at his place, grab his laptop, and meet him at a cute little Italian deli he's told me about for years but that I've never actually been to. He tells me I look skinny, and that makes me feel good, although I suspect it was said more out of concern. I buy a salad and an Americano, and he gets a sandwich and a latte. We sit in the sunshine at a cute little outside table.

He reassures me repeatedly that I will be OK. I am strong and good and I will find the things I want in life eventually. I don't believe him. While he talks, I search his face looking for traces of the man I married, and they don't elude me; they're very much there. Who could have possibly known this far down the line that not only would he and I be friends, but that he would be a source of support for me while I rebuild my life, again. We both struggled so hard after our separation. We fought, we cried, we went months without speaking, we spoke all day, we did every possible messy thing until we arrived here, today, two people who once shared a life and a future, a home and two dogs, and who are now sharing fancy Italian coffees.

It's odd, though. When I look at him, I see so much more of the good than the bad, and I know, without a trace of doubt, that the ending of our marriage was not a matter of fate or inevitability, but instead a choice. No matter who or how the events were set into motion, there were choices along the way; we stopped fighting for each other. When Wes and I made the decision to "do it differently this time," I think that's mostly what I meant, to always always choose him. Maybe I didn't get it right each moment; OK, not maybe, I **know** I didn't get each choice right in the moment. Hell I got it flat-out fucking wrong. Dead wrong. But choosing him over not him, he would have always won. No matter what. I still choose him right now.

I see now that the choice to stop fighting for someone, the illusion that we can be better with someone else, the mindset that with the "right" person it'll just be easy—are all false. You can make it work with any person so long as you always choose them, unless they stop choosing you. I had certainly thought about breaking up with Wes prior to things going totally south. I'd heard that little voice that whispers doubts to you, and every time it was met with a "No! I would do anything for him and those kids, and even if I'm not getting it right, I'm going to try." He was the person who, after I had failed at marriage, I promised to never fail by choosing not to choose him. And so I chose him, and chose to express to him the things I was struggling with, and I tried to give him what he needed. I didn't get it right. I failed him. I didn't understand or properly hear how to help him. I did it as differently as I could, I pushed myself to the brink of insanity trying to get it right, and it was still not enough for him to keep choosing me. I must be the worst. I must be so ridiculously unlovable for a person to look at me, knowing I love them, knowing I would do **anything**, knowing I'm not getting it right but "holy shit, is she still trying," knowing I would always always always choose him, and for him to have thought, "I want not this." The burden of that failure weighs so heavily on me, not only now, but on my hope for the future, because if trying your best is not enough, then what is the point in trying?

The coffee and lunch are pleasant, James is kind and supportive, we share a few laughs before he has to head back to work. I go to his house and nap.

When I wake up I'm filled with nervous energy. It feels terrible knowing right now, while I'm alone in this little suite, there are people at my house packing up the life we had together. I can't just sit here. These poor dogs, they don't get a moment's rest. I load them up again, and we head back to the trail. I walk for hours listening to music and podcasts. I stare at my feet and focus on just moving. I name natures as I pass it to try and be present and keep my thoughts from Wes: "Flowers, bumblebee, creek, rock, pretty leaf, bird, snail."

It's well into the evening when I head back. Lucy has a friend over and has invited me up for charcuterie and drinks. The three of us sit on her porch under two large umbrellas protecting us from the onslaught of rain. We talk about life and love, we talk about failed relationships and boys we used to date, breakups and marriages and weddings and children. I cry a lot, about the kids. Lucy and her friend are both mothers. They are part of a club of which I never was and never will be a member . . . but they know and understand what kind of person I am, and the leap I made to open my heart to those two beautiful little souls. I smoke a lot of cigarettes, but only drink one "nude" vodka water drink. I haven't been drinking since the infamous microwave-smash attempt. I want really badly to get wasted, but I know it's just a temporary fix to a very long-term problem. After my one drink and several hours I excuse myself to the basement. Lucy gives me some all-natural sleeping medication in pill form as well as a spray that's supposed to help me sleep. I seem to always be needing medication of some kind these days. I hate that. I pass out.

## June 30

All I want is to go home. I pace anxiously in James's kitchen. I haven't heard anything from Wes about when they're supposed to be done moving stuff out. Lucy's home is beautiful and James has been so nice in letting me stay here, but the dogs are unsettled from being kept out of their home and, let's face it, so am I. I dread the thought of having to walk back into the house and face the emptiness that will lie in front of me, but the waiting seems even worse.

I hike with the dogs, I tidy up James's place. I rip through a drive-through for coffee, twice. By lunchtime I can't take it anymore and I text Wes.

"Hey, I'm gonna head home pretty quick, I didn't wanna bug you but I just hadn't heard anything and I need home now."

He doesn't respond. I take a shower and fifteen minutes later I follow it up with, "Is that OK?"

Why am I asking him if it's OK if I go home to my own house? I guess because I don't want him to feel I'm being invasive or rushing him, but I'm not sure what else to do. I load up my things and start driving. Just before I get home, he calls. He explains they had a late night yesterday and a slow start this morning, and they're almost done. He tells me it's cool if I come by so long as I'm OK with it. I now haven't seen him in a full week, and my heart starts racing. I look like shit and I am nervous to be around him. I wish I looked better, but I don't have it in me, and how weird would it be if I got dressed up? I say out loud over and over again as I drive to the house, "You can do this, you can do this, you can do this." I pull in and there are several cars in the driveway; one is Greyson's, one is Wes's truck, and I'm assuming the other must be Wes's brother's vehicle. He had tried to return the money I'd sent him to come for Wes's birthday, but I refused. I'm so glad he still came to be with him. I toss the dogs into the backyard and head inside.

Asphyxiating, that's what it feels like. The absence of air. The breath sucked up inside of me in one wave of shock, and then there wasn't any more. It's so, so, so, so empty. It's quiet; they must be downstairs. The coffee maker Wes had bought us that I had pulled out for him to take remains on the counter, as well as the speaker I gave him as a move-in present, and the blue teapot Fox had given him as a housewarming. It's happening again. I'm being left with all the little pieces of a life someone didn't want. The very few specific things I'd hoped he would take stare me in the face, aggressively present in the absence of everything else. He has taken the table he bought for me, though, which is good. When we first met I didn't have one, and to have to eat at it alone after so many meals with him and the kids, would be hell.

Footsteps, and Greyson appears. I'm glad it's him and not Wes. Greyson has this extremely genuine smile that radiates reassurance. His presence seems to always have a calming effect on me. He hugs me. Wes's brother appears and hugs me too. I feel sheepish. I don't know what Wes has told him about me, but I'm sure he knows about the microwave smash attempt. His eyes, while they cast no judgment, make me incredibly nervous. Can he picture me trying to smash the microwave? They both look worse for wear; they've obviously been going hard, but they're friendly and warm and I appreciate that.

I hear Wes before I see him, and I can feel my face whiten as he comes up the stairs and around the corner. The walk across the kitchen feels long, and I'm not sure if we're going to hug but we do. He looks . . . *oh my god; he looks like absolute fucking shit.* The worst I've ever seen him. There is no joy in this for me, there's no small part of me that relishes for even a second in how awful he looks. His eyes are red and puffy, brimmed with black circles. His normally muscular physique looks thinner and more fragile, his face is sullen. *Who is this person?* I'm overcome with worry and sympathy, sadness and regret. We talk quickly, and he explains there are just a few more loads, then a tidy and they'll be gone. All three disappear back downstairs and now

I'm not sure where to sit or stand or what to do. I head to the master bedroom and lose it. His bed is gone—we'd moved mine downstairs. His dresser is gone. There are two under-the-bed storage totes in the center of the room, two dog beds, and two bedside tables that look ridiculous without the bed in the middle. I sob, but I sob into my sweater to try and muffle the sound. With no furniture and paper-thin walls, I don't want the guys downstairs to hear. I sit myself on top of my short dresser and wheeze and snot into a sweatshirt. Downstairs I can hear them laughing, making jokes. I know they're allowed to find the humor in this, I know humor is probably the best thing for the situation. I know Wes is just doing what he can to get by, but the sound of his laugh hurts my heart endlessly.

A soft knocking on the door.

"Come in!" I say frantically dabbing my eyes and my nose.

Greyson wordlessly enters and wraps me in a huge hug.

"Hard day. It's gonna get better from here." I don't believe him. Everyone lies to me with common platitudes these days.

Wes comes up next and Greyson excuses himself to keep loading.

I'm surprised when he moves in close to where I'm seated on the dresser. For two weeks or so prior to our breakup, he barely seemed to want to touch me, I never knew why. He reaches his arms out and begins to rub his hands on the underside of mine; just up from my elbows he strokes me. It feels so good and it might be the last time he ever touches me, so I revel in it. I cry, then apologize and tell him, "I'm sorry, I shouldn't have come. I just wanted to be home."

He tells me it's OK. We talk for a bit. I tell him he seems to be doing well, he says he's not. He tells me about a house he plans to buy. I am genuinely excited for him and the kids to potentially have a place where they can really settle; they all deserve that. He says he has to get going, but we can talk mid-week. It feels so formal, his phrase, "I'll call you midweek," but it's something. He hugs me goodbye and heads out the door. A minute or two later I hear the door reopen. It's

Greyson. He wordlessly slips his arms around me, and we lean on the banister of the stairwell in my front door. I sob all over him; I put my weight into his body collapsing into him. We stay like this for I don't know how long. When I right myself he offers to lend me his air mattress. I can use it to sleep in the basement during my parents' visit so they can have my bed.

Greyson slips away and I text my parents, who are en route, to let them know the coast is clear. I didn't want them showing up when any of the moving was going on, because it's embarrassing. I don't think I could take it. I don't think I can take them watching my life fall apart again. I wonder if they think to themselves secretly, never daring to utter it out loud to each other: "Where did we go wrong with her? How did we raise a woman who no one wants?"

I'm alone in the house now just waiting, just stunned at the empty. One could think it's absolutely ridiculous that a six-month relationship has caused this level of devastation. I know that. What I've learned already, though, is that it's not the time—it's the commitment and the level of emotional investment that will determine the weight of the loss and grieving. Time is irrelevant. I went through an almost two-year period where I had given up on love. I didn't want children and was convinced that their being part of my life was off the table. The heart leaps I made to be with Wes, the sizes my heart grew from loving those kids, the doors in my soul I opened to him? They were unparalleled to any other relationship in my life. Ultimately, that has been my downfall. The time is irrelevant.

All of my previous relationships came inadvertently second to my work, but because of the transition stage I was been in when I met Wes, that wasn't a factor. We spent almost every minute together for half a year. We travelled, fished, camped, cuddled, created, laughed, and cried. It was because of him that I came to picture the type of life I had never ever in a million years allowed myself to dream of. It is hope that dies with this relationship, not just love. All my hope is gone, truly. The cracks in me where I'd allowed the love to sink in are replaced by the paralyzing fear that I have lost the three most important people in the world, and that nothing will ever repair that. I perceive that for Wes, this was a learning experience of what he didn't want. It is a footnote on his trail to post-divorce self-discovery. It was an attempt that went awry. We didn't have the same affect on one another. His certainty that this was wrong shouldn't cast a shadow on my memories . . . but it does. He saw in me what he didn't want his life to be, and he moved away from it. I found what I wanted, and ruined it. No one wants to be left; no one wants to be discarded. I am a stepping stone to greater things for him. He and those children were my mountaintop. The glorious view at the end of an arduous trail I never thought I'd see the summit of. Now I am back down at the bottom of the valley staring up at the jagged rocks I'd climbed to the top and thinking, "I will never get there again."

So yes, to some, it will seem absolutely bizarre, dramatic, ridiculous, insane, or unfathomable that this much shorter relationship broke me more than the end of my marriage. More than the death of my best friend. More than the elevator accident. But it has, and so he and I will grieve this differently, and I try to tell myself that's OK.

When Mom and Dad walk through my front door my mom hugs me, and I hug her back, probably the tightest I ever remember doing, and I spit out, "I'm just so glad you're here," before silently bursting into tears. I'm not overly concerned about food these days, my weight continues to plummet, and so I'm a bad host. I have nothing prepared for them. I've also decided to reveal to my mother that I currently smoke like a chimney. I have hit that no-fucks-given point so hard. They sneak out to Superstore to grab a few things. Dad uses Wes's barbecue to make us salmon and salad. I feel guilty we're using his stuff. I'm snappy and short with my parents. I feel myself being shitty, but I can't seem to stop. We're always the worst to the ones we love. It's an early night for all of us because Mom and Dad are tired from the travel, and I'm emotionally exhausted.

At 3 a.m. my phone dings. It's a message from Greyson, drunken, nonsensical, and vague, but it leads me to believe the guys are getting into trouble together and it makes me furious . . . especially because he doesn't respond to any of my follow-up questions about what the hell is going on and if they're OK or need a ride or something. Just a complete asshole move, as far as I'm concerned, and so I tell him.

"Asshole move, dude, honestly. Now it's 3 a.m. and I get to be up again even though sleeping is like the only break I get from crying...and you know my brain is doing that thing where whatever it's imagining is a million times worse than what's actually going on, so thanks for that, glad you guys are having fun."

His response comes right away: "You're right. Sorry. We will chat soon."

I cry myself back to sleep.

## July 1

Dad hands me a mug full of coffee, a small morning gesture I have been missing more than I knew. Wes used to always set the coffee maker for me and leave sweet notes in a mug he'd set out. I cup my hands around it, enjoying the warmth.

"Get any sleep?"

"Not really." I explain about Greyson and the text and how pissed I was. "I was up pretty much all night wondering what those idiots got up to."

"Huh, sounds like you guys are going to have to chat about some boundaries if he's going to move into the basement suite still, hey?"

I verbally walk my folks through the pros and cons of letting my ex-boyfriend's best friend move into my basement.

Pros:

He is reliable and I know he will pay his rent on time.

He loves my dogs and has a dog and we can help each other with dog stuff .

A somewhat awkward situation with someone you know, if it goes south, is better than a fight with strangers.

We enjoy each other's company and hiking together and he could be a great source of friendship during a difficult time.

Financially this would be a big assist to me.

Cons:

The incestuous nature of having your ex-boyfriend's best friend live with you has the potential to get problematic really fast.

I don't want to rely on my ex-boyfriend's best friend for friendship.

It could mean more Wes hurt.

What if he's here often to see Greyson and not me? What if Greyson's never here because he's always at Wes's and I'm not invited? What if it extends the hurt more by keeping me tied to Wes?

I'll have to think about this more. I've already told Greyson he could move in down there, but I'm riddled with uncertainty about the wisdom of this decision and its potential to make this situation much, much, much worse. I'll have to just have a really clear chat with him. He's easy to talk to and generally, from my limited knowledge, pretty mature and receptive to honesty, so it should be OK. I want to remain optimistic.

My dad gathers up willow branches from the recent storm and loads them into "The Beast." He rakes leaves, and I stand on the deck smoking and chatting with Mom.

"Sorry there's only one rake," I jokingly yell to him across the yard. My mom laughs. I know I'm not showing them very well, but having them here means everything to me. We take "the Beast" on a run to the dump and Home Depot for supplies so dad can tackle the "dad list" I've made him. It's things I need help with around the house that I don't know how to do. One of the items Dad is going to tackle is that downed fence Wes had built me. He wants to reset the cemented post, which requires taking the old cement off of it first.

"Bert!" he calls me by my childhood nickname, "come out here!"

He has the original post down on its side with the chunk of cement still attached at the bottom, where I can see it, a heart with our initials on it that Wes drew in the cement. Dad hands me clear safety glasses and a mallet.

Never in my life have I been as envious of Wes as I am right now. He's buying a new place and will be creating whatever he wants with it. I'm here, with the remnants of things, with all the broken abandoned bits. With dents the kids made in the walls—dents I'll never want to fill. With their little plastic cars still in the yard, his daughter's rock garden still piled near the back door. With a post of cement with our initials in it that he actually joked I'd come to hate if we ever broke up. I was so naive, so stupid, and so foolish. I hate myself so much right now.

"Swing it away from you, gonna take a couple hits," Dad tells me.

I lean down with the mallet, swing with all my might, and the entire block shatters into nothing in one go. Funny how easy it was to destroy something that looked and felt so permanent.

My mother shares my love of a particular brand of jewelry that can be difficult to find. We locate a store that carries it about twenty minutes away and decide to go see if we can find me something to replace the protection necklace Wes had bought me. Each of these pieces has a special reminder and comes with a meaning that the wearer would like to embody. The amount of times I've purchased these items in hopes that it would make me feel one of the many messages is staggering. After my divorce I bought a "new beginnings" ring. When I struggled with fear and loneliness I wore a "neither fearful nor wanting" medallion. When I felt broken I wore my "unbreakable" ring. I find myself wondering how often I'll return to a store, sadly trying to rebuild, hoping to buy some inspiration for my next battle.

I settle on one that represents self-care and, oddly enough, putting your own needs first. It has a sun on it too, representing the rising of a new day where I can successfully "tend to my own garden." It's an entirely different message than any of the others I've tried. Mom buys it for me and I hug her right there in the store.

"Thanks, Mama. That's so kind of you."

She buys a hummingbird for herself, a representation of joy, and we head back home.

We spend the day tackling things around the house, drinking lots of coffee and chatting. In the evening we go for dinner at Whitespot and then watch a movie my brother-in-law recommended called *Ingrid Goes West*. I go to bed dreading that my mom and dad have to leave tomorrow.

## July 2

The morning is moving too quickly for me. I know as soon as Dad finishes reassembling the fence they're going to leave. Mom and I sit in the kitchen sipping coffee and I tell her I don't want them to go.

"We will see you again in just a few days," she reminds me. I have to head down to the coast and the island where I'm from for that wedding.

"That feels far away." I start to cry, and this time it's not sobs or tears, it's this silent awful inward cry. I cover my face and shake. My mother breaks the silence.

"Perhaps you should look at some medication if you're really having trouble with this. I hate seeing you so sad."

"People get sad when people leave them, Mom!" I snap at her and instantly regret it. Why am I being so shitty? She's only trying to help. I busy myself with cleaning up the kitchen and she gathers her things. Dad finishes the fence and they start loading up the car. I hug Mom on the front porch and follow her and Dad out to the car. I hand Dad a bag that he places in the trunk. He hugs me super hard.

"I love you so much," I tell him. "I'm so sorry I'm so shitty to be around right now."

"It's OK; I'm no peach myself some days."

"I'll see you Friday."

I walk back up to the porch and wave as they pull away. I go back inside and I don't cry, I simply walk to bed, pull the blankets over my head, hug my knees to my chest, and sleep.

I wake up feeling groggy and shitty. I recall Greyson's advice to "just keep moving." It is true that there's a healing quality to simply being in nature. Moving and going outside is the last thing I feel like doing, but I change, lace up my runners, and drive across town to the site of a steep hike.

One of my favourite podcasts features people sharing stories from the worst moments of their lives. It sounds depressing, and sometimes it is, but it also shares the stories of how they've overcome adversity, or how they're at least trying to. Knowing other people's struggles, most of them much worse than mine, helps me realize this pain will pass. I listen to an episode called "Best Friends Forever," about a woman whose best friend died suddenly. It's a pain I know all too well. I lament missing Tese, I lament that Wes had become my best friend and I'm missing him. I reach the summit, where a group of people are gathered at the lookout. I sidestep to a little rock, and I weep. I'm so fucking sick of crying, but it just keeps coming. I'm probably the most dehydrated person on the earth.

I hike back down and drive home. I've got a Facebook message from Greyson, apologizing for his message the other night that I was so mad about. We go back and forth, and I let him know that the situation has the potential to become too complicated. I need to stop dumping all my sad about it on Greyson, and he needs to understand that even though it's foolish, I'm still hoping Wes might want me back one day. He's super receptive to it. We agree we can still make the living arrangement work and, ultimately, we are friends. We can continue to develop our friendship around the things we enjoy, like our dogs and hiking and each other's company. I feel relieved, but I'm still not 100 percent sure this is a good idea; in fact, I know Fox vehemently thinks it isn't. I don't know. I don't know what I'm doing but I know I dread the thought of strangers downstairs worse than the potential for some awkwardness with Greyson, so I'm going to see how it goes.

My phone rings and Wes's name displays. My heart knocks. It's only Monday and he said we would speak mid-week, so this is a welcome surprise. I'm especially glad when he tells me he would have called sooner but he's been busy with the kids and trying to sort his stuff out. It's a quick chat, and it's a bit choppy. At times I accidentally talk over him or we both start talking at the same time. Regardless, it's nice to hear his voice. We make plans to hang out on Thursday before I leave for the coast. The hike has exhausted me, so I crawl back into bed and pass out.

## July 3

I hit the gym first thing in the morning under the mindset that if I keep moving, maybe today I can avoid the sad. It catches up with me on my second set of deadlifts. I don't cry, but I fight every single rep of every single weight for the whole workout. The entire thing is a grind and I leave physically exhausted, probably only having completed forty minutes of activity.

At home there's still so much to do. Our podcasting studio downstairs was dismantled during the move, but all of the sound baffling remains on the walls. The air mattress Greyson lent me is still inflated and covered in blankets that need laundering. The whole house needs an epic clean, and a lot of stuff needs to be moved back upstairs to get the suite ready again. I blast music and attempt to get some things sorted. Upstairs, downstairs. Upstairs, downstairs. I tread back and forth lugging office chairs and coffee tables and dishes. *This sucks.* It sucks so bad I can't finish. Why am I rushing this? Greyson isn't moving in for a few more weeks; my body is tired; I don't want to be doing it. I crawl into bed and watch TV. I have a hair appointment today with Meesha and I'm excited about it. It's the first thing I've been really looking forward to in a while, and honestly, shallow as this is, looking good helps me feel good. I grab an Americano and head to the salon. Over the last year I've basically destroyed my hair. It used to be my pride and joy, extremely long and coloured a fire engine red. It was my signature, my most identifiable feature. When my life took a hard turn I did the thing I shouldn't have done and started fucking around with it. First I let some other stylist in California bleach the absolute shit out of it while I was on vacation. It turned strawberry. Then I spent several subsequent months having Meesha correct it and cut it shorter and shorter each time to remove the damage. Three months in to dating Wes, I coloured it back to the bright red, except the colour wouldn't hold because my hair was so damaged. It turned pinky orange. In the spring Meesha had corrected it to a dark colour just to override the red and stop it from seeping every time I have a shower. Now I have no clue what we're going to do. Her salon is one of my favourite places in the world. She launched her own business when she was just twenty-seven, and the pride I feel about all she has accomplished in the seven years we have known each other is huge. This is a good place for me. Meesh sees the beauty in both my soul and my exterior when I cannot. Her gift is that she can help people take all the beauty they have inside and make them feel equally beautiful outside. I've never known someone who had such a talent for making people feel so special, gorgeous, and confident. I need this.

I'm at the salon for a good five hours, but it's awesome because I get a chance to catch up with her. The end result is . . . I can't believe it. I have no clue how she's done it, but after all the fucked-up shit I've done to my hair she's managed to make it look beautiful and natural and sun-kissed. It has the finest streaks of blonde through it, but an ashy undertone like my natural colour. I've never had my hair this particular way before, but I feel so like *me*, and I feel pretty for the first time in months.

"What do you think?" she asks me, pulling the cape off as I stare into the mirror. My face, it's smiling back at me. It's thinned out substantially since Wes broke up with me. I'm struck with the thought that I look like me before I met Wes. The thinner me, the lighter-haired me, and the me that's closer to the me I want to be than I was five hours ago. My eyes well up with tears of joy.

"Don't cry!" she says

"I'm just so happy. Thank you." I embrace her so hard. "I love you so much."

Greyson shoots me a message to let me know he's going to hike this evening and would the dogs and I want to join? I feel oddly jacked about it, although he's forewarned me the trail is a steep one. I tell him as long as he is patient with my short-person steps and smokers' lungs, I'd be glad to come with. We meet soon after and tackle the trail. It is challenging, and we don't talk a ton on the way up because, to be honest, I'm huffing and puffing and trying to make sure my stupid dogs don't wander off a cliff edge.

It's not a particularly long hike despite its steepness, but the view from the top is stunning. You get an almost 360-degree view of the city, encompassing a bridge, beautiful lake views, a forest, and the downtown. We take pictures at the top, even a selfie of the two of us, which for some reason I hadn't really pictured Greyson doing. He barely uses social media. We get photos of each other with our respective dogs. On the walk back down I talk more, blabbing endlessly about my friends and my visit with my family. When we're done, I'm starving and I tell him so.

"Wanna drop the dogs off at my house and go get some food?"

I'm happy when he agrees. We go to my favourite restaurant and I plow through a giant salad with chicken. I have two beers, which for me these days is a lot. We talk about relationships and people and friendships. We come back to the house and talk in person a bit about the boundaries for living together, and how we think that will work. I'm getting excited now for him to move in, and I'm really just hoping this doesn't blow up in my face. He heads home, and I go to sleep.

# July 4

There's no pallet sign you can buy that erases the memory of being not chosen. There's no scented candle or new lamp that will make it OK to know that someone looked at you and decided: "Life is better without her." No matter where I put things it doesn't feel quite right. Move a picture here, change a decoration there, can any amount of redecorating ever replace the sense of emptiness? Doubtful. This house has become a shrine to my pain over the last few years. Horrible things have happened to me here, and yet I have no appetite to sell it, as so many people have suggested. I'm not sure why. I'm a nostalgic person, that's for sure, but it can't quite be called nostalgia when most of the memories bring me pain.

Is that true, though? Yes, to some extent, I have a few particular memories in this house that will haunt me forever and be the fodder and cash cow of therapists for years to come. I have some that used to hurt, but that time has healed. I have great memories here with Fox and Lucy . . . too many to count, and then there's the last six months. I pray to a God I don't really believe in that one day, time will soften the edges of these memories so that I can see the beauty in them again without the sting. Most of all, though, I recall both James, and Wes, saying kind and loving things to me. Both telling me I am the nicest, kindest, most loving person in the world . . . and telling me this as they are leaving.

I'm happy when Greyson messages and says he's hiking again today. It's a trail I've done before and really like, except he's hiking it the opposite way I normally do, which means more up instead of down and a different view. We meet up with the dogs. At the top of the hike I go to take a picture and realize I've either lost my phone or forgotten it. I'm really hoping I left it in the Jammer and haven't dropped it along the trail, because I normally—stupidly—tuck it into the hip band of my workout pants. It's sad that my first thought is, "I hope I haven't missed any messages from Wes." When we make our way back to the parking lot, my phone is sitting on the back bumper of my vehicle, where I placed it when I was leashing up the dogs.

"Finally a lucky break," I say. We give the dogs water and sit on some rocks.

"What else you got going on tonight?" Greyson asks me.

"Nothing, I don't think . . . you?"

"I gotta head back; Wes and I are having chicken wings for dinner."

"Nice!" But secretly I'm sad and envious. I give him a hug and tell him I hope he and Wes have a fun night. I was supposed to have coffee with Jer in the morning, but on the drive home I get a text from him telling me his morning looks a little insane, and would I wanna swing by tonight instead after the kids crash.

"Cya den," I write back.

Just before 8 I get a text from him saying, "Kids are down. Hit it."

I shoot him back, "awesome cya in a few minutes" and I drive to his place up the street.

I have a grapefruit Radler, and we sit at his patio set outside. I fill him in on everything I've been up to, which really isn't much, other than hiking and the gym. I tell him about my parents' visit, and about my hikes with Greyson. He's curious about the Greyson situation, so I explain it at length. I tell him I know Greyson's moving in is complicated and I know it's a weird friendship to be having right now, but we get along and it works and he's good company. I suspect he wonders if there's more to it than that. We talk about his relationship and what's been going on in his life. I want to support him the way he supported me during my divorce, and the way he supports me now through this with Wes. We discuss at length how we'd both like to be in our next relationships, and I'm not sure if it's wishful thinking or stuff we can actually accomplish. This stuff has taken a toll on both of us, and whether you want it to or not, it changes you. We're both grieving not just our relationships but our formally hopeful selves. It makes me sad to see him doubt himself this way, because I know someone is going to love him like crazy. We laugh about his potentials; there's no shortage of women who would kill to be with this guy. We discuss every possible outcome and pontificate on who we'll end up with and how and when. It's nice; to be in a daydreamy place with the outdoor gas fireplace glowing, talking about what the future might hold instead of our pasts. I try to tell myself that all of the good that I know is going to come his way, all the things I can see that he can't, will come to me one day too.

I get home and message Greyson to see how the chicken wings were. This is my life now: I'm so boring I inquire about other people's dinner. He says they were good and asks what I've been up to. I tell him I was hanging with Jer. He asks if that's "a thing." I'm straight up with him and tell him that Jer was clearly wondering the same thing about him! I explain it's so curious to me now how the world works; is no one just friends anymore? He tells me with guys and girls that's usually not the case, but we can be friends. I write back, "no sorry I didn't mean that as a slight against you, we ARE friends, I'm just so out of the loop with the current culture I guess." My mind has no room for anyone but Wes.

I lie in bed and think about the people closest to me. I think about how hard and scary the current dating culture is for me, and why I never was good at it and don't want to go back. I think about sex, and how much it takes for me to trust someone enough to get there. I think about the fact that since my marriage ended two years ago I have had only two real boyfriends. One was only for a couple of months and I ended it when I realized I wasn't ready, and the other was Wes. How can I go back to a culture that doesn't align with what I'm capable of? No one is going to want me, because I take things so seriously. But I can't and, more importantly, don't want to play fast and fancy free with my heart. I wish I was built to be colder, I wish I was built to not care so much. I sometimes even wish I didn't place the value I do on friendships, because then maybe I'd be more open to wrecking them by considering some of the men around me as potentials. I can't be what I'm not, though. I know the road ahead will be tedious and sad and lonely. I know I'm so far away from dating that these can be later Roo problems, but no matter how long I postpone them, these problems will come back to haunt me.

## July 5

I'm anxious about seeing Wes tonight and it eats away at my tummy. It's like reverse-excited butterflies. I kill as much of the morning as I can with mindless housework, until it's time for me to train with Hendrik. At training my mind is elsewhere, although seeing him does have a calming effect on me, as does the lifting of heavy things. I haven't been this nervous to see him since our second date. Most people say they're the most nervous on the first date, but the first date I wasn't really nervous because I didn't know how much I was going to like him. Preparing for the second date though? Different thing.

True story, and ironic and ridiculous to look back on now, but both Fox and my father can back me up on this one. After I went on my first date with Wes, I called them both and said the exact same two sentences to each of them:

1) "We have a fucking problem."

2) "This one's gonna do some damage."

I KNEW, I knew right from the start that I was wild about him, filled with reckless abandon, and was going to hand over my heart to him in a way I'd never done before. I've never said anything like that about anyone after a first date, and a part of me wonders now if I shouldn't have seen that as the positive and funny thing I took it for, but rather some sort of warning bell for impending pain. At the time the words were only connected to my mind. Logically, I could see it coming a mile away, but my brain failed to connect those sentences to my heart, and so pain was just a word and not a feeling. It felt fun and exciting to know I was taking a risk.

My girlfriends ask what I'd like to do with him and I don't really have an answer for that, at least one that's appropriate. I know a lot of things I'd like to do to him, that's for sure. *Not helpful. Focus.* I perseverate on if this meeting will be positive, if I'll feel better or worse afterwards, if I should even be seeing him. I spin. In the end I decide on jeans and a black tank top, just usual Roo clothing that won't seem out of the ordinary. By the time he's off work, I'm vibrating with a combination of nerves and excitement. He texts to ask if he should swing by the house and then maybe pop down to the local pub. I tell him that's great.

I sit at my kitchen bar and read a book. Oh, who am I kidding? I don't read; I try to read. I reread the same page over and over. I wonder if he will knock when he comes in, or just open the door like he used to. When I finally hear the door open, I'm panicked. My heart is pounding, my hands feel sweaty, and I feel a little sick to my stomach.

"Hellooooo," I call out trying to sound casual.

I hear a "hey" back.

I walk around the corner to the front door and see both the dogs accosting him. Ducky jumps up, and her claws leave a large red scratch down his forearm.

"Sorry," I say. He pushes the dogs down and maybe I'm imagining it, but I sense a slight bit of relief on his part that he doesn't have to deal with them anymore. He looks so good, but I have this weird sensation I'm seeing him differently than I did before, and I can't quite place my finger on why. I find myself scanning to see if he's lost weight, or if he's cut his hair. I don't think anything is that different, but he just looks different to me. It makes me uneasy, especially because whatever it is is not unattractive; if anything, I find myself already resisting the urge to grab hold of him.

This pub is down the street from us. It just reopened, and we quite recently rode our bikes down and back. We are going to the same place, but it's not at all the same, because everything is different now.

We keep the topics light at first, but there's a heaviness between us. He shares some things about how and what he's been doing that make me sad and very worried about him. I am, however, impressed he's so forthcoming and honest about it all. We talk about his birthday weekend and what I missed. I hold it together quite well until we get to the topic of the kids, when I spit out, "Listen, I'm going to say this really fast so I don't get emotional, I'm not sure what that looks like but if there's a way where I could see them that would be awesome because . . ." I feel myself choking up and I turn my head to the side to avoid his eyes. "It's killing me how much I miss them."

"Hey, if we're all cool then I don't see any reason why that can't be a thing."

That sentence is everything to me, and I resolve mentally that things between him and me will just always, always, always have to be some version of OK so that I can still see the kids from time to time. There's a few times during the discussion that my eyes sting with tears, but I don't ever full-on cry and that feels like a win for me. Toward the end of the meal a stranger approaches, a grey-haired gentleman who seems to know Wes, and they chat.

"Oh and this must be your beautiful girlfriend." Neither of us corrects him.

"I'm Roo, it's nice to meet you," I shake his hand.

"Oh, I know who you are, I've listened to your show and the show you guys have been doing . . ." He natters on for a bit, wrapping it up with, "Didn't mean to interrupt date night, I'll leave you to it."

When he walks away we both burst out laughing.

"Of course," Wes says rolling his eyes, "that would happen to us."

When we finish dinner he drives us back to my house. Inside, I ask him if he wants a beer. He says yes, but first he disappears to tackle a wasp nest that we had never gotten around to. It's quite close to my front porch, so I'm relieved and thankful he wants to deal with it. After smashing it down with a fishing pole, he sneaks around to the back deck and we sit.

The details of this conversation, I'm aware, are so subjective, open for interpretation. We each have our own perceptions of our, and each other's, faults and flaws. We head down a painful path. We get into the minutiae of who did what; who could have done what, who understood or didn't understand what was being asked of them. It's a sad talk, at least for me, and it makes me want to hold him. I move my Adirondack chair closer to his and put my hand on his leg. He leans in closer to me to talk and when his face gets near I run my fingers through his hair and pull his head in. He rests his forehead into my body, and then against mine. I'm crying now, but it's because I'm happy he's so close to me, and I'm sad I'll never get this back. A noise, half-laugh and half-cry, escapes my mouth.

"How could a person who loves somebody so much have gotten it so wrong?" I hope he knows I mean that about myself. I hope it sounds like the apology I want it to be.

Our faces are so close and I'm hoping he'll kiss me. He does, although to be honest maybe I kissed him? I'm really not sure. His tongue shoots sparks through me, and the kissing goes on and on. I know this is not advisable. I know this is probably a horrible idea, but more than anything, I know myself. I know that I want things to end not how they ended the microwave-smashing night, and that this is my chance.

I pull away from the kiss and with my hands on his chest I look him square in the face and say, "I mean . . . we never got to have breakup sex."

He seems surprised. Hell, I'm surprised. I've never had breakup sex in my life.

"Is that really what you want?"

"Yes," and then I kiss him again.

We head inside, making out like our plane is going down. I tell myself over and over again to hold onto this moment, to enjoy every second of it, to memorize the way his tongue feels in my mouth, and the scent of him, and the way his hands feel on my ass, and the feel of his hair and his face and his beard against my cheeks and lips. I bathe in every little detail of him I've been missing and will always miss. *This is goodbye. Make it good.* We break momentarily so I can grab a glass of water, then I open my bedroom door, inviting him in.

"Can you lay here with me, for just a second?" I ask.

He climbs right on top of me and wraps me in his arms. It's silent. I wrap my hands around his head and lean into his ear and whisper, "I miss you so much." What I really mean is, I'm going to miss you so much. What I really mean is goodbye.

"I should get going before this gets sad," he says, and starts redressing.

It's a funny turn of phrase to me, as if it isn't already sad. That's us, never on the same page. "OK."

I follow him to the door, we kiss goodbye, and then he's gone. I sleep well for the first time in weeks.

## Week Three

## July 6

The intelligent, rational part of my brain had whispered to me as I fell asleep last night: *you might have made a mistake.* I did catch myself wondering how I'd feel come morning. It has arrived, and oddly enough, I feel weirdly good. The decisions I made last night still sit well with me, and in some roundabout way I think they have left me feeling empowered, like I went out on my own terms. I've overridden the microwave-smash attempt as the last night we spent "together." I've replaced it with something more meaningful and gentle, and satisfying, even when I know it might not have meant anything to him. It doesn't erase the sting I feel when I think about our last night as a couple, but it helps put something else in the windshield and moves the bad night to the rear-view. I continuously search my chest cavity waiting for some delayed ache, some smouldering regret, some new pain I've created by doing that, and it just doesn't come. Not only has no new pain appeared, but, miraculously, it seems to have softened the edges around the now-familiar daily ache I've been fighting since he broke up with me. It was the right decision for me. Do I actually feel a bit lighter? Could that be possible? Am I just in denial?

It's 4:30 a.m., and I'm not supposed to leave to go to the coast until 8, but I know I won't be able to go back to sleep. Feeling even remotely better than the day before is a win for me, and it gives me an almost itchy sense of anticipation and energy. I'm anxious to get going, even though I'm somewhat dreading the trip. There's a weird peace that's settled over me as I drive. I listen to podcasts and a bit of music, but I drive mostly in silence for the three hours until I reach an area to gas up. I text my dad and let him know I'm only about forty minutes away. He is surprised, because I wasn't even supposed to leave for another forty-five minutes, but he's happy I'll be there soon, I can tell. I'm so happy to see my parents when I get there. Something about the comfort of being around them makes me realize I'm exhausted after all the driving. I curl up in a little ball on their couch, dad throws some giant pillows all around me, and I pass out.

Something has changed recently in my relationship with my folks, and I can't quite pinpoint how or what, but it's different. I love my mom and dad so much, but I've always felt the need to protect them from anything I've done or am doing that might disappoint them. I've always had a very open relationship with them, but lately I've blown the doors wide open. There's a certain liberation in losing the most important things to you; it's freeing to know I don't have anything else to lose. Combine that with the fact that I know my parents will always love me, and well, you get a Roo who's probably more forthcoming than my parents need or want, but it feels so real to me, and I love that something good has come out of this.

My mom asks how it went with Wes last night.

"Well . . ." I laugh and my face blushes. Me seven months ago would have dodged the question; now I can't hide my shit-eating grin when I tell her "the chemistry is still intact" and give a cheeky little "click click" noise with my tongue to emphasize. I explain some parts of the conversation I had with him last night, about how I might still get to see the kids from time to time if he and I can be friends, and how we'll look at the possibility of getting the podcast going again, as it's something we both truly enjoy doing. My mom makes a motion in the air to me like scissors.

"Cut the cord Roo."

Let the record show her advice is the best advice. Hands down, coming out of a relationship this is the cleanest, simplest, least hurtful, most self-protective, sensible way to conduct oneself. However, I'm the girl whose ex-husband lives in her best friend's basement. I'm the girl who moves her ex-boyfriend's best friend into her own basement.I'm the girl who, less than a year ago, drove four hours to have dinner with her high school boyfriend and his new wife and their child. I'm the girl who will always choose a complicated relationship with someone I value, even when it comes at a cost to me, over peace.

I make the snipping gesture back at her in the air with a genuine smile and say, "Wish it were that easy, Mama."

The pub they've chosen for dinner is called "Roo's," which amuses us for obvious reasons, and we all pile in. My brother and his husband are there. The food is slow; my mom has to ask for a new glass because the one her wine came in had lipstick on it already. We all joke around with one another. My brother's husband in particular makes me laugh a lot. I'm a little embarrassed to see the boys, though. Unlike my parents, they'd had the chance to spend a bit more time with Wes, and to meet the kids. I wonder if they ever wonder what's wrong with me that makes me keep winding up alone, or, maybe worse, if they know. It's rare that all five of us are able to get together; I hope it will become less rare now that my parents have moved off the island, but the evening still feels special, so I ask the waitress to take a picture. The ones she takes are blurry and the lighting is bad. We laugh and redo it again ourselves as a selfie. I love the photo. I'm smack dab in the middle of the five of us, and I'm happy, really truly happy. It's the first post I do to social media since Wes broke up with me.

That night, though, as I lie on the pull-out couch in my parents' spare room, I look at the picture again, and I see it differently. My mom and my dad on my right, married forty-one years this fall. My brother and his husband on the left, married five years and together for the last decade. Then there's me. Right in the middle. Alone.

## July 7

I wake up extremely early to catch the ferry to Vancouver Island for the wedding I will be attending. Since Tese passed away, I've stayed very close with her family. Over the years I've raised over $50,000 for epilepsy research and education in her honour. Her little sister is the bride, and I'm so truly honoured to have been invited, except . . . I'm mortified. This family has always held me in such high regard and shown me more love and support over the years than any human deserves. They've taken such pride in my work, and my career, and my progress and development as a human and as a woman. I feel embarrassed to show up and have to tell them I have no job, I'm a wanna-be author, and I'm alone again. I know, without a shadow of a doubt, that they would never judge me, and that my embarrassment says only things about me and not them, but it doesn't ease my shame.

I'm also not especially great in giant groups of people I don't know, and this will be mostly that. Since the only people I'm close with are the bride's immediate family, I anticipate spending much of the day alone, as I know they'll have their commitments and priorities and family craziness on a day like today. I missed her little brother's wedding two years prior when my marriage ended and I had just had my breast reduction. I wasn't able to face them then, mostly because of the recovery pain but also because of the embarrassment. Not being there for him on his special day was something I've always regretted, and while the struggle is real, I refuse to make the same mistake twice.

In line at the ferry I call Fox and she dives deep into a story about a ridiculous over-the-top fight she and Clive had. We laugh a lot about it; we're all so fucked. When we load onto the ferry I gather up my laptop and head to a workstation. It's a little cube with a power supply and a desk, and it hints at privacy but really provides next to none. I sit down and work on this writing. I try not to write about the writing of this book for two reasons:

1) It is a little too *Inception*-y for me.
2) Writing is a largely uneventful process that for the most part need not be chronicled.

Today is different, though. The writing is painful, the recalling of it all hurts too much, but my fingers fly anyway and I type and type and type. The words are pouring out of me, and with them come tears: big, round, full-sized, two-year-old in the throes of a tantrum, don't ever seem to stop tears. I walk to the on-board cafeteria and snag myself a handful of napkins to blow my nose and blot at my face. For the entire two-hour trip, I am head down, engrossed in my laptop. I tell myself the tears are a cathartic release; it's been a few days since I cried, and this is just my way of letting it out. It's an emotional time returning home for the wedding of the little sister of a deceased best friend right after a breakup. Jesus, even saying it I think you'd get why I'd be crying. This isn't a backslide, I'm OK, everything is alright. This is normal.

When the ferry unloads, I hit the highway but then take the first possible exit off of the freeway. Instead I decide to follow the much slower, meandering scenic oceanside route. When I was a kid, this was the only highway. It winds along sandy and rocky beaches, following the Strait of Georgia. It's a gorgeous view, and it's a beautiful day. I stop several times to take pictures. I try calling the motel I booked for myself several times to see if I can arrange early check-in but I can't get a hold of anyone. I'm not supposed to check in until 3 and the wedding is at 3.

Just before lunch I arrive in my hometown, which is still another half hour from where I need to go. I pull into my favourite coffee shop. It used to be called Joe Read's Bookstore and Internet café, but I couldn't for the life of me tell you its current name. It'll always be Joe Read's to me.

My brother is three years older, and when he started coming here to hang out and have coffee with his friends I thought it was the coolest place on the planet. When he got his driver's license I used to beg him to let me tag along. On the evenings he did I remember feeling extremely sophisticated at thirteen. Later this would become mine and Tese's favourite hangout. It's situated next to a beach and a small pathway-style park where we would have our coffees and sit at one picnic table in particular. I grab a coffee from inside and then wander around through the back to our table. It's peaceful here, and when I'm in this place I feel "with" her. I stare out at the ocean; I watch couples and children walk by and I leisurely consume my coffee. It's so strange to be back in my hometown for the first time since my parents moved and since we laid my nana to rest. What's here for me now? Nothing, really. This place does not belong to me anymore. It doesn't give me the comfort it used to. I walk back to the car and drive to the motel.

I arrive at noon, and leaving my things in my car, I head to the front desk to speak with the attendant about early check-in. The girl is a huge bitch and cuts me off before I can even explain what I'm asking.

"Last name?"

"Phelps, but I was wondering . . ."

"Ms. Phelps, your check in is not until 3."

"Yes, I understand. I've come from out of town for a wedding. I emailed you guys earlier this week. The wedding is at 3, and I don't have a place to get ready. I was trying to find out if there's any way I could check in even a tiny bit . . ."

"Check in is not until 3," she repeats.

"Yup. Got that." I stare at her blankly and don't leave. I put on pretty much the meanest face I have to offer but I say nothing. I figure if I stand here long enough she will realize I'm not taking her response for an answer. I raise my eyebrows as if to say: "Now what, bitch?"

She sighs and flitters some papers around dramatically. "I guess I could see if we could get you in at 1:30, so come back in like an hour and a half."

"Wonderful, thank you so much." I smile at her but I'm extremely irritated. It should not be this much of a thing to arrange an early check in.

I head back to my car and drive out toward an ocean-view point where I pull over and park. My phone dings. It's a text from a friend, more an acquaintance really, that reads, "So sorry to see you and Wes broke up. Xox"

See? What does that mean? How does she know?

So I write her back, "thanks super appreciate that. How'd you know?"

Her response is a gut punch. It's a screenshot of Wes's updated dating profile. In the photo he has chosen, he's sitting at the table of a breakfast diner in Toronto. He has one hand resting casually on the table, aviators adorn his bearded face, and he's looking off into the distance out the window. It's edited to black and white, and he looks devastatingly handsome. It is my favourite photo of him. I took it that day when we were having breakfast together in Toronto. I edited it to black and white. I used it as the screensaver on my phone until just a few days ago. He promised. He had promised he would tell me so I wouldn't be blindsided.

*Can't breathe.* I scramble frantically to pull at the door handle gasping for air. I open it just in time to throw up my coffee. I fall onto my hands and knees out of the vehicle into the dirt, where the vomit lands in front of me on the ground. When I'm done throwing up my coffee I retch and gag, but there's nothing left for my stomach to expel. I can't get up, I'm dizzy and my heart is racing. I wonder if I'm having a heart attack, but I realize it's a panic attack. I stay on the ground, perched above my own vomit on all fours like a dog. Eventually I'm able to pull myself back into the vehicle, where I fight to get my sweater off. My body is revolting against me and now I feel like I'm a million degrees. *I can't, I just can't breathe.* My hoodie is cutting off all my air. I manage to rip it off over my head and I pull it into a little ball and push it against my face and sob. This, this is more than just Wes now. **This has nothing to do with him**. This is me splitting in half. This is me breaking open. My mind deals me card after card after card of all the images that hurt. Wes's children's beautiful faces. The day James took his last bag out the front door. Wes's face lit up by the glow of one of our many backyard fires. Kissing my nana's cold cheek before they zipped the body bag over her face. Wes's sons saying, "I want Roo to do it!" Tese's mom at her funeral. Wes's toothbrush on my bathroom counter for the first time. Lucy's face that day on our drive. The birth of my first nephew when I was married to James. The elevator door closing on my hand. Wes's daughter casually climbing onto my lap while I have coffee with Fox. The first time Wes told me he loved me, the first time his son told me he loved me, the valentine his daughter brought me home from school. My shoulder dislocating as I pull against the elevator door followed by the dislocation of all the knuckles on my right hand. Jeremy's face when he told me he was getting divorced. James's dating profile being sent to me by listeners again and again. Wes rubbing my arms the day he moved out. My backyard filled with people and children and laughter. The Sea-Can.

Someone has created an album of all that I have lost, all that the people I love continue to lose, and they're flipping it in front of my face, rapidly screaming, "Loss is what life holds for you!" It's undeniable after this much loss. I am the problem. I hurt people. There's a pier nearby that I used to go to as a child, and I'm struck with a very clear thought. *I am going to go and walk off of it*. I'm terrified of drowning, but I'm more terrified of more endless pain, and continuing to hurt and lose the people around me and watch them hurt. *I can't keep going. This will be a relief.*

I'm scaring myself. I try Fox and can't get a hold of her, so I message Greyson, who's getting ready to leave for a camping trip. I tell him I'm having a full-on meltdown, and he tells me maybe I should reach out to Wes. This seems like the exact opposite of what Wes would want, as my emotion was always too much for him, so I'm hesitant, but fuck it, I'm walking off a pier in a bit so what do I have to lose? Maybe he will call and I can hear his voice one last time . . .

I don't even really think before I write it, I simply summarize the message I got and why it upset me. The text is really long but I don't reread it before hitting send. His reply comes instantly and is not at all what I expect. It is empathetic, kind, apologetic, and explanatory. It's vulnerable and thoughtful and understanding. He is just a person in the world, trying the best he can to live life the same way I am. I tell him it's OK, and I find myself wanting to alleviate any guilt or bad feelings I may have caused him about this. When I go off the pier I don't want him thinking this was because of him. His words ease the sting of the initial blow, but they don't quell the storm that's started, because it's too late. This isn't him, this is everything. I have gone to the dark place. I wish I could call him. I wish he could call me. There are so many people I want to say goodbye to but I want none of them to be saddled with the guilt or knowledge that they were the last one I spoke to.

*Don't do this, Roo. Do it. End it. Don't do this. Be brave. This will end your pain. Now, before you chicken out. Stop! Don't do this to your family.* I fight myself, I don't know how long. The first thing I do is take my keys out of the ignition and place them in my purse so I'm not tempted to drive closer to the pier. I take deep breaths. I make a list of the things that tether me to this world. My mom and dad. I actively picture what hurting myself would do to them, and I feel embarrassed and ashamed and selfish. *Good.* I think of James and Fox, Lucy and Jeremy and Hendrik. My brother and his husband. I think of my two dogs, Atticus and Ducky. I think of all the people I would hurt. I tell myself pain cannot be the answer to more pain. I tell myself I'm not thinking clearly. I tell myself anything and everything I need to tell myself to be convinced that if I put the key in the ignition, I will drive back to the hotel. It sits in my bag; I don't trust myself to start driving. *I don't want to hurt anymore. I don't want to fight anymore. What did I do that was so bad that I always wind up alone? Why is this so hard for me? Why can nobody who loves me stay? I can't keep doing this.* I close my eyes and lean back in my seat. I breathe deeply over and over again trying to stop sobbing. *End it.* I Breathe in. *Don't do it.* I breathe out. This goes on and on. When I'm certain I'm not going to do it, I don't feel relief, I feel . . . disappointed. Like I'm too useless to even kill myself. I go back to the hotel, I check in, I play music like everything is normal and I put on a beautiful dress. It's time to go and celebrate "everlasting" love.

The venue is a whiskey distillery I've never been to. I pull into the lot and sit in my car, unable to get out. Thankfully, Tese's little brother, his wife, and their new baby girl arrive right next to me. The welcome is so warm, and I'm elated to see them and meet their baby. I'm more candid about what's going on with me than is probably appropriate under the circumstances, but I've decided that's a better route than being dishonest. I try and smile when I tell them my life's a bit of a mess right now. I laugh through parts of the story, but I know they can tell I'm hurting. It feels good to not have to hide it. They let me hold their baby girl, and she is perfect and beautiful, and oh good god it feels amazing to hold a child in my arms again. I don't ever want to put her down, and yet something is off. It's her weight; she's so young and too little to perfectly satisfy the weight I long for in my arms. Wes's children are older, and heavier, and feel different against me. Tears sting at my eyes. I am aching with the longing to hold them. To hug them. To read one of them a story before bed. To feel them run at me and jump into my arms. To hear their voices. I haven't seen them since Monday, June 18. Wes has sent no pictures, and whenever I ask about them he tells me they're good. I often find myself wondering if he even knows how much I truly love them. Does he not speak about them to prevent hurting me, or does he really just not know how much losing them is affecting me? Does he know what it would mean to me to see their little faces on my screen, let alone ever be able to hug them in person again?

The ceremony is absolutely stunning: the bride is beautiful, the groom is handsome, everyone is happy. I fight my natural bitterness, and instead try to remember a time when I believed in true love. I try to see the day through the bride's eyes, and I try so hard to remember what it's like to believe so strongly that someone will stay for life. During the ceremony, three eagles fly overhead and call out. It is an unimaginably cool moment. Many people at the reception make a point of speaking to me and telling me they appreciate the work I've done for Tese, or that they've heard stories about her and me together. It lifts me up. The speeches are funny and heartfelt, the dinner is beautiful, the first dance is amazing. Six hours after arriving, I slip out without saying goodbye to anyone. I know it's rude, but it's for the best. I'll follow up with notes of thanks in the coming days.

My motel has really poor cell reception. I'm not ready for bed, so I drive up the coast and park along the water. I wait for the cruise ships to go by, a favourite pastime of mine when I lived in this area. I told Wes I'd check in with him later, so I shoot him a text to see how his day has been. He's just putting the kids to bed and says he'll call in a little bit. When he phones we speak for just a few minutes, not about anything important. Our conversations these days feel short. There doesn't seem to be a whole lot to say to each other, even when there's so much I want to tell him. We keep saying each week we'll look at getting the podcast going again, but we haven't so far—he always has a reason to cancel. I leave tomorrow and I'll only be home for a few days before I leave again for California. I'm hoping I'll see him again before I go, but who knows. I have to be up crazy early to catch the ferry back, so Wes tells me to get some sleep, and we say goodnight.

I drive back to the motel and use the Wi-Fi to video Fox. There's a filter on Facebook that allows it to appear as if there is a cat on your head, and whenever one of us is away from the other we use it, especially when we're having a serious talk. We call it "cat hatting" or "cat hat chat." So on goes my cat hat, on goes hers, and I tell her about how low I got. I tell her about my full-on meltdown and puking. Tearfully, I tell her how close I came to going off the pier.

Her reaction is maybe one of my favourite things she's ever done, and it's not what I'd recommend someone do to anyone else, yet it was perfect. Cat hat on, glass of wine in hand, she extends a beautifully manicured fingernail toward the camera and taps delicately at the screen.

"Heeeeeeeeeey," she sing-songs at me, still rapidly and comically tapping at the screen. "Sounds like someone's finally hit rock bottom."

I laugh a bit, and she laughs, and then we're both losing it, hysterically laughing and I'm sobbing at the same time. I laugh until my sides hurt and I can hardly breathe. "Just get home," she tells me. "We will get it all figured. You're going to be OK." We say goodnight, and I crawl into my uncomfortable motel bed.

## July 8

I wake up at 3 a.m. and drive two hours south to the ferry terminal to catch a 6 a.m. ferry back. It seems last night's laughter was not a cure-all, because as we're loading the boat I'm struck with the eerie thought that I could drive my vehicle right off the ramp. The idea of it is less of a pull than the pier, but the thought crosses my mind nonetheless, which bothers me. I don't even go up this time—technically you're not supposed to sleep in your car on the ferry, but I don't care and decide they'll have to forcibly move me if they really want to argue about it. I push the driver's seat as far back and as low down as it will go, I ball my hoodie into a little pillow, and I sleep for the entire crossing.

When we unload I drive in a zombie-like state toward home. I have a good four and a half hours ahead of me, plus I'll have to cross town when I arrive to pick up the dogs and then circle back to my house. I am not in a good mood. About an hour and a half into my drive my mom calls me; she can tell I'm unsettled.

"Sounds like you're really missing him. I'm sorry."

"Today, Mama," I choke out the words, "I'm just really missing the kids." I cry so hard on the phone with her that I have to take a random exit and pull over to get my shit together.

It's lunch time when I pull into town and I'm grumpy and my back hurts from driving. I text Fox "Back, can I come by for a coffee on my way to get the dogs?"

She says yes and I head over. I don't stay long, just long enough to show her I'm back and I'm OK. I drive across town, grab my dogs, and head home. I feel bleak and dismal and autopilot-y. When the dogs and I arrive the first thing I see is the wasps nest Wes knocked down still buzzing with activity on my front step. *Fuck.* We enter the house by climbing up over the garden bed to avoid the nest. I open the door, get them some water, and then head directly to bed.

Post-nap I feel as if I could immediately go back to sleep. This isn't good; I have to keep moving. I force myself to go to the grocery store and grab a few basics. I pick up a can of Raid; I spray the wasp nest from a distance, which seems to have no effect other than really, really pissing them off. I leave the swarm of wasps behind me, shut the door, and go to bed unreasonably early.

## July 9

I have a plan. You know those beautiful garden goddess parties where all the women wear flower crowns and look like they're a sponsored Instagram post come to life? Yeah, this will be the opposite of that. We're calling it the garden goddess flower crown bullshittery, and it's basically just an excuse for all of us to get together and let loose a bit. Lucy and I could use it. I have to make plans like this to convince myself there are things worth sticking around for.

I text Lucy to see if she wants me to bring her a London Fog. I'm trying to make sure that in the midst of my own self-absorbed misery I'm remembering to be there for her struggles the way she's always been for me. She says yes, and I head over. It's nice to see her kids; they bring so much energy to the room, and we need it.

We're both struggling on completely different sides of the love spectrum, her in a marriage and me with myself. We laugh a bit about how outside the world we feel, like everyone else got sent this email to some rulebook we aren't privy to. Mostly we just ask each other questions and listen to the answers, which is rarer than one might expect. We give each other permission to have the struggles we're having. We reaffirm to one another that neither of us is crazy, that you love who you love. That we are the type of people who don't give up easy, who really mean it when we commit, and that that will come at a cost to both of us. We talk about how to any outsiders the solutions to our problems appear simple and cut and dry: Forget him. Cut contact. Move on. Meet someone else. These sensible ideas don't make sense to us, and we remind each other repeatedly that it's just time. Time, time, time. She is the strongest woman, and when I look at her I see the best and most generous side of what love has to offer.

After our visit I decide to wander down to her basement to pay James a visit. It feels weird to be in here at the same time as him. I've stayed here a lot, but we've never once been together in any dwelling he's lived in since he moved out of my house. We sit on the couch and catch up. He's eating a somosa. He takes a bit out of it and hands it to me. "I see you eyeing it."

I smile and laugh because I was eyeing it, and he does know me so well. We laugh a lot during this visit and it's really nice. We talk about stand-up comedy (a mutual love of ours) and our families. It's a short visit and then I head home to curl into bed with the dogs.

I'm just about asleep when my phone dings. I still have a large following on social media from my radio days and this message has come through on what could essentially be described as my fan page. It's a message from a listener whom I've never met before. She's writing to inform me that while she's struggled with whether or not to tell me, she wanted me to know that Wes has reached out to her on Tindr. Screenshots included. *Fucking awesome.*

This is the mega downside of having lived so much of my life in the public eye. I feel very, very, very fiercely protective toward Wes's reputation, though, so I'm quick to write her back and thank her for her concern. I inform her we broke up a while ago and while it's not my favourite thing to see or hear about, he has done absolutely **nothing** wrong in terms of anything regarding me. I feel a great need to make sure she doesn't think anything bad about him. The worst part is that I send James a screenshot of the woman's photo because she looks so familiar and ask him, "Do we know her?" Turns out it's a woman he dated after we split up. God damn, this town is too small.

Wes is a good person; there is nothing on the planet that will change my mind about that, not even the several similar messages I receive from other women in the subsequent days. Each message breaks my heart a little bit more, each screen-shot of the things he's said to them hurts my soul. This cannot be a person who is missing me. . .but every time I pretend to be unfazed. I clarify he isn't cheating on me, he's the best dude, we're no longer together, and I thank the women for their concern. Every message slowly confirms to me that he is moving on. I tell myself one day I will too. I fall asleep wondering if he's speaking as kindly to the world about me, as I am about him. I believe in my heart he is. I wonder if some small part of him still wants to protect me, the way he used to, the way he promised he would. I believe in my heart he does.

## July 10

I've arranged to have a cleaning company come today to do a deep clean on the whole house. This will be good for when Greyson moves into the basement suite downstairs, and also I'm sadly hoping it will have some energy-transforming effect on how I feel when I'm at home. The dogs and I head out into the woods to be out of the way of the cleaners. For several hours we wind through the hills and I listen to podcasts. When we get back, the cleaners are still there but my room is done so I toss the dogs in there for a nap and to keep them out of the way. I head to the gym. I lift weights mindlessly, but it feels good on my body. I don't feel super connected to my actions, but I try. When I finish, the cleaning company is still there. *Jesus, how dirty was my house?* I lock myself in my room and nap with the dogs. I seem to always be tired these days, which is ridiculous because everyone else around me is working way harder and doing way more. What do I even have to be tired about?

I'm starting to dread going to California, which is extremely unusual for me. At the height of my career I was often placed in situations involving crowds, which I was never comfortable with. Hosting charity events, music festivals, concerts. I always found so many people overwhelming. Palm Springs became my escape. It was where I would go on my time off to disappear. Granted, it's a place that broke me once, essentially where James and I had the final fight that ended our marriage. It took a long time after that before I could go back, but when I was ready to face it again, it became my strong alone place. My healing place. Now I have no desire to go, but if you're going to be miserable anywhere, why not be miserable in California? Maybe I shouldn't even go. I search my phone for events in the area for the thirteenth, the night I'm supposed to arrive. A SIGN. My all-time favourite band is playing about forty minutes away from the condo the night I get in. I do not want to go to a concert alone, at all, but this is 100 percent the universe telling me I should. I look down at my forearm where I have lyrics from The Counting Crows tattooed on me. *Guess I'm still going to California.* I swing down to the grocery store and buy myself a somosa for dinner because I haven't stopped craving one since James gave me a bite of his.

I'm excited when my phone rings and I see its Wes.

We have a really good talk, the best one we've had since we broke up. He asks if I've given any thought to getting the podcast going again, and I tell him I've thought more about "can we be friends" than the podcast itself, because without that, the podcast won't work. I know he wants to uncomplicate his life, and for things to be simple and easy.

"I still love you," I admit. "I'm still in love with you, and that in and of itself makes things complicated. I can't guarantee I'm even going to be good at being friends."

"I know," he replies. "I care about you a lot."

His response feels like a punch to the shoulder from a friend's older brother.

We don't dwell on the past, although he does summarize our time together as having been "an amazing six months." We talk more about how neither of us has a clue what we're doing with our lives, and that expectations for anything are a bad idea. We discuss allowing a friendship to unfold "organically."

"I get you want it to be simple, but you also have to be a friend if you want to have a friend, so not everything can be on your terms. Base minimum, you'd have to do me some friendship back."

"I know, and I want to," he says. We talk about some of the things we enjoyed about our relationship, like going to the movies, and maybe that's a way we can start spending time together. He seems to like the sound of that. In general, the tone is "let's not look back, let's look forward, let's do activities together every now and again, and let's just fucking see what happens." The call is just over an hour long, and I hang up the phone feeling cautiously optimistic.

I call Fox, who's bummed she can't come with me to California because of her schedule. (Side story, here's what a good person she is: Before I met Wes I was at the peak of my ability to be alone in the world. I had booked myself a trip to Palm Springs to spend New Year's Eve alone and was really excited about it. Fox surprised me by telling me she was coming, and I actually told her no because my alone time was that important to me. Now, seven months later, I have the balls to turn around and beg her to come with me because I don't want to be alone down there? What in the actual fuck is wrong with me, and why is she my friend?)

Fox and I decide to book another trip to California in September. We coordinate flights, we screen-shot schedules, we throw down our credit cards, and all of a sudden I have something I'm really looking forward to. I just have to get through this trip alone first. In bed I stare at the ceiling, thinking of Wes's words over and over again. "An amazing six months."

## July 11

I open my eyes. Something . . . oh, man, something is different! I wake in an amazing mood for no reason I can pinpoint. It's 5 a.m., and I'm full of beans. I throw music on in the kitchen and dance while I make coffee. I dance at the dogs and they eye me like I'm crazy. I have that happy, giddy feeling you get when you realize a guy you like likes you back and it's all flirty and adorable, only there's no flirting and no guy and no reason for it. The day is beautiful and the sun is coming up, but it's not hot yet, which is perfect for a pale, sun-burnable girl like me. I move my laptop out to the deck and write for several hours. Time disappears around me and suddenly it's just about 10 a.m. and I realize I'm supposed to meet my friend Seamus for a coffee.

Fuck! I toss the dogs out for a quick pee, swipe a brush through my hair and then dash out the door. Seamus is a law enforcement officer who I met several years ago at a country concert. I don't see him and his wife and kids as often as I'd like, but they're very dear to me. He's a badass-looking dude, a former rugby player with broad-set shoulders, a stern face when he's all business, but a shit-eating grin when he's off the clock. He has a loud, boisterous laugh that always makes me smile. The coffee shop is right by my house and when I pull up I see he's already there. He's in town working a case that will see him here during the day for the foreseeable future. He waves to me but motions that he's on the phone and will be right in. When he walks in, his hug is huge and just a little longer than normal. This is the first time I've seen him since Wes and I broke up. We order our coffees and go sit outside.

"So, what happened?" he asks.

I sigh deeply. This has nothing to do with Seamus, but in general I'm a little sick of summarizing everything for people, especially when I haven't wrapped my head around it myself. I try my best to give him the *Coles Notes* version. Seamus is, as I mentioned, a cop, and so he has a natural tendency to see things in very black and white terms. Good, bad. Wrong, right. Yes, No. He's also very protective of me and admits he has been concerned. In his summary, it's somewhat uncomplicated. The relationship was having a negative impact on me, on both of us, on my self-confidence, my drinking, now it's over, this is a good thing. If the house is painful for me, sell it and get a different house. And so forth. Nothing he says or advises to me is untrue, or even said without empathy. It's just such a linear way of thinking, and be it wrong or right, it's not how my mind or my heart works. This is the clarity other people have that Lucy and I were just discussing. It's always so easy when you're not the one living the situation. I explain that I feel selling my house would simply be evading working through my fears surrounding loneliness and putting off the grieving I'll need to face in terms of the kids.

"So what are you doing then? Are you writing the novel still?"

I tell him that the novel has come to a standstill in the wake of my new *11 weeks* project. I explain the concept.

"So . . . will there be a chapter about how you meet with a devastatingly handsome badass cop, then?"

"Well, if I meet one, I guess I'll throw it in."

He laughs. "While I'm up here for work, you want to try and get a standing coffee time going? Wednesday maybe?"

"Sure."

He has to head back to the office, so we hug again and off he goes.

Back at home, I'm about to continue writing when I get a series of text messages from Lucy. She's having a tough day and is planning on leaving work. I tell her I'll come into town and meet her for a coffee. I drive to the coffee shop when Lucy phones me to tell me she's in line at the drive-through getting our drinks.

"I'll meet you in your vehicle and then we can smoke."

"Perfect, see you in a sec."

Minutes later she hops in the passenger seat.

"I've turned you into a monster," she says handing me my order. When Lucy and I first started hanging out I drank only plain coffee and never from anywhere fancy. Now, with her influence, I have crafted possibly one of the most pretentiously revolting specialty coffee orders in history. Venti Americano Misto made with almond milk and three pumps of sugar free cinnamon dolce.

I laugh. "You did this to me! So what's up, not feeling the work vibe?"

Her face intensifies and she looks out the windshield. "You know, I just, got up from my desk and said, I'm going home now. And I left."

She is riding the "wavey ocean," as Jer likes to call it. It's that emotional state when the highs are high and the lows are low, and fucked if you know which one you're going to get hour to hour minute to minute, let alone when you wake up in the morning. She vents to me about the things she's thinking and feeling, and I reassure her that no matter what she does or thinks or feels, it's OK and I support her and she is justified. She does the same for me.

"Look at us," she says. "Quite a fucking pair."

"Yeah," I laugh. "Just a little matching set."

For an hour we joke and we listen and we swap stories of the things that are pissing us off, and when the time rolls around that she has to leave to go and pick up her kids, I'm happy to feel like on the whole we've done a lot more laughing than anything else.

"Hey before you go, can you take a picture with me?" I ask her. "I'm trying to send my mom and dad lots of pictures lately to show them I'm life-ing and stuff."

"Sure."

The photo turns out hilarious because the A/C is blasting in my vehicle so her hair is blowing in the wind like a goddamn supermodel. She looks so stunning; she is such a beautiful woman.

"Hey, thanks!" I call out behind her. "Weirdly I feel super good after that chat!"

"Me too," she yells back. "Come out with us tonight, I'll text you later!"

At home I water plants and do yard work; I keep music rolling all day. I still feel really great, possibly even better than I did in the morning. I hadn't planned on going out with Lucy and some of her other friends, but I kind of want to now. I'm back to my pre-Wes weight, and I try on outfits I haven't worn or felt good in for a long time. I text Lucy, "I think I'm gonna try and make it out tonight, what's the place and time."

She texts me back with where to meet.

My confidence had slowly been dwindling the last few weeks I was with Wes. I dressed up less and less because I felt I couldn't get it right. Wes and I had very different nutritional habits and I have an admittedly really unhealthy relationship with food. When we were together I'd slowly been packing the weight back on until I was up about thirteen pounds. It wasn't just the food either, it was the booze too. Fuck, I'm glad the weight came off so quickly after he dumped me and I went back to my regular eating and way, way, way less drinking.

It's liberating that dressing up tonight is only for me, and I really don't give a shit what anyone else thinks. As a result I put together one of the most blatantly ridiculous outfits I've ever worn out in public. It reminds me of a much younger me. I used to just absolutely not give a shit. My ex-husband called me "Boots" for years because of my penchant for wearing cowboy boots no matter what. That doesn't sound too ridiculous, until you see someone do it with fleece sleep pants, with a pencil skirt, or with a wedding dress. My closest friends know my secret favourite clothing item is an oversized men's reflective safety jacket I've had for years. I would go out in public wearing the most horrific combinations you've ever seen, safe in the knowledge that work would soon require me to throw on a ball gown for an awards show and I'd get to live another extreme. I felt so balanced back then.

I stare at myself in the mirror. I look like a complete fool, and it makes me insanely happy. I have on black dress shorts and a black shirt, with a spiked belt. I'm wearing intense black and flesh-coloured leggings, and motorcycle boots. I have an excessive amount of black eyeliner on and an unnecessarily messy ponytail. I smile at myself. I walk out to the driveway about to hop into the Jammer when I eye The Beast instead. It just sits there never getting used these days, even though I used to love driving it. Why did I buy a truck with Wes when we'd only been living together for 3 months at the time? A testament to how sure of one another we used to be. Now it's just a daily reminder of my consequences for believing in love. What an absolute waste of money. What an embarrassment. It's been too painful to use, so other than the load of yard waste to the dump with my folks I haven't been in it. It calls to me now. I run back inside to grab an adapter cord from the shop radio so that I can play music in it. Climbing up feels so good. It's a huge truck, totally unnecessarily large, and I could not look more ridiculous wearing what I'm wearing seated behind the wheel of this thing. Oh, wait. Yes I can. I light a cigarette. *Fuck, I feel so good right now. I wonder if this is what people who take drugs feel like?* I crank music so loud it literally hurts my ears, and I'm driving the tiniest bit faster than I should be. I sing at the top of my lungs. I try to crank the music again only to find I've maxed out the volume. I roll the windows down and let the summer evening air hit me in the face. I can't remember the last time I felt this good, this free, this happy. And I'm alone. I remember this. I remember being not just OK, but truly happy in moments of solitude. I notice my own word choice when I think it. Solitude, an entirely different thing than being alone.

As I fly down the highway I think of Wes's choice of words when we spoke the other day. "An amazing six months." I think of some writing he shared with me recently where he referenced his failed marriage and "a string of broken hearts in his wake." I think how different our relationship was to each of us. He is a novel to me, and to him, I feel, I am a nameless footnote rolled into a sentence . . . a "string of broken hearts." One of many. Not even singled out from the crowd. No significance amongst the others. Just another un-notable woman on his path to find himself.

"An amazing six months." These words reverberate in my head but I feel differently about them today than I have before. I am making peace with the fact that we will not remember each other and our time together the same way. I'm starting to recognize that his level of grief has no bearing on my own. I'm starting to give myself permission to suffer what this loss means to me, regardless of what it means to him. The two are undeniably mutually exclusive, and it's not about one of us being right or the other being wrong. It's about the fact that it truly is possible for two people to have been in the same relationship and have had entirely different hopes, goals, dreams, investments, and emotional connections to it. Why then would I ever expect him to grieve it to the same degree that I do? As if that might give me permission to be as sad as I am? "Nope," I think to myself. My experience was the truth to me, and his to him. How he will remember me has nothing to do with how I will remember him. The thought is so powerful and strong; I am overcome with a sense of epiphany that adds to the fiery joy I'm already experiencing. This, I tell myself, this is the work of being alone. This is the progress of facing the shit you don't want to face head on. Today I believe, for the first time, that I am going to be alright.

I have dinner with Lucy and two of her friends, who are both lovely. I don't stay long because, to be honest, the high I've been riding all day is maybe starting to fade. I'm still happy, I'm just coming down a little and the overstimulation of a pub is taking a toll on me.

I Text Fox. "I come by on my way home?"

"I'm not wearing pants. Deal with it." I'm alone laughing.

I reply, "Wait til you see what I'm wearing . . ."

"I hope it's reflective . . ." See. I told you, the safety jacket, it was "a thing."

I let myself into Fox's house, where she and her husband Clive are on the couch. True to her word, she has no pants on and she's eating ice cream with a spoon.

"I can has some?" She hands me the spoon.

Her husband grabs me a drink. I excitedly tell Fox about what an amazing day I've had.

"I'm so glad I'm finally fucking starting to . . . I dunno, just make peace with some stuff, and myself. Like a few days ago I was ready to jump off the pier or drive off the goddamn ferry, and tonight I had this whole realization when I was driving in about how he and I can think super differently about this, and it doesn't matter. Like, we were in the same relationship but we weren't, because what someone feels is real, and so my feelings about it are real no matter what and I don't have to feel crazy or bad or embarrassed about that. It was real to me, Fox." I want so badly for her to understand what I'm trying to say, but I'm talking so rapidly I'm not sure she's following me. "Two people can be in a relationship and have a completely different experience of it . . . they're both real, you know?"

She puts her spoon down, sets the ice cream on the table, and leans toward me, her eyes welling up with tears. "I know. I know exactly what you mean. There was a summer when I was a teenager, and I made friends with this guy. I met him through a guy I was dating at the time. Well, he had been injured in an electrical accident and, Roo, he was so hurt, he was horrifically disfigured in this accident. So he was off work, and I wasn't working, and we spent every day together. Not romantically. We'd hang out, we'd watch TV, we were just together all the time, for months, and he was like, my best friend, just the best. So time passes and I move away and we sort of lose touch but there was nothing bad about it, like I thought we were still amazing friends. I just cared about him so much and that time was so special to me, especially because he was recovering during it and whatever. So, I go to Mexico for this wedding and I see him, and I'm so excited and so happy! But he's weird, he's like, not being an outright asshole but just not nice, ya know, just dismissive. I don't know if it's because since then his buddy and I had broken up or what, but it's just off. So I call him out on it, right, and Roo I'll never forget this, so long as I live I will never forget what he said to me." The tears are blurring her eyes and I can tell just from looking at her that in this moment she's not even seeing me, she's seeing his face clear as day. "He looked me right in the face and said, 'I am sorry if our friendship meant more to you, than it did to me.'"

My heart breaks for her, because this, this is exactly what I was falling all over myself trying to explain, and I didn't need to use so many words, because she obviously knows.

"And I was like…" she shrugs sadly. "OK. Because obviously, yeah, it did."

We're quiet for a second.

"He died later and I wondered if I should go to his funeral, but I didn't, because I wasn't that important to him."

I crawl up onto the couch. It's divided into two recliners each designed for one person, but I sneak myself in next to her and she throws an arm around me. To be understood is beautiful, but the experiences that get us there, man, there's always a cost.

## July 12

The Fog is lifting. All the hurt is there, but now I'm starting to notice the world outside of it and beyond it. I'm anxious about California. I'm not sure if being alone is the best thing for me right now, but I know being alone has this magic way of providing me clarity and insight, and I could use that now more than ever. I text Wes to ask if I can borrow the GoPro for my trip in case I do any cool hikes or cycling, and he says yes, but it's at Greyson's place, where he's been staying, so I'll need to coordinate with him to go and grab. In the time I've known Greyson I've parked outside his place to pick up Wes or to swing him by to go and grab something, but I've never been inside. I bring him a coffee, which, along with my own and my purse, I precariously carry down the path that leads to his suite. He comes out to greet me. His place is stunning, there's a beautiful view of the water, and a swimming pool and a hot tub.

"Oh my god, this is so nice, why would you wanna come live at my dump of a house?" I say it jokingly but I am curious.

"Yeah, it's nice but just so expensive. Come on in, I'm just doing some work. Check this out." He slides over a book about the provincial park we've decided to go camping at in a few weeks. It's a place he's been to before and I've always wanted to go, so when he mentioned he was heading there I basically invited myself along.

"Awesome! I'm so excited!" I really can't wait. I know just being in nature will be good for me.

We sit at his kitchen table and I tell him all about yesterday and the high that I was riding.

"You were in the zone! It's a real thing." He proceeds to tell me about the "zone of proximal development," and I am fascinated. He tells me being "in the zone" was first noted by a psychologist in the early 1900's. I'm excited to read more about this.

I hear all about his recent camping trip and the beautiful waterfalls he saw and how much his dog loved it and how the company of his female companion on the trip was. He tells me about cold-calling for his line of work and makes the hilarious observation that he's perpetually concerned over contacting someone in a professional capacity and then accidentally reaching out to them via a dating app later. "So, what if it's like, you want neither my professional services, nor my 'personal' ones?"

I laugh super hard. I hadn't even thought about that. I could sit and chat with him forever, but he is trying to work. We make plans to hike later so I tell him I should hit the road.

I head to the drugstore to buy a new SD card for the GoPro, Wes said there wasn't one in it, but when I turn it on the first thing that comes up is an image of him and me in Cuba. We're in the ocean, my arm is draped around him, and we're smiling. Ughhhh. That girl had no clue what pain she was in for. I feel sorry for her even though she's me.

I can't even figure out how to get the damn camera out of the case to remove the SD card, so I let the lady in the store handle all of that. When she takes the case apart some sand falls out and she looks at me quizzically.

"Cuba," I say.

"Wonderful!" she smiles.

Not wonderful at the moment, I think.

At home I FaceTime my dad while I fold laundry. I tell him all about the concert I'll be going to tomorrow night when I arrive in California.

"They were just so bad last time, so if this time it's good it'll like be a sign or something . . ." I stop short.

"Bert?" he asks. "What's wrong?"

It's like someone has stabbed a screwdriver through my heart and cranked it.

I stare down into the laundry basket and then carefully, slowly and gingerly I hold up to the camera the source of my expression. A sock. Just one. A teeny tiny little sock, belonging to the most adorable three-year-old boy.

"Wonder how long I'll be finding stuff like this for."

"I'm sorry. California will be good for you."

I sure hope he's right.

I pack all afternoon and find more Cuba sand in both my carry-on and my giant checked bag. It feels oddly metaphorical to me, this sad sense there will always be these little granules showing up in places I wasn't expecting to see a reminder. Do other people feel like this ever? Or do they just go, "Shit, there's sand in my suitcase" and carry it out to the porch to shake it off never even acknowledging the source of these traces. Is the way I view the world always going to be so marred by emotion and sentimentality? I feel it's one of the things Wes least liked about me, and I wish I could change it. When I'm as packed as I can be, I load up several bottles of water, smother myself in sunscreen, leash up the dogs, and head out. The day is an absolute scorcher and the steep terrain of this hike will make it the most challenging one I have undertaken with Greyson so far. I hope I'm able to keep up. In the first five minutes I'm already dying. I feel sweat beads running down my forehead and my back. Thankfully he stops frequently in the shade so all of us, dogs included, don't get too overheated. We reach the summit over an hour later.

"We'll wanna tie the dogs up here," he advises me. I follow him down a narrow path and I can see why. We are so high up it makes me dizzy.

"This'll be a good view point." He moves closer to a rock right near the edge, and my feet freeze while I fight the instinct to move backwards away from the cliff.

"It's OK, there's one more ledge right below us so even if you fall it'd be bad but you're not going right over."

I step a little closer. "I don't know why this makes me so nervous . . . I'm actually dizzy." I force myself to sit next to him on the rock and once I'm there I can see what he means. I have no ability to estimate distance, but right below us is another ledge probably fifty feet down, and then beyond that is a drop off of certain death. (Later I'd ask Greyson his best guess of the ledge distance and he said only ten feet, so point proven.)

"Wow. It's beautiful, we're so high." We both take some pictures and then sit back down on the rock, perched above the world. Greyson points out the vantage point we did from another hike that seems so far below us now, to think it felt staggeringly high at the time.

"You know, it's weird right now," I say. "I know I'm supposed to be alone at the moment, and I know I'm not ready to 'relationship', but I just can't believe ever that life is intended to be lived alone. Doing life is just more fun with somebody else, you know?"

He nods. "Yeah, we all crave that companionship and contact."

"And all this thinking and sorting through I'm trying to do, it's like, sometimes I feel, why? What's the point of all this thinking? Sometimes it seems really self-serving."

We chat a bit longer and eventually I say, "We should probably go get those dogs, tied to a tree is cougar meal waiting to happen."

On the way back down we talk about some of the girls he's dated since his marriage ended and why it didn't work. One in particular is seeking more contact than he's comfortable with post-breakup. It's my assessment that some of these women are, or have attempted to be, more casual than they're really capable of.

"I can't do the casual thing," I tell him. "Sex takes so long for me to get there and it's so personal to me, so I just know myself well enough to know I'll get attached to someone when I do that. Think about it physically, guy vs. girl, for a woman you're actually letting someone straight up inside of you, and for me that has this huge emotional price tag." We talk about some of the more non-traditional approaches I've had in terms of my current friendships and the people I choose to keep in my life, in particular James.

"I think there's something about you, Roo, some way you have of being that makes these 'shouldn't work on paper' types of situations function."

I think about that for a second. "Ya know what, I don't tell a lot of people this, but Tese and Iwere fighting right before she died. The last thing I said to her was 'square peg round hole, I'm tired of trying to make this work,' and then she fucking died, and I hadn't meant it at all because she was so important to me. Whatever it was we were fighting about seemed so big at the time and was literally meaningless. So with James when he left, I had this weird relief that he was still a person in the world, and that as long as he wasn't dead that would always be better than what I'd already been through. No matter how mad I was at him, I just wanted him to be in the world, and still in my world."

I don't think often about how that experience with Tese shaped me. I do think often about how her death affected me, but now I'm seeing and wondering, did her death impact me anywhere near as much as how I had treated her when she was alive? Until I said it out loud to him, I hadn't really connected the dots on why I might be so good, for better or worse, at holding on.

When we get back down to our vehicles Greyson asks me what else I've got going on for the night.

"Nothing, wanna drop the dogs back off at the house and go for dinner?"

"Sure."

We ditch the pooches at the house where they can cool down and head to a pub just down the street. It's the same one Wes and I rode our bikes to, it's the same one I went to with Wes the night when we slept together. The patio is open for the first time of the season and after a short wait at the bar we sit outside. We talk about our upcoming camping trip and some of the hikes we can do. I'm a bit worried because my foot has been giving me some grief and is aching really bad. I hope it's better by then.

I check my phone and see I missed a call from Wes.

"Oh I missed a call from Wes."

"Yeah me too."

I text him and tell him: "sorry just having a post hike beer with Greyson." Wes had a special event for work, so I assume he's still there.

"I left cuz it was dead, need beer and food."

"I'm gonna tell him where we're at," I say to Greyson.

Wes writes back, "Perfect, see you in eleven minutes."

When Wes arrives I feel immediately self-conscious, and it's nothing he says or does, I'm just aware that I'm a sweaty gross makeup-less mess. Somehow, the camping trip comes up. I search his face for a sign he disapproves and then force myself to stop because, really, what would it matter? I care so much about his feelings and I don't want to do anything that would bother or upset him, but I also have to live, and this trip is one of the very few things I'm looking forward to lately. There's some laughing and some joking, but I mostly feel uncomfortable and I can't put my finger on the cause. Is it just that I feel I don't look good? Is it the fact that three weeks ago we could have been doing this exact same thing only all of the dynamics would have been different? I can't tell, and I guess I don't need to know right now. It's not bad, it just feels . . . different. When we go to leave Wes walks to his truck, and Greyson and I walk to his car.

"Hey," I hear Wes behind me. "Have a great trip." He opens his arms for a hug, which I accept far too awkwardly.

"Thanks." Greyson and I get in his car and leave.

I Text Wes that night before I fall asleep.

"It was nice to see you tonight."

"Same have a great trip."

"Thanks, I'll prolly call ya while I'm there if that's ok?"

"Ya ya, get some sleep before your flight."

## Week Four
## July 13

I am so happy when I make my way into the waiting lounge of the airport and spot a friend of mine. Two years ago, when James first moved out and I had my reduction surgery, I paid for a friend of a friend to come and live in my home for two weeks to care for my dogs. The idea was that since I was out of commission she would simply sleep in the spare room and look after the dogs. What ended up happening though was this incredibly deep connection whereby we bonded at one of the weirdest times in my life. She took as much care of me as she did Atticus and Ducky during those two weeks.

I wander up and throw my purse down next to her.

"Hello gorgeous, fancy meeting you here!"

She lets out a cry, delighted to see me, and we share a long hug, rocking back and forth.

"It is so fucking good to see you," I tell her.

"Oh my god you too! What's been going on?"

She and I don't live close and we both are always wrapped up in our own shit, so it's been months since we caught up. I regale her with my tail of heartbreak and low and behold if she isn't in the exact same boat. Oh my god do we laugh, and we aren't laughing at the guys, we're laughing at ourselves, and our behaviours, and the crazy the breakups bring out in all of us. She sees my microwave-smash attempt and raises me some late-night parking outside his apartment followed by a full-on cuss-out of a woman she believed him to be sleeping with. We fill up the whole somber early morning airport departure lounge with laughter. To see her riding the same wave as me—God, I don't wish it on anyone, but somehow it normalizes the experience for me. Even the best are sometimes broken, and laughing about it in that moment with someone who I love, it just feels perfect. Her flight departs slightly before mine and I'm sad to see her go, but I'll see her again soon at the garden party at my place.

The first flight is short and uneventful. I grab a coffee on my layover and then we load up again. On the second plane I'm seated next to a mother and daughter, and for some reason it makes me teary-eyed. I have no desire to "unpack" that emotion while on the plane, though, so I push it out of my mind and bury my face in a book. When I arrive at the condo I busy myself with the work of "opening it up." Turning the water, A/C and ice maker on, reconnecting the car battery, and a host of other small tasks to get it set. I drive to the store and get a few groceries, primarily craving a type of iced coffee I can only get in the U.S. When I'm home I throw on a bikini, pour myself the iced coffee, and sit on the pool deck. I listen to a podcast that Greyson has sent me the link to. It's about being "in the zone," and he attached a message saying he thinks it might speak to me in regards to my question about why we think, and where we find meaning in life.

The podcast does speak to me. It's a psychologist discussing how writing is the most demanding form of thinking, and how writing forces you into the zone of proximal development. There we are most able to self-examine, grow, analyze and learn, which in turn makes us better people, which in turn becomes "an antidote to the catastrophe of life."

It makes me feel as though all of this inward looking I'm doing through my writing isn't as selfish as I sometimes feel it is. Maybe pawning it off as selfish is another way to simply avoid having to confront the uncomfortable feelings we'll often find when we look too hard at our own behaviours, thoughts, actions, and feelings. I send Fox the link too. I think she will think it's really rad. I Facebook video her.

"What's going on?"

She's in her bathing suit as well, enjoying a beautiful day by the lake where she lives.

"I sent you a thing you gotta listen to from this podcast. Also, I need you to tell me to go to the concert. I'm very much in a don't want to do this alone mood . . . and if they suck, I'm gonna be pissed."

"They won't suck, and you got this."

Each minute the concert draws nearer my anxiety builds. I force myself to get ready, throwing on jean shorts, a tank top, my black motorcycle boots, and an abundance of makeup. I drive forty minutes out into the desert, my stomach riddled with dread the whole way. The show is at a casino, and I'm worried I won't be able to find where I'm supposed to go. I'm doing the thing where I worry about things before they've even happened. It's a specialty of mine. Fortunately, parking is readily available and easy. But now what if I can't find what part of this maze the concert is in? The concierge at the hotel part of the building gives me clear directions slowly and precisely, which I am bound to screw up. I don't, and I find the venue easily. So far so good. There are people milling in the foyer and I can't quite bring myself to go in yet; it's too crowded in there. I find a shaded palm tree and sit on the grass to smoke and people watch. Everyone here is with someone; I don't see another person by themselves. I recall telling James I'd be coming to this alone and was happy when he told me he once went to a concert by himself in his early twenties. The way he spoke about it I could tell it was impactful, although he admittedly said it was weird and he didn't stay for the full thing but he felt cool about it afterwards. I smile trying to picture a young James alone in a crowd. OK, if he can do it, I can. I stand up and walk to the line of people waiting to enter. When I'm let inside I'm happy because my seats are really good, but I'm choked because the most awful woman on the planet is seated directly behind me. This show has an opener, but she was under the impression there was a second act on the bill. I laugh to myself when she references a terrible '90s band she thought would be here. For the next thirty minutes she complains vehemently behind me, lamenting their absence. The absurdity that this person would be concerned with that act over the one we're here to see allows me to find it mostly comical, but her voice is like a drill in my ear hole. I have to get away from her. I leave to pee and grab myself my one beer for the night. On my way back in I spot a merch table with a beautiful black hoodie I'm dying for. I pick it, and a blue T-shirt. The guy managing the table looks at me oddly as he's processing my payment.

"Only person tonight who's bought a hoodie in 104-degree weather."

"Yeah well, I like to buck the trend." He smiles at me.

"This is there walk-on music, you should get in there."

I grab my stuff and walk back toward the doors. *Please God, just let this be good, I need this to mean something.*

They start with the song whose lyrics I have tattooed on my arm. I've never heard it live before and it's . . . oh God it's better than I knew music could be. I don't even go to my seat, I walk right down one of the aisles and stand as close as I can get, spellbound, captivated. I sing along at the top of my lungs, and when I know my favourite words are coming I turn my phone on and record the line. In person. The words, just hearing them for real, hearing it live, being here. I put my phone in my back pocket and I start to cry. The lights, the sounds, the people, the music, the guitar, everything just seems to have meaning right now, this experience feels so profound. I know in this moment, that this is exactly where I am supposed to be, and I am supposed to be here alone. Why? Why is this amazing experience something I won't get to share with anyone that I love? Why am I meant to be so far away from everyone that matters to me, experiencing something I've always wanted, something so special to me, by myself? For two full hours I am in a trance. I cry but I feel my cheeks stinging from how hard I'm smiling. All of the lyrics, even the ones to the few songs I've never particularly liked, now seem to be significant and powerful. My heart is wide open and every note, every word just hits it again and again and again.

Before I leave I text Wes a photo. His responses are short and sporadic; he's busy with a work thing. I tell him I'll let him go get at it then.

"Glad the concert was awesome."

Why do I keep reaching out to him? Is the sense that he's always busy or not really interested in talking real, or is it just in my head? I want to believe that he and I can be friends and that maybe the podcast will still be doable, but my hope is fading each time he seems indifferent to my efforts.

On the forty-minute drive home I ponder my life and my choices, and the decisions that have led me to be alone here tonight. Wes was never going to come with me on this trip, and perhaps even that itself should have been a telling sign. I'd told him over and over again how important this place was to me. I'd gone on two trips he'd chosen the location for, one of which was Vegas—a place I had zero interest in, but it was important to him and so I truly wanted to see it. The trips were fun and amazing, and we'd had a wonderful time together, but my trip sat un-booked, undiscussed. So I had booked to come alone and he had seemed OK with it at the time. Hell, I was OK with it at the time. All these little details, little choices, little decisions, so under-thought in the moment, and now I feel I will be scrutinizing them to death for years to come. Was that the wrong choice that made him he realize he didn't want to live his life with me? Or maybe he realized it when I didn't attend a cabin trip with him and some of his friends a few weeks before we broke up. Worse yet is the idea, and probable reality, that it was a series of mistakes I made that all added up to his one clear thought: "I don't want this person in my life, or my children's lives."

I facetime Dad when I get back to the condo to let him know I had a great time at the concert and am home safely. I have one beer out on the pool deck, and then I head to bed. Weird the places the memories live. Wes has never been to this condo, but when I was here back in January we were newly dating and Facetimed a whole bunch, from the master bedroom. I walk in and flip the switch, staring blankly at the spot on the floor where I sat so my phone could reach the charger, talking with him late into the night and laughing and laughing and laughing. *Nope. Fuck this.* I shut the light off and sleep in the spare room.

## July 14

I wake up assuming it's near or around 6 a.m., only to discover its 8:30. Unusual move for me, I must have really needed it. I'm irritated with myself, though, because these dessert days get hot really quickly and the only way to sneak in physical activity is to do it early before the staggering heat makes it impossible. I load up one of my dad's backpacks with water bottles, slip on my shoes, and drive toward a hike that ends in a waterfall, which Lucy and I have done before. It's my favourite in the area. You have to pay to do this hike and the woman behind the counter smiles and greets me.

"Meeting someone or hiking alone."

"Alone."

"Oh see, you're doing it right, you'll really get to enjoy the trail the way it's intended to be enjoyed."

"Yeah, I guess so. Thanks."

She puts a yellow wristband on me and hands me a guide book, which I don't need because I know the way. The trail makes me nostalgic for the hike Wes and I did in Nevada together. The landscape is really similar. When will everything not remind me of him? It honestly makes me feel like such a loser. I wonder if he has these hints of me everywhere, or if he just goes about his day able to forget I exist until my name pops up on his phone or there's a specific reason for us to have contact. I don't "enjoy the trail the way it's intended to be enjoyed." It is beautiful, and I stop to take the odd picture, but the sun is blistering and the heat sweltering, and I find myself pushing to the brink of exhaustion to reach the top, where I know it will be shaded. When I hit the summit almost an hour later, I'm irritated that the falls are overrun with couples lounging in the water. It's much shallower, and the fall runs much weaker than when last I was here, in January. I peel my clothes off down to my bathing suit and put my toes in the water. It is beautiful, and the shade feels so good. I dread having to hit the sunny trail again to make the descent. After a good half hour of chilling out, I decide I should make my way back down, and I do it in record time, almost three times as fast as I made it to the top.

The day is filled with listlessness. No matter what I'm doing I have this odd sense that I'm neglecting some important responsibility. Each time I open the sliding glass door to go on or off the pool deck, I have the sense that a child or a dog should be right behind me. I am riddled with this inexplicable anxiety like someone or something needs tending to, and I'm not there to help. I think on this feeling and I know that it is me missing the kids. I haven't learned to turn off the part of my brain that subconsciously analyzes their safety in each situation. I still feel a twinge of panic when a car drives too fast in a parking lot, reaching out to grab a shoulder that isn't there. I still get a knot in my tummy looking at the deep end of the pool. I still apply my sunscreen and then feel like, "Who's next?" even though I'm alone. I'd honed a skill that I no longer needed, but it's there still, searching for them. I know they are safe, I know they are ridiculously loved, but it's not just my heart that's aching for them these days, it's literally my mind. It has yet to comprehend. *Put those skills to rest, my dear, no one needs or wants them now, and you were never that good at it to begin with.*

Wes texts me early in the evening and we exchange a few messages about a painting he wants to buy for his new place . I tell him I really like it, and I do. It's so incredibly him, but it feels slightly off discussing furnishing for the home he's buying and the new life he's starting that I'm not part of. I am absolutely shocked when the next image he sends me is of his son. *Oh my God, oh my hear*t. It feels like it's been forever since I've seen his little face. He has his beach bucket in hand traipsing through the water at the lake. He also sends me a selfie of him, shirtless, ball cap on, lounging in a yard chair, eyes squinting into the sun and brightness of the day. He looks fucking amazing. Kind of cruel, I think, but know it was well-intentioned. I don't want to see what I can't have. I keep staring at the picture of his son. I want to scream at him, "Thank you, thank you for letting me see his little face! I've been dying inside, I've been fighting myself every day to call you constantly and ask about them."

Instead I write back: "Omg thank you so much for the pic of him, you have no clue how much I miss them. Great pic of you!! Looks like its smoking hot there!!"

Another picture comes through and it's his daughter dressed as a superhero. Oh god, she's just . . . there's no words for how these pictures of them make me feel.

I write again "Ahhh frick she's so gawd damn adorable."

No more responses come from him, and I "Roo" hard. Have I said the wrong thing? Probably. Time to spin out. I re-read what I've written, and be it wrong or right I think I spot where I've gone wrong. What idiot in their right mind would tell a single dad who has struggled so hard with the moments when he can't be with his children "you have no clue how much I miss them"? Of course he knows, he knows it in a way that I never will, and I feel like an idiot.

I send another message: "Also I think that sounded wrong...you know what it's like to miss your own kids obviously more than anyone facepalm* I just mean I miss them tons is all...didn't mean it to sound as weird as it came out."

Fifteen minutes later when he still hasn't replied I send one more text: "Sorry."

A minute later comes: "it's ok no worries."

Fucking text messaging. There's no tone, there's no way for me to know if I have in fact stepped in it, and if my messages are making things better or worse. *Chill the fuck out Roo, you're doing the best you can.* Wes loves avocados so I send him a shot I took of one this morning.

"May I present you with a giant avocado as a subject changer?" The photo is one so big I can barely wrap my hand around it. I get an

LOL and one or two more messages and then another LOL, which leads me to believe I need to stop bothering him. I chuck my phone in my suitcase so I'm not tempted to text again.

I promised myself that while I was here I would not hermit in the condo like I normally do. When I worked a public job, it made sense for me to disappear to what is essentially a ghost town this time of year. Most of the snowbirds don't come to this gated community in the dead heat of summer, and it's normally eerily silent, like a scene from some post-apocalyptic film. Now, though, it doesn't make sense. I need to push myself to "people." In my suitcase I have several beautiful dresses that Fox lent me, so I sigh heavily and begin putting one on. It's gorgeous really, a stunning beaded bodice that transitions into a fuchsia full-length gown. I pull half my hair up, allowing the rest to fall down across my shoulders, and apply some makeup. I throw on cute pink flip flops that match and I head to the main strip. I drive myself because I have no intention of drinking, and I'm happy that I find a free parking lot right along the main strip. Now to find somewhere to eat. I wander, aimlessly, observing the people and the establishments. I keep hoping some place will "feel" right and I'll want to go in. I'm not feeling it. Every patio I pass seems overwhelming, the people already grouped up and paired off, tons of empty seats but somehow it feels like nowhere will have room for me. When I've walked for almost forty minutes I realize my feet are killing me, as long walks in flip flops are less than ideal. Not only that but now I have to walk another forty minutes back, and I'm still starving. I feel oddly embarrassed passing many of the same people on my way back to the car. I'm not exactly inconspicuous in this dress; do they think I'm lost, that my date stood me up? Almost two full hours later I make my way back to the condo and scarf down a bagged salad. I tear the dress off and put my bathing suit back on. My feet are blistered really badly, on the bottoms of each and in between my big toe and second toe on each. It's really painful and I'm mad at myself because I've probably put myself out of commission for more big hikes while I'm here, let alone the impact this might have on my pre-existing foot issues and the hikes Greyson and I were gonna tackle on the camping trip. *Fuck*. I Facetime my dad and explain my failed mission to dine alone.

"You'll get it tomorrow," he tells me.

I throw myself on the couch and just lie there watching the overhead fan spin.

My phone dings. It's Wes. That's a positive sign; I'm really surprised to hear from him again today. He has a suggestion of a show he thinks I'd like. I write him back and tell him I'm embarrassed to admit it but I've already watched it all; however, I'm making up for my show consumption by hiking lots. We go back and forth a bit. I send him some hiking pictures, one of a super disgusting bug I saw on the trail. Around 10 at night he doesn't reply further, so I toss my phone in my bag and crawl into bed.

## July 15

I wake up extremely early and decide I'm going to try and go for a bike ride, but fucked if using the pump to get it ready to roll doesn't seem like way too much work. I'm just not in the mood to have to do shit to be able to do shit, so instead I Google another hike and drive 20 minutes out into the desert to the trailhead. There's a multitude of trail heads here actually, and I'm a little uneasy because I'm totally alone, this place feels remote, I see no other cars, and I have a propensity for getting turned around. Just go, I tell myself. I pick a route whose name includes the word "loop" because, logically, I figure worst case scenario I'll stay on the trail and it'll bring me back to where I started. Right away I sense my feet are going to be a huge problem, my blisters are killing me and every step I take is painful. I'm curling my toes weirdly to try and keep the blisters from making contact with the material in my shoes, but I know the weird way that makes me walk is going to end up making my hips or my back sore. Fortunately the loop is short and I'm back at the car in under an hour and a half. I take my shoes off in the car and look at my feet. The blisters are slick and red and hurt like absolute crazy. *God damnit. Why did I have to wear those stupid flip flops out?* I bargain with myself that while I hate not hiking I'm going to be more mad if I can't hike when I camp next week and that I need to just take it easier so they can heal.

When the evening rolls around I've worked myself up for "go out alone" attempt number two. Again I get dressed up, colourful leggings, high heels, shorts and a black tank top. I drive to a local brewery nearby that serves food and order myself a chicken salad. I still feel conspicuous sitting alone at a high-top table sipping my water waiting for my food. (Maybe it's the neon leggings.) I tell myself that's just my ego talking, because no one is actually looking at me. Funny the things I see now, not glued to my phone, not with anyone. I have become an expert observer. A man with a much younger date who he's clearly trying to impress—it works a bit when she sees he knows the bartender. Ah, to be young and impressed by such bullshit again, I'll pass. A mother and father out on a date night, and she keeps anxiously pulling her phone out of her purse to look at it.

"Sorry, last time I promise, just making sure the sitter hasn't sent anything yet." He rolls his eyes each "last time" she checks. An entire family of people wordlessly eating, all engrossed in their phones. They don't speak the whole time I'm there. My salad arrives and the chicken is pink but the waitress has already wandered away. I stare at it. Wait a few minutes until I can catch her eye again to get her attention, she wanders back over.

"What?"

"I'm so sorry, I never do this, but I can't eat it like this." The petite waitress looks irritated but grits her teeth and tells me, "I'll get them to remake it."

Great, there's totally going to be spit in my food now.

It comes a second time and I eat bits of it but mostly just shove the food around on my plate to create the illusion of consumption. I pay; tip generously for no reason in particular and drive back to the condo. I text Wes to see how the rest of his weekend has been, he's busy helping Greyson load his stuff for the move into my suite. How is this all happening? What a weird weird life I'm living. I tell him: "Well... this, then your move...then hopefully everyone just stays where the fuck they at for a looooong time" with a little crying laughing emoji face. I get an LOL back, which to me is code for, "I have nothing else to say and I'm busy." Greyson and I chat on messenger and he tells me about getting everything loaded up. I ask him about the most recent camping trip he's been on, and he sends me some unreal pictures. I decide its vodka time for some reason. We talk a bit about supplies for our trip; primarily me explaining I'll be good as long as we have coffee and I don't get too hungry, then I'll be terrible to be around. I heads him up that I've fucked my feet up even worse than when I left, but that I'm hoping it'll be all good by the time we're supposed to go. He tells me we can keep the hiking less intense too if needed. I'm relieved because I really didn't want to be a killjoy but I'm not sure what I'm going to be capable of.

I drink more vodka alone in the dark. I sit on the pool deck scrolling through Instagram, a friend of mine posts a story of his daughter. She's speaking to one of those automated phone systems asking it to play a song. Her little voice squeaks with excitement on the few occasions she can actually get it to register.I think of Wes's kids calling out to the automation system in his new truck. I think of their car seats and how I'd finally gotten good at doing them up without help. I picture tiny shoes, and tiny clothes, and tiny socks. Tiny little moments, tiny little items, tiny little people . . . the world's biggest loss. I crawl into bed hugging my pillow, determined not to cry, but I do anyway. I just miss them so much.

## July 16

It is my "un-aversary." James and I ended our marriage on the same date that we were wed, years later, so that's fucking awesome. Why not make that date a double whammy. I sip coffee at the kitchen table staring blankly at the wall waiting for time to pass so I can head to the spa. I've booked myself for a massage, an updo for my hair, and a French manicure. I wonder what James is doing today and how he'll pass the time. I genuinely hope he's with his girlfriend or at least family so he has some company. After all this time I still feel so protective of him. I will still always always care what happens to him and worry about his happiness. There's a stillness to this morning that's unsettling. I never expected I would face another "un-aversary" alone. I think of waking up next to Wes, I loved that so much. I'd hear him moving, and look over. He'd be eyeing me sleepily, hair messy, so incredibly sexy in the mornings. He'd give me a boyish grin and say,

"Sup?" always followed a few minutes later when he was more awake by, "How'd you sleep?" Having someone to ask you how you slept is so underrated. It's like "I just laid next to you for eight hours, but the first thing I need to know still is how are you, if you're OK." I miss that so much, and this morning I miss my life with Wes so much.

When I head to the spa I tell myself it's going to be a good day. I love the place where I'm going, and I've been a frequent and good customer over the last few years. It becomes a clusterfuck. First of all, there's been a miscommunication regarding the type, start time, and length of massage I'll be getting. Whatever, fuck it, a massage is a massage so I'll be happy either way. It is a really good massage. I lie face down on the table to start and with each forceful stroke I will myself to let go of all the sadness I'm holding onto. It doesn't work, but mentally I try so hard to get there. Every time I catch my mind wandering to Wes and the kids I remind myself "just focus on how this feels on your muscles." I fight every step of the way to be present in my body enjoying the moment instead of trapped in my head. After the massage I was scheduled to get an updo from one of their hair stylists. I figure I can wear it out tonight along with a really hot dress of Fox's. Except they only have me down for a wash and a blow dry and the stylist doesn't have time to actually style my hair.

"Don't worry," he assures me, "I can set it with a blow dryer in a way that will make you look like a Victoria's Secret Angel." This proves to be a lie. The hair washing is admittedly nice, but when he blow-dries he pulls much too hard on my hair, and I can smell it burning. It's too hot on my scalp.

"That's pretty hot," I say more than once, and then finally, "Ouch, you're burning my head."

"Oops, sorry," he giggles. Well, I'm glad he's having a good time. When he is done, I look just fucking awful. The blowout is less Victoria's Secret Angel and more *Real Housewives*, or *Stepford Wives*, or some bullshit type of wife that looks nothing like me. It's got volume, but not the good kind, and he's blown it into these weird curls that jut in toward my face. It's like a child's beauty pageant hair, like some fucked-up doll style.

"It's great," I say, because I'm me, and I know I'm going to pay regardless, and it's already done.

He smiles, thrilled to death with himself, and I want to punch him and his paisley shirt right in the face. I should have known not to let him touch me, because his hair is stupid and people with stupid hair like to do stupid hair to other people. I can't believe I'm paying like 100 bucks for this bullshit. At least I still have my French manicure . . . which the esthetician then balks at doing.

"I didn't have you down for a French manicure."

"Well, I have it right here in my email." I hold up my phone and show her, she squints at it emphatically and disbelieving.

"Nails aren't long enough for a French."

"Pretty sure they are, cuz I've had them a million times before and this is the longest my nails have ever been, I grew them out specifically for this."

"Won't look good, you want other colour? Something sparkly maybe?"

She has one of my hands in her hand and she's already rubbing cream on it.

"You know," I snap and pull my hand back. "I'm done here. Like, this whole thing hasn't been anything of what it was supposed to be, I'm already paying for stuff I didn't want, and now I just wanna go home." I storm out of the manicure station and up to the front counter.

"I'd like to pay for everything now, please."

The woman behind the counter looks concerned. My eyes are tearing but I'm not sad. I'm pissed off.

"You don't want your manicure."

"Nope, just want to pay and go please."

The esthetician follows me up.

"I'm sorry! I can do French for you! Don't cry!"

I put my hand on her shoulder and say "this," motioning to my tearful face, "this has nothing to do with you, so don't feel bad, just a bad day."

I throw down my card to the tune of $265, absolutely furious about it.

I skip the tip option but hand the woman behind the counter a twenty. "Please give this to the massage therapist, she was really good." I say the words, but there is zero delight in my face.

"Sure you're OK? You don't want to stay?"

"Yes, and absolutely not." I angrily jam my credit card back in my wallet and walk out.

I call my mom on the drive back and tell her about it: "I'm just so fucking irritated because this was supposed to be my big super-relaxy distraction from it being my un-aversary day, and I left there so much more mad then I went in."

"Well, how bad is the hair?"

"Oh Mom . . . it's fucking awful."

"Maybe you can fix it? You're pretty great at doing your hair these days."

"I don't even know if I brought my flat iron . . . the worst part is, if I didn't bring it, then to fix it I'm going to have to wash it, and Meesha just did a whole bunch of highlights and stuff so I'm really not supposed to wash it that often, too hard on the hair. I'll just have to put it up somehow or something."

"Well, there are some curling irons under the sink and some rollers and stuff so use whatever you need. We're off to another show now so we should go."

She and my brother are in New York and are seeing multiple shows a day on their trip.

"K sounds good, love you."

"Love you too." I hit the condo, crawl into bed and pull the blankets over my stupid hair.

When I wake up I stumble into the bathroom, fighting to shake off post-nap grogginess. My hair has somehow stayed exactly the same. Exactly. *That firm hold hair spray using son of a bitch.* I sigh and stare at myself. This is not gonna work for me. I dig through my bag and finally come up with my flat iron. *Yes! I can work my magic.* I manage to smooth out the giant rolls he's done in the middle portion, split up some of the giant barrel curls into smaller waves, and work my mane into a sleek style that has a bit of bounce at the bottom. It's still not my favourite look but it's much better. I decide I'm going to catch an Uber back to the strip and make myself eat and drink at one of the establishments, no backing out, no hole in the wall place nearby, full on public situation. I'm going to do this right. I grab my favourite dress of Fox's. It's sleek and tight and really flattering, it looks amazing on her, and I'm hoping tonight the dress will lend me some of her foxy mojo. I'm bigger in the bust than she is, though, so I have to remove my bra altogether to sneak into it. How in God's name I manage to get it done up, I couldn't tell you (I'd needed her to assist me with it five days ago when I tried it on) thank god for stress weight loss. It goes on like a glove. I do my makeup and listen to music, humming along while I paint my face. When all is said and done I check myself in the mirror and I feel like I look really good. I take a selfie against the mirrored closet door in the master bedroom. Hmmm. I want a picture that isn't a selfie, it seems less pathetic. When Lucy and I were here this time last year, the only other people we saw, or have ever seen in the condo complex, were two douchey young frat boys blasting terrible music. I noticed them again out in the pool earlier today. I wonder if they're still there. I wander through the condo and can hear them before I see them as I approach the sliding glass door. They're blasting rap music riddled with "N" bombs and a shudder runs through me. Why is it always the whitest most privileged looking dudes I seem to notice listening to this type of music? I slide the door open. There are actually three of them today, the two original frat boys, tatt'd and muscle shirt-ed out, and one very sweet kind-faced chubbier Hispanic young man. He meets my eyes with a smile.

"Hi guys!" I wave.

The frat boys jab each other in the ribs and laugh and whisper and laugh some more.

"Hello," says the kind faced young man.

"Look, this is really embarrassing, but I wanted to get a photo before I head out for the evening, and I don't have anyone here to take a picture. Would one of you mind?"

This sends the douche bags into stitches. God, I'm only thirty-three, is the site of me dressed up really so laughable? Am I such a fucking joke? I feel like I look pretty good. The kind-faced kid stands up from his pool lounger and wanders over. "No problem."

He takes the camera and I back up toward a palm tree.

He takes two pictures.

"Thanks so much," I say as I grab my phone back.

He looks at me with what? Kindness? Sympathy almost? Then says much too softly, "Anytime, anything you need."

Weird. I wander back into the condo, their laughter echoing across the pool behind me, and grab an ice coffee to perk myself up more before I leave. I screw around in the kitchen for several minutes, grab some jewelry, and touch up my makeup. I wonder how the picture turned out, if it's good I'll send it to Fox and Lucy.

I unlock my phone to look at the image, and recoil in horror. OH MY FUCKING GOD. The dress is made of material that, when dampened by sweat, is very visible. The sweat from my boobs, and my lack of bra, has accumulated right where my nipples sit, just below my own line of site when looking down. It appears 100 percent as though I have lactated through my dress. I start laughing, like really hard. No wonder they were laughing, I legit look like my milk leaked everywhere. I'm honestly not sure what's worse, if they thought I was lactating or if they knew it was just sweat. I brace myself against the counter, I'm laughing so hard. Any other place, any other people, maybe I'd care, but at max I'll see these guys across the pool once a year, and I have no desire to impress them anyway. It makes me laugh to think they'll get to go home telling their friends about the crazy chick with the leaky nipples who asked them to take her photo. The moment has been immortalized, I hope. Somewhere in my crazy wandering while laughing I put my phone down and now can't find it. I Facebook message James from my tablet and ask him if he could call it for me so I can phone Uber. He does. It's back in my suitcase and I dig for it frantically.

"Hiya!" I exclaim. "Have I got a story for you!" I explain what just happened with the photo and the leaky nipple shot.

"Oh my god, Roo," he laughs.

"I know, right?" His laughter perks me up.

"I'm going to change, obviously, and then head in for dinner, but can we talk when I'm back?"

"Yeah, for sure, try me when you're home."

I slip into a black non-sweat-revealing dress. Thank god Fox lent me such an assortment. It's like a black tank top that attaches to a layered frilly mini skirt with lots of playful colours. Much better, I tell myself. I walk out to the condo gates and catch an Uber. The driver is originally from Brazil but relocated to Palm Springs for his wife's work. He is very pleasant and seems like I person I would actually like to know. Maybe that's why I decide to explain to him.

"Look, I'm forcing myself to go out, but I don't know the area super well. I'm hoping to find an outdoor place with live music and pretty patio lights. I only say live music outdoors because I'm deaf in one ear and I can't hear anything if the music is too loud. When it's outdoors it tends to be a little less overwhelming for me." I actually think it's kind of funny I'm worried about being able to hear. Whom exactly? Whom will I need to hear while dining alone?

"I know just the place . . . you like Mexican food?"

"Love it."

"Oh, this place is perfect then."

We talk politics while he searches for the establishment. He knows he's seen it, but he just has to find it. He keeps intermittently apologizing, telling me, "You're probably annoyed, I swear I'll find it."

"Honestly, this is the only good conversation I've had in person since I've been here so I'm seriously OK, take your time."

We are deep in discussion when he excitedly proclaims, "Aha! Found it!"

It's stunning, it's perfect, it's better than I could have imagined. The whole thing is shaped like a circle with the exterior of the circle a covered bar. The interior of the circle is a stone terrace open courtyard with vines growing all around and a small stage. It feels private from the street but is packed inside with every different type of person you can imagine. There are families with tiny little kids, there's a young couple on what appears to be a date that's going very very well, there's two bros in ball caps sipping beers. My eyes are so happy to take it all in.

The hostess is a beautiful young black woman with a showstopper of a smile. "Just you?" she says, seeming genuinely shocked I'm alone.

"Just me," I beam back at her, for the first time on this trip not feeling embarrassed about it.

"Get it, girl." she winks at me and leads me to my seat.

The waiter brings me chips and salsa, and I order a beer. The atmosphere here is perfect. I wish there was something like this at home. Actually probably a good thing there isn't because I'd be there all the time. My beer comes and it goes down much too easily. The band starts to play and, amazingly, it's the perfect volume. *Holy shit, am I in the zone again?* I think I might be because things are just feeling right. I text Lucy a picture of me sitting alone.

She replies, "I wish I was there! It looks amazing, and you look amazing too! Did you cut your hair or did they just style it differently?"

I write back, "They styled it differently, it was a whole thing. If I'm not back too late I'll call you."

I take pictures of the garden terrace and the stage and the band, and then, again, I make a conscious decision to put my phone away until I'm done with the evening. The food is delicious; I drink beers in rapid succession. I get overly enthusiastic when the whole crowd sings "Happy Birthday" to a patron named Glenda on her seventieth.

The keyboard player from the band makes eyes at me while he sings. I'm not being crazy he definitely is. Possibly the lead singer too. OK, I must be drunk then. In between the next two songs the lead singer says right at me

"Come dance pretty lady" and I shake my head no and laugh. Several songs later they play one of Fox's favourite songs, and it makes me miss her so badly . . . I know she'd want me to dance. Inspired I get up there and giv'er. I don't dance with anyone in particular, and I mostly just sway because my stilettos don't allow for much more movement than that on a stony floor, and my feet hurt, but it does the trick. When the band takes their first break the lead singer comes over and chats with me. He is mid forty-ish, handsome and funny, but has an air about him like he probably chats up every woman who ever sits alone in this restaurant. I let him know I'm leaving soon, and he scribbles his number on the back of a business card.

"That's my personal one," he emphasis. "Call anytime."

No sooner does he leave than the keyboard player wanders over. I knew I wasn't crazy. When I extend my hand to shake his he pulls it in close and kisses my hand.

"How come such a beautiful woman is here dining alone?"

"It's a long story," I tell him. He too gives me his number and suggests I come back again tomorrow night.

"I'll be back in fall with a friend," I tell him. I know Fox is going to absolutely love this place, and I'm so excited to bring her with me in September.

As I'm heading to the street to get in the Uber I feel myself doing the walk you do when you've had a little too much to drink and you're specifically trying to walk like you're not drunk. In these heels this is a deadly game. Each step is careful and calculated and while I think I look OK I know I probably don't. Inside the Uber I remove my shoes and rub my feet. My blisters are horrible now; I'm really making any chance at hiking on my camping trip difficult. *Idiot.*

Back at the condo I video-chat James. He seems off, though, and I'm not sure how deep into it I should look or if he even wants to acknowledge it. I shoot him a text after our chat.

"Just because we didn't talk about our un-aversary doesn't mean I wasn't thinking about it. I think not saying much about it made you think I didn't care and that couldn't be further from the truth."

His reply reads: "Its fine, seeing the condo in the background of our chat really brought back a lot of bad memories." He means that final fight we had.

"Shit yeah," I tell him. "Just remind yourself you're with the right person now...and I will find someone...someday hahaha."

"I don't know what to say to that" comes his reply. "It implies you were the wrong person and I don't think that's fair to the time we had together. Not a matter of wrong or right, just a matter of making it work."

This makes me sad, and it's because I know he's sad, and I hate that. I hope at least one of us ends up ridiculously, gloriously happy with someone. I think for a minute before typing

"I love you James, always have and always will, just want you to be happy, it makes me happy."

"Thanks I want that for you too."

I notice he doesn't say he also loves me. It strikes me as odd, although it's not an emotional reaction, it's a logical one. I've never ceased to tell James over the years that I love him, because the reality is it's true, I love him and I always will. Is it that same "build a life together, stare out into the same sky, hold-my-hand-while-I-die love" that I used to have, well no, but it is still very much a type of love. I think about the idea of "hold-my-hand-while-I-die love" and part of me wonders if years from now it won't still be James doing such a thing for me in that moment. I don't foresee anyone else wanting to be there when the time comes. I'm marred by people's inability to allow love to transform. If it was romantic love and that is gone, then there must not be love anymore. It's not so one or the other for me. Love to me is simply this: the willingness to show up for someone. I don't keep people in my life that I wouldn't show up for, or that don't show up for me, so yes, you'll often hear me telling basically everyone around me that I love them. I wonder if Wes and I will still "show up" for each other.

## July 17

I wake up much too early—it's just before 5 a.m.—and I am filled with the awful awareness that I will not be able to fall back asleep. I throw on some sunscreen because it's already boiling hot, lace up my shoes, and walk around the block. I can't go far because my blistered feet are killing me. I need to buy new shoes for this hiking and camping trip, but I hate shopping and feel entirely unmotivated to go. The drive to the mall is not far, and I realize I actually somewhat know where I'm going as I've been here once before with Lucy. I enter through a large department store and find myself smack dab in the middle of the children's' section. I bee line for any other department. Tiny clothes, man, they just fucking kill my soul. Will that ever go away? I wander through store after store and nothing appeals to me, it's like everything is food but I don't feel hungry. I was hoping to at least find a manicure bar here to kill some time getting my nails done, but there isn't one. I'm bored, truly and utterly bored. I search the name of a shoe store on my phone and drive a few blocks away. This is a little better. There's a bigger selection than at home. Trying on new trail shoes gets me excited for camping and hiking. I hope my dogs won't be too much of a handful on this trip; they're both kind of disasters. I miss my dogs a lot. I'm looking forward to getting home and seeing them, but at the same time the house energy will be all different when I get back. Greyson will be moved in downstairs, and I'm adverse to facing yet another step in the reality that my life has changed, and is still changing. I wish it was not now, I think for the millionth time. I find a pair of hikers I'm excited about, but when I pull out my wallet to pay I remember it broke while I was travelling here and it won't stay closed. This place has some. I don't like any of them, but what does it matter. I throw an earth-toned one into my basket. Another passing of time, another small change that feels huge. I shopped for my wallet with Wes and the kids, and his daughter had selected it, as well as begged to buy a matching one. Wes decided against it because he thought that might be insensitive to her mother. "Roo and I have matching wallets," it just felt a little off somehow so Wes had redirected her toward a watch. I remember thinking how kind it was he wanted to be so considerate of his ex-wife's feelings. He really is such a great dad, truly the most loving, kind, silly, gentle, conscientious father I've ever met. I'm starting to worry that he feels it in the kid's best interest to not have contact with me, as he still hasn't arranged any chance for me to see them. A wave of shame washes over me, and my face flushes. I sit down on one of the stools meant for trying on shoes and stare at the wallet thinking of the kids. I think of trying to smash the microwave, something I never would have done had they been home. However, that justification sounds pathetic even to me. I feel ashamed for having let myself get to that point. That was me when I was twenty, when I didn't have communication skills, when I didn't know how to express I was struggling. How then, with all the expression of my struggle a decade later, had I let the old Roo out of her cage? Not only had I let the people I loved down, I'd let myself down as well. I am better than that night, and it stings knowing if I could have controlled myself better the outcome of all this could have been different. But it happens, sadly, I came unhinged. Would have not coming unhinged that night prevented the breakup? No, certainly not, but I could have kept a lot more of my dignity intact. I had used all the words and tools and sharing skills I had to no avail, and when that didn't work I'd let it all come out through my fist in a fiery drunken act of complete desperation. I silently vow to never let it get that bad again, to never let myself get so far away from me that I become a person I don't recognize anymore both physically and mentally. The shame of my actions can't be ignored. It need not be dwelt in, but I can't ever let myself brush it under the rug, because it's that heavy shame, that uncomfortable squirmy unsettled place inside me, that will make me better in the future. *Wow, how the fuck did the wallet bring all that up?* I pay for my shoes and my new ugly wallet and drive back to the condo in silence, no radio or music playing.

I video-chat my dad: "Dude, I couldn't spend money if I tried today, was not feeling a shopping vibe, but I got hikers and a wallet." I hold them both up so he can see.

"Couldn't quite stimulate that economy, hey?"

"Nerp...just wasn't feeling it." We chat briefly, and he recommends an Indian place for dinner. "If you don't feel like going out again it's really good, Mom and I love it, might even be a takeout menu in the drawer." He gives me instructions on where it's located.

I kill a few hours writing and tidying. I can't believe I am going home tomorrow. I've struggled really hard this time; it's been such a different trip for me. Normally I'd lock myself up in here, a little hermit barely leaving the complex; this time I pushed myself to get out a bit more. I wasn't feeling like I had enjoyed myself a ton, but now I desperately don't want to go home. What if it's weird living with Greyson? What if once I'm back I run into Wes all the time? Back home means back to facing my life, which I'm not currently enjoying. I am, however, very much missing Fox, Lucy, Jer and Hendrik, so I'll be excited to get back and see them, plus the dogs.

I shoot Wes a text: "Hey you, wanted to call but I'm never sure when a good time to catcha is and I don't wanna bug you while you're at work. Hope you're having an awesome day, gimme a shout later if you feel like chatting."

He writes back about how crazy busy his work is and some of the events he has going on. I tell him I hope he has fun, and he says, "Chat tomorrow?"

I tell him that sounds good and let him know what time I'll be in the air travelling home.

I don't think we will actually "chat tomorrow." I'm noticing when I reach out I always end up feeling like I've caught him at a bad time. This could mean one of two things:

1) I've caught him at a bad time
2) There isn't really going to be any "good time" for him and me to talk anymore.

Almost a year ago to the day, I was here in this exact same condo alone, doing what I'm doing now. The work of self-discovery. The huge realization I had back then was this, silence speaks to you. No reply is a reply. People will "say" everything they need to say to you, even if that comes in the form of lack of communication. We will put our energies toward that which we feel is important no matter how busy we are, and we will never seem to "find time" for the things we do not deem a priority.

That realization was before I even met Wes and had nothing to do with him, but it's creeping back in now as something that may pertain to my situation with him. I'm disappointed because I had really hinged my hope on us still finding a way to be friends. Is he trying to slow fade on me, and if so why wouldn't he just say he doesn't want anything to do with me? I am still so baffled at how much or how little contact he'd like to have. I know he's told me time and time again it's up to me, but that just doesn't seem fair. His intention is that he knows he hurt me and therefore to prevent further hurt he will allow the relationship to exist on my terms. That should make sense, but really it doesn't because you can't leave the girl who didn't want you to go at all in charge of how often she invites you over. People don't break up with you because they're looking to spend more time with you. I remind myself he jumped right back into the dating game. I remind myself that he does not want me, and that sometimes people just say they want to be friends out of guilt or a misplaced sense of responsibility. I don't do things by halves, the few friends I keep are the "call at 3 a.m. and help you with anything" type pals, and so I honestly have no idea what a reasonable level of contact with him should be. Regardless of the love I have for him, I'm not so stupid as to continue making a fool of myself trying to cling to a cord he has severed, and if he doesn't want to "show up" for me, then I have no business trying to "show up" for him anymore. The propensity I have for being warm and unyieldingly loving and forgiving is matched only by my ability to shut down when I sense it's not wanted or appreciated by its receiver. It may be time for me to start letting him know it's ok we don't have contact, and to offer him some assistance in cutting any of the ties that he still feels obligated to fulfill. I think of the hot tub and The Beast. Going to have to get those sorted. One thing is for sure, I can keep neither. The last thing I need is him feeling like he got robbed by me, or that I took everything, or that I made out like a bandit and he got screwed. Not gonna happen. I promise myself I'll discuss selling The Beast and moving the hot tub when I get home.

I order the take-out Indian food and Dad's right, it's delicious. The portion for one is massive, and I eat myself sick without making a dent in even half of it. I send Fox a picture of my devastation with the caption "so I'll probably barf later."

"Looks so good, and would it really be a vacation if you didn't puke?"

She's referring to the fact that once on a work trip to Nashville I ordered and ate a giant plate of ribs, followed by a piece of pecan pie for dessert. It was so delicious that when the waitress asked me how it was I said, "Amazing, I'll have another." She laughed and started to walk away and I was like, "Wait no, I'm not joking, please bring me another piece of pie." And thus was born my puking while on the road reputation.

After eating I throw my new hikers on and decide to start breaking them in with a walk around the block. I listen to a podcast that addresses why we pick inappropriate, inadequate, unfulfilling, problematic partners for ourselves. It does not resonate with me at all. The general idea is that we inadvertently seek out what is familiar to us even when it's unhealthy, because familiarity is comforting to humans and requires no growth or change. OK, I guess that makes sense, but then it draws on examples of people who witnessed toxic marriages or relationships from childhood and where the pattern is formed. This just simply isn't the case with me. My mom and my dad bicker, what married couple doesn't, but they have an incredibly loving, committed, exemplary marriage that's spanned decades. They truly are best friends.

What does it mean to have picked an inappropriate partner, anyway? Is the breakdown of the relationship ultimately the only reason we deem them an inappropriate choice? Clearly at one point we thought it was a great idea. I'm hard pressed to see patterns in any of the three relationships I deem to have been my serious or important ones. All of them came from extremely different socioeconomic backgrounds. Their levels of education and intelligence were completely different. They all had different religious, or lack thereof, upbringings. Their habits in regard to alcohol or drug consumption were totally different. Two had parents who were still married, one did not. Some had parents that were deceased; some did not. Height-wise we're all over the map, hair colour not the same, eye colour, different.

Do multiple breakups over decades actually indicate a "history of choosing inappropriate partners"? I'm apt to think no. I refuse to believe that I "chose" Wes poorly, and I hope he doesn't think that way of me either. God, I really hope that. We both made the best decisions possible with the information we had at the time. OK wait, that's a lie. Maybe we didn't make the best decisions, we rushed like crazy, but we both felt sure of one another. I refuse to allow myself to doubt that now based on information I'd have had no way of knowing at the time. I also don't have a history of rushing with people, so this isn't some weird established pattern of mine I need to break. I foolishly viewed its departure from the norm as a good thing. I don't fucking know. The evening is beautiful, and I decide fuck it, I'm going to go enjoy the hell out of my last night here. I pour myself a glass of vodka mixed with flavoured water and leisurely sip it on the deck listening to music. Time slips away from me, I do nothing, but I think all the things. On drink number I-don't-know-how-many I find myself in the kitchen pouring more vodka into my red cup.

"Just a little," I say out loud to no one as I pour what was supposed to be a shot. I misgauge and more than I expected comes out. "OK, that's a lot," I laugh alone.

Morning light is breaking now, and the birds have started to chirp. A deep sadness overtakes me. I don't want to go home. I think it again and again. This place, this magical place has always sent me home different. It's always challenging, and it's always unique, but each time I find magic and inspiration and insight and healing here, often never realising its full impact until I've returned. I just don't want to go back. I focus on the party coming up with the girls, I focus on the dogs, I focus on Fox and training with Hendrik and all the things I know I need and want to be home for. I sigh and peer into my empty cup. Bedtime, Roo.

## July 18

I clean the condo from top to bottom all morning and then order an Uber to take me to the airport. En route I hear the driver gasp. I look out the window to see a homeless man crossing the street. He is dragging a sheet and crying. He has draped the sheet around and over whatever it is he's pulling inside, and upon close examination I see a tail, a dog's tail, poking out the end. It's an unsettlingly similar scene to a painting I have at home; a homeless young man leaned up against a power pole cradling a dog that has passed. Angel wings rise up from behind the man and the dog, a raven sits on the power line above crying out "all dogs go to heaven." I used to have it in my office at work and people would often remark on its darkness, but for whatever reason I've always found it beautiful and uplifting. Seeing it unfold in real life, my eyes sting with tears and I can't wait to be home to hug my own dogs.

The travel back is boring and riddled with delays. One of my flights is late by several hours. I was supposed to pick my dogs up from daycare tonight, but it's getting too late for that to make sense. I'll have to grab them tomorrow morning. It's about 10 p.m. when I get home, and it's not very welcoming. Forest fires are burning very close by and the air is thick and heavy and dry. The night accentuates the fires and the flames pop out of the darkness like ominous angry eyes. I hate this season; it's the major downfall of where I live. Even if you don't get evacuated, the smoke makes the summers scary and sometimes unbearable for activities. Several years ago, James and I and our two dogs and two cats spent many nights shifting from friend's house to friend's house, not knowing if our house was still standing. I'll never forget the feeling of returning home to find it was still there but realizing how close it came and how powerful a force Mother Nature is to be reckoned with.

At home I throw my bags down and text Greyson, who should by now be officially living here. "I'm home, you come up or I come down?"

"Place is a mess still unpacking, I'll come up."

Several minutes later I hear the door that divides the suites open, and when he rounds the corner up the stairs I hug him super hard. *Wow, it's actually super nice to have someone I know at home.* We decide to go for a drive down to the beach to watch the fires. I know this sounds like a morbid screwed up activity but when you live in a community like this it's a real pastime. As is proven by the point that we're hard pressed to find parking along the narrow beach road we drive to. Everyone has the same idea. We lean on the back of his trunk and just stare.

"Fuck, this is unreal," I say in awe. "It looks like a volcano."

There are two fires burning in close proximity to one another, one directly across the lake and another just south of us. The magnitude is sickening.

"Look there," Greyson motions across the water. "If you watch one spot really closely you can see individual trees going up." I follow where he's pointing and make out one tree going up like kindling.

"Jesus," I reply. "Look how fast it spreads to the next tree."

We pontificate on why they can't do more controlled burns ahead of time, why water bombers aren't going right now, why this that and the other thing. That's also a pastime where we live.

"You think of it, though," I tell him. "Nature wants this to happen, like if we weren't here this would just go until it stopped and then the forest would grow again eventually."

"Yeah, it's cyclical, in the '60s there was the big 'only you can prevent forest fires' stuff, and so much burned it wasn't as bad for a while and now apparently we're in another phase of it."

It's unsettling to watch but I can't look away. "I kind of feel guilty watching this," I admit. "Like it's a show or something, but no houses have been burned down yet. Plus, to my credit, I did the same thing when it was my neighborhood that was one fire."

For a while we don't talk; we just stare wordlessly captivated by the volatile display of nature.

Greyson has to work in the morning so eventually we head out. As I crawl into bed I think of the fire, and of nature. Sometimes everything has to burn to ashes, so the cycle can start again.

## July 19

I roll over in bed and hug myself. Begging, pleading to stay in my dream just a little bit longer.

She has a white dress on with little popsicles all over it. There's chocolate around the edges of her mouth and it's stained the front of her dress and the hem as well. She has a headband on, which gives her an adorable unicorn horn. Across the room she motions to me: "Roo, come see!" She's pointing to a present from her mom and Wes. Her mother is standing next to her, beautiful, radiant and beaming proudly at her little girl. Wes is crouched down on the floor beside her and she drapes one arm over his shoulder. He rubs her back lovingly as, wide-eyed and grinning, she eyes the gift. He scoops her up and kisses her cheeks, so she giggles and her hair flies everywhere.

"I love you I love you I love" he's saying each time he kisses her. The unicorn horn falls off and I catch it before it hits the ground hand it back to Wes.

Turning to her I say, "Happiest of birthdays to you, Madame," bowing emphatically. She giggles again and he puts her down.

I feel a hand in my hand and look down to meet his perfect gaze. "Little sir," I say and I crouch down to his height. He jumps into my arms and I catch him at the last second hoping he didn't hit his head on my belt buckle like he's done so many times.

I smile at their mother, she smiles at me. I smile at Wes and he beams at me, slipping an arm around my waist. "I'm happy you're here for this," he whispers into my ear.

Except I'm not there. I'm in my bed, and I am missing her birthday. I lie still for so long, hoping if I just don't move I can get back there. But I cannot. I am soured for the day with the longing of this dream, and the knowledge that there's nowhere else in the world I'd rather be than with them on her birthday.

This is my first morning with someone else in the house so I creep carefully around, unsure how much noise will be annoying to Greyson or what will make his dog bark. Mine are loud lunatics so there's not much I can do to keep them quiet other than head outside to the back deck and let them play. I bring my laptop out and sip coffee. It's not long before Greyson and his dog emerge.

"Can I ask you a question?" I say to him as he brushes twigs off a patio chair.

"Yeah, for sure."

"I've been doing a lot of thinking about relationships and patterns and stuff. I listened to this podcast in California about how we seek out familiarity, and I'm just not seeing any patterns in the men I've been with. There's also the whole notion of deeming someone an inappropriate choice just because it didn't work out. That's flawed, right? Like, I'm not crazy?"

"No not at all, you're totally right."

"So, did your ex-wife or any of the girls you've dated have things in common?"

He thinks long and hard, and I can tell he's racking his brain. He comes up empty-handed.

"Nope, all the girls I've dated have been completely different. Education, income, background, kids no kids. I think that was a big thing for me after my marriage ended and I started to date, was just to try and meet all kinds of different people."

"Huh," I say. "I feel like with all this processing I'm doing I should be seeing some sort of pattern and it's just not there. The only one consistent thing I can think of is that, financially, I have never allowed a guy to solely take care of me, I always take at least my share if not more in that regard. But I think that says more about me than it does about the men I choose. My mom says I have a hard time letting people take care of me fully, and I'm not sure why that is."

"Have you heard of the theory of why?"

"Nope."

"It was designed by an auto manufacturer for diagnosing problems, but basically you take any issue and you ask why five times and just see where that takes you to help sort it out . . . maybe try that."

I tell him I will and he heads off to pack up before leaving town for a wedding. I won't see him again for a week until we rendezvous for camping. I stay seated on the deck. Well now here's a problem, what problem am I even trying to diagnose? Is the fact that I won't allow a man to become financially responsible for me a problem? Let's say it is. Here we go.

I won't allow a man to be financially responsible for me. Why?

Because I take great pride in my independence. Why?

Because it sets me apart and provides security. Why?

Now I've divided myself into two sets of answers, but the security thing is probably the most interesting. Why does not allowing a man to be financially responsible for me allow me to feel secure?

Because if someone leaves me and I can't take care of myself that would be the most humiliating thing.

Why?

Because I don't ever want to need someone so much that I can't go on without them.

Hmmmmmm. This is an interesting tool for sure. I could see this being a huge breakthrough if I'd been financially dependent on my husband and then useless after he left, but that's so far from the case it's laughable. Clearly the need to be OK alone goes way back to even my high school boyfriend.

I wonder if it works for other things.

I want to be friends with Wes still. Why?

Because he makes me laugh, he's my best friend, and I feel there were a lot of ways that we brought out the best in each other. Why?

Because together sometimes I felt invincible. Why?

Because we were shaping our own world. Why?

Because maybe neither of us liked the world as it was for us when we met. Why?

I don't know. I don't know yet what this stream of thought means. I still haven't heard from Wes, which is disappointing but no longer surprising. His "chat tomorrow" text on a Tuesday gave me false hope, but now it's Thursday. I'm irritated. This weird middle ground is really hard for me; I have no skill at flippant friendships. Mainly, now I just want to talk to him about selling The Beast. I'll need to get him on board as it's in both our names, but if I can, we can split the money and it could be a really good thing for both of us.

The Garden Goddess Flower Crown Bullshittery party with the girls is coming up in two days, and I'm ridiculously excited about it. Lucy is super jacked about it too, she's coming over later to hang and get ready. When she rolls up I am so ridiculously happy to see her. I have always felt a deep connection to Lucy, but our bond over the last seven months has been further solidified in a way I never knew was possible. The year my marriage ended, without her and Fox, I could not have made it.

I never could have imagined us being closer, but then . . . kids. Lucy is, oh my god she's an amazing mother. When Wes's children came into my life I had no clue what I was doing, and she was there every step of the way to encourage and congratulate and now console. I remember one night probably four months into my relationship with Wes we sat together in my shed, our special hang out spot, smoking and drinking and I confided in her my worst fears. I am failing these kids, I get tired, I'm not good at this, I get frustrated, I get worried, they make me want to laugh and cry at the same time. I think I suck at this. It scares me how much I love them. I was in tears when I told her, and she leaned down to where my head was hunched into my lap and patted my shoulder, which for her is huge because she's not a touchy person.

"I feel like that all the time and they're my kids. Congratulations, this is what it's like. You are doing amazing."

It was the first time anyone outside of Wes had complimented me on my skills with them, and it was certainly the first time I'd heard from an actual mother that it's OK to be overwhelmed and feel like you're failing. Let alone hearing this from the best mother I know.

The kids played together, and I came to have a much better glimpse into what her life is like and how her love for her children and family shapes everything she does. My love for Wes's kids had helped me understand such a fundamental part of who she is, and that is such a gift. Now, with each of us facing our own unique relationship battles, I am firm in the knowledge that we face them together. Her problems are mine, and mine are hers. We are such a united force these days, and the strength and comfort it provides me is beyond words.

She climbs out of her Jeep with bags of stuff, and I'm already laughing.

"Wings, I brought wings!" she laughs.

At first I think she means the food, but now I can see she's talking about literal fairy wings. She has bags and bags of decorations and ridiculous shit for the party. Fake flowers overflow from the corners of each one.

"Oh my god you're amazing." She hands me a coffee to boot.

"Beer?" I ask

"Do you still want the coffee then?"

"A world of yes."

I drink my beer and my coffee, and she sits at my kitchen table crafting her flower crown while I organize my kitchen. Greyson had left me several boxes of junk that were still in his suite when he moved in. Some of it is mine, some of it it's Wes's, and all of it is annoying me.

"I just keep having to deal with shit, like literally stuff. I'm so over it," I tell her as I jam cooking supplies I'll never use into my kitchen cupboards. "I'm gonna get back to my minimalist ways, starting with . . ." I eye the fancy coffee maker Wes and I had bought. "That," I point. "It needs to fucking goooooooooooo! And look!" I pull my old one out of the box. Simple, plain, black, nothing fancy. "I still have my original. Ya know, Fox told me she associated this coffee maker so strongly with me that if I died it would be the only thing she would want."

Lucy laughs.

"What are you going to do with the fancy one?"

"I don't know. Put it on a shelf somewhere. See if Wes wants it if I ever hear from him."

I set up my old coffee maker and it brings me a weird serene feeling. It's sitting next to the speaker that Wes still hasn't taken. "I'm really gonna miss that thing." I say.

"You're giving it to him?"

"Well, I bought it as a housewarming present for him, and I just really want him to have it, even though it's one of the few material objects in this house that really means a lot to me. He left it the day he moved his stuff, because he wasn't sure if he should take it, which was nice. But I mean, really, a gift is a gift and he should keep it. Plus I'm just really on this whole thing of being . . . I dunno, weirdly worried that he's going to feel, or people will perceive, that I took him for something. Need to make sure he gets what's fair so it's not like 'Oh, look how hard I got fucked over by her' or something. I'll get myself something else."

"Yeah, get something you really like."

I tell Lucy all about the five why situation and we apply it, and some more beers, to her relationship questions.

"Wow," she tells me, "that's a bit terrifying."

"Yeah, it's a good tool to have, even if you're not exactly sure what the outcome means, and when it's feeling-based instead of facts it could change day to day, but just another tool we can using for our coping kits. Our large large coping kits."

We move to the front porch with our beers. I tell Lucy how I haven't heard from Wes and we pontificate about nearing the cut-the-cord phase.

"I just didn't want it to go down like this, but I'm also not going to keep trying to insert myself into someone's life. Not my style . . . well, at least once I hit that point; let's face it, two weeks ago I was practically begging. Now it's just gotten, like, sad and tiresome. I dunno, maybe it has to be a thing like me and James where if it even happens it'll be a several years long road to friendship . . . and at this point is that even what I want?"

"Yeah, you eventually hit a wall with trying with people. I'm just done, like my trust with everyone is fucked. It's you and two other people in the world I trust and no one new gets in."

I admit I feel the same way. "I don't have the energy to pump myself back up to people."

We talk a lot about my living situation with Greyson and the wisdom or stupidity of it. The absurdity of it all has become somewhat of a hot topic with my friends and family. I don't think anyone thought it was strange until I told them I'd be going camping with him soon too, then the sideways looks started.

Here's the thing . . ." I start to say, and then laugh because I always know I'm being ridiculous when I break down my thought process like this. "He's my friend and he was here often anyway, and you know I don't do well with strangers. I know my own intentions, and while everyone else around me seems to think I'm a fucking incompetent idiot at 'life-ing,' possibly with some proof to back that up . . ." We laugh super hard. "I feel like having a friend nearby is going to be really good for me, even if your ex-boyfriend's best friend in your basement seems fucking ridiculous to everyone else. As far as the camping goes, I'm gonna get Fox's tent, so it'll be a separate-tent scenario, and why can't I go have a good fucking time with my dogs and my friend? I mean, Christ, Wes was the one who suggested he move in here. It's like everyone keeps forgetting that. He knows better than anyone else how small I keep my circle and if someone is in they're in. Greyson has been in for a while. If Wes can be not just OK with it but suggest it, then who the actual fuck has a right to have an opinion to the contrary? I want to make the most of this time, and that includes doing shit I wouldn't normally get to do, like just taking off to camp. Fuck, some people . . ." I place heavy emphasis on the some so she knows I mean Wes. "Just hop right back onto the meat market even when they've explicitly said they wouldn't or would at least have the respect to warn me . . . so why, why can't I camp and move in whoever I wanna move in, and throw dumbass fucking parties with my friends, and wear a flower crown and train my face off with Hendrik and write a book . . . ya know?" I'm starting to realize I'm drunk, but it feels good. It's the energetic positive laughey kind of drunk.

"Exactly," she agrees. "You don't owe anyone any explanations. As long as you are happy, I will always support your choices, and come to your ridiculous parties. I'm going to drink myself under the table on Saturday and I mean that literally."

"I feel like I'm doing good at being social . . . in terms of me."

"You totally are," she reassures me. "I couldn't believe you came out that night with us before you left for California." This is the thing about my friends. They know I would do anything for them, but they understand my limitations socially and my weird anxieties around group activities with people I don't know. I know Lucy and Fox can see how hard I've been pushing myself even when others cannot. It's the same way I see Lucy's strength lately even when other people don't know she's struggling.

"I'm really proud of you." I beam at her. "You're so strong, and the way you've been handling things lately . . . just when I thought I couldn't admire you more, you inspire with your ability to . . . I dunno, ride the wave."

"Thanks, I have a lot of respect for your ability to just get through things too, the same way you did with your divorce. You handle big things so much better than most people I know. You just do this thing where you make it seem like everything will be OK somehow. You deal with your emotions so intensely and so intentionally and then you hit a point where you just seem to cure yourself."

"Yeah, you were a big part of that," I admit. "Would not have been able to without you and Fox. And now with your situation and even mine too, it's just like, the non-action that's hard. I'm taking these eleven weeks to heal and just stay focused on self-care, and you'll just need time to see how things unfold too. It's like Jer always says to me: 'wave-y ocean.' The hardest 'work' for us right now will be the act of not acting. Letting time pass, sitting with the discomfort, and not making any big moves until we're more certain."

"I hate the not knowing."

"Me too," I say.

The night blurs on into a lot of laughing and a ton of cigarettes. We hold court on the front porch for several hours and drink pretty much all the beer in the house. A giant bug flies at us and we scream uproariously, remembering a similar incident with a disgusting desert bug on one of our many trips to California. We talk about guys from our past, dudes we know now. We discuss women we admire and women who failed us, failed as friends and as humans. We shit-talk mutual enemies. We laugh so hard my cheeks hurt. I climb up beside her on the Adirondack chair and we take a selfie. I caption it with "Thursday Schemes and Saturday dreams. Pre-party party with the tribe."

It's funny Lucy and I call ourselves that. It stems from a necklace I bought her at Christmas and has since blown up into our name for the special bond we share. A tribe of two. Matching palm tree tattoos. Matching necklaces. Matching need to have that one fucking person who you know will always tell you "I see you try. I'll be there if you fail. I will not disappoint you the way the world has."

## Week Five
## July 20

A sobered-up Lucy drives herself home in the morning, and I head to the gym. I'm giving more and more thought lately to Hendrik's suggestion that I go balls to the wall on my fitness goals. It would be a really great investment in myself. I mean, what could or should possibly take a higher priority than yourself when you're alone? It was so easy to make excuses when my life was full, but now there's really nothing stopping me. Financially, I'm sure I can swing it, especially now that I'm not eating out as much or drinking every day.

When I plug my headphones into my phone I see I missed a text from Wes last night. I don't think I've ever just missed a text from him before, but Lucy and I were so riled up that I wasn't paying any attention. It's basically an explanation of how busy he is right now and how problematic his schedule is. It doesn't ask any questions or invite any type of response. Feels a bit like some sort of brush off. I'm not sure how to respond or if he even wants me to, but I do need to ask him about selling The Beast. I tuck my phone into my pocket, throw my music on, and decide to deal with it later. The workout feels good. I go for a long time to avoid having to go home and deal with things. I've spent a lot of time lately "cleaning," but for the most part I really haven't been keeping up with other facets of my life. It feels like I have five million phone calls to return. I've got financial stuff I need to be dealing with regarding investments and making sure I've set myself up properly for this year. I haven't checked the mail in a very long time and I still need to deal with the bill for the epic hole-in-front-lawn incident. I check the mail on my way home from the gym and spend time sorting through all the junk and a few things for Wes. I text him back: "Shitty. Lemme know when ya can spare 5 minutes to chat some logistics about The Beast and hot tub, had some things I wanted to run by you." I busy myself with sorting paperwork and shifting money around from one account to the next.

Twenty minutes later Wes calls. I explain to him that after a lot of thought I'd like to sell The Beast, and that we can split the funds and then he can use the money from his half to move his hot tub to his new home.

He assures me repeatedly that The Beast was intended for use on my large property and that he would happily allow me to keep it if it's important to me. The hot tub can stay if it makes me happy too.

I hope I don't come across as too blunt when I tell him, "Nah, it really doesn't. As for The Beast, it doesn't make sense now for me to have two vehicles. With the bill from the waterline and hole in the front yard and covering expenses when you left . . . July legit turned into like, a nine thousand dollar month for me out of nowhere. Also, I just really have it in my head that I don't want it to be a thing for you or anyone else to say like, she kept that truck and his hot tub and stuff."

"I would never say that" he tells me, and I want so badly to believe him.

"Listen, I know you would let me keep The Beast, I 100 percent know that, and that's so ridiculously kind of you and I really appreciate it. It just probably makes more sense now for each of us to try and get some many back out of it."

He assures me again he can think on that idea, but only if it's what I really want to do.

"It is," I tell him.

We talk a bit about logistics for the paperwork, and he agrees to get back to me after he's had some time to sit with the plan.

"As for the monthly cost for when I moved out I will totally give you money for July, we just hadn't talked about it yet but 100 percent I want to do that."

That is kind of him, but I wish I hadn't said anything now, because I'm trying to show him I don't want to take any of his money or goods, not that I feel he owes me more.

"No no no, sorry that's not what I meant at all, I totally don't want anything from you for that month, I just meant that goes towards why it makes sense to sell The Beast."

"Well, we can always build that money into whatever we get out of the truck too."

He gets busy again at work so he has to jet, but we say we will catch up about this again soon. I let him know I have some mail and some boxes of his stuff too.

When we hang up the phone, I feel relieved but also sad. I don't care about the money, I just want him to be happy, and I want me to be happy too. I miss him so much. How . . . how how how do I stop?

## July 21

I jump out of bed. Today is the Garden Goddess Flower Crown Bullshittery Bash. I am so so so excited. I have a lot of running around to do. I need some more decorations and I have to buy some food and booze. It's Saturday and there's only so many stores in this little town. There's a fair chance I'll run into Wes. I throw on jeans and a tank top, I don't bother doing my makeup but I make sure my hair looks decent in a high ponytail. I'm still very conscious of running into him and having him see what a mess I am. It's not an ego thing, or a try and impress him thing, it's a "save myself from the shame of letting him see how destroyed I am" thing. I hit pretty much all the major stores: the big box ones, the grocery store, and the liquor store. I'm amazed that I don't run into him anywhere. Lucky break, finally. At home I switch into comfies and set up solar lights all over the front yard to get them charged for the evening. I clean and sweep and vacuum and wash the floors, which is kind of stupid really because I know all of us are going to be traipsing in and out all night long so I'm just going to have to do it again tomorrow. I take the dogs for a quick walk around the neighborhood to try and tucker them out before people arrive. Fox and Lucy are supposed to come over earlier to help me set up.

I look at myself in the mirror and I'm a gross sweaty disaster now. I have a little bit of time before people get here. I have a girlfriend who works at the drugstore down the street who does makeup, and I wonder if I swing by there if she would throw some fake eyelashes on for me. I decide there's no point in changing to go out since I'm about to change into my dress later anyway, and I leave the house a total disaster. I have green sweatpants on, a red workout shirt with no bra, my face is sweaty, and I'm wearing flip flops. *Whatever, I'll be 15 minutes max.* I see my friend at the cosmetics counter the second I walk in.

"Hey Roo!! How was the event?"

*Aw fuck I did not think this through.* The last time I was here was the night before Wes and I broke up. She had done my eyelashes and my makeup for the event we were at.

"Well . . ." I wander right up to the counter. "Not so good, he broke up with me the next morning."

"Shut up! What happened?" she is genuinely shocked and no wonder because about a month ago I sat here with a shit-eating grin smiling like a fucking idiot talking about how in love I am and how him and the children give me purpose in life and how I've learned to love in a way I never thought I could before. Fuck, I was so stupid and naive.

"Well . . . we fought, I flipped out . . . not my finest hour by any means, and the cumulative effect of that was him breaking up with me the next morning . . . so . . . yeah. Super embarrassing, definitely not proud of myself, but it was bigger than just that night or whatever."

"Oh that's so sad, you were so happy, see this is why I don't date."

"Yeah, gonna be a long time for me now. Hey, can someone do my lashes?"

"Yeah sure, in like fifteen minutes?"

"Sounds good."

"So tell me more, like, what was the problem?"

"Oh I dunno, I'm still trying to sort all that out. Mainly we moved too fast, but, it was a whole bunch of things . . . there was a lot to it. He just hit a breaking point where he realized I'm not the right person for him. I'm still processing it all." I'm vaguing a bit because I don't want to get too personal out of respect for Wes, and honestly sometimes I don't even really know the answer.

"So, what happens to the podcast now?"

"Oh fuck I dunno, we keep saying we're gonna do it but . . ." I'm caught off guard when my throat catches and I hear my voice cracking.

Guess I'm missing doing the show with him more than I thought. I've told Wes multiple times I'd like to keep going with it, but he has so much on his plate right now, and while I sense he'd like to as well, it just really isn't a priority for him at the moment, which is fair. I feel my eyes blurring a bit and I promise myself I'm not going to let the tears out in the middle of the store.

"We just haven't been able to make it work yet, but hopefully." I don't even know now if I only mean the podcast.

"Aww sweetie" she leans down to rub my arm. "It just wasn't your time. Hold on a sec, the guy behind you is looking for something."

I turn around and mother fuck, it's Wes. *Oh my fucking god.* I know I look terrible. Why, why would I see him now after making sure I didn't look like a total disaster when I was running errands earlier. Fuck my actual life, this is mortifying. He looks amazing as always, casual and devastatingly sexy. Beard and ball cap, flip flops. He shows no hint of the embarrassment that's written all over my face.

"Oh hi!" I say too loudly out of nervousness." I was just gonna see if I could get my lashes done before the party. What are you doing here?"

"I'm getting candles for her birthday party." Oh man, my heart feels like someone thrust a hunting knife into it. Do not cry. Do not cry. Do not cry. Do not cry.

"Nice!" I ask him a few questions about his daughter's party and then as quickly as he showed up he disappears casually in search of candles.

I lean my head against the counter.

"Was that him?"

"Yup." My reply is muffled because my face is tucked into my arms.

"Wonder how much he heard us saying."

"I dunno . . . but . . ." I raise my head. "Fuck the lashes . . . I need to go home and curl up and die now."

I exit the store as fast as possible and call Fox on my way home.

She is dying laughing, we both are, but it's sad, painful laughter.

"Ohhhh Roo. Just can't catch a fucking break, can you."

"Like what do I even do now?" I ask her.

"Ummmm . . . do nothing. This is totally a do-nothing situation. It happened, it was embarrassing, let it go. I'll see you in like an hour."

We hang up and by the time I reach my house I'm crying. This day, this night, was supposed to be all about letting loose and forgetting and being silly. Now a neon sign points over my head that says "not invited," and all I can think of is her birthday party today. Am I really such a bad person that I couldn't have even been invited to swing by to give her a gift and a hug? I crawl into bed. My mind does not want to do my party now, which is really sad to me because I've been looking forward to it for weeks.

Nope, this isn't going to work. I need to snap myself out of it. Talking out loud to myself seems to really work; it's a habit and method I've honed in on during large sums of time when I've lived alone. I stand in front of the mirror looking at this tear-streaked shit-bag version of myself. I channel Hendrik and say a phrase he uses with me all the time before explaining the plan.

"Here's the game . . ." I start. "You are going to set a timer for ten minutes, crawl into bed, and cry about her and the party and how much you miss them and wish you could be there, but only for ten minutes. Then you're going to get your ass up, do your hair and makeup, and have an amazing time with people who are so special they've all agreed to do something so stupid with you. You are not a shitty person; this is just a shitty time. You are not a fuckup, you've just fucked up, and that's OK." I stare at myself. I look so pathetic. "Also, you really do look like shit, but we will fix that." I call the dogs to come and cuddle, I slip into bed and set my timer. For ten minutes I sob, oh god horrible wretched sobs just thinking of her beautiful little face and her laugh and her brother and her party. I cry so hard my abs ache. I cry so hard the dogs stare at me with great concern. The timer sounds with a much too cheerful little song. I throw the cover off of myself forcibly and jump out of bed. Hard reset, let's do this.

There's no real plan for the evening other than that everyone was going to bring some food, wear some crowns, drink, and enjoy each other's company. I'm excited for it to get dark out so that all the solar stuff will come on. Better still the Christmas light laser I have for the holidays. I'm certain that when it's dark if I aim it at the willow tree in my backyard the effect will be stunning. I throw beers into coolers and set out paper plates and napkins. Fox arrives, and I switch between two dresses asking her opinion.

"Second one," she yells up to the porch from her car, where she's hauling stuff in.

"Belt or no belt?" I holler back.

"No belt."

I bring her a mound of supplies to start making her flower crown.

"Beer?"

"Yup." We crack them and cheers.

"Lucy will probably be later than she thinks." I explain she's gone into the fabric store for something she needs for a decoration and that essentially that place is a black hole where she will lose time. Fox's crown looks awesome when it's done, it alternates between pink and white. Funny, because Lucy did hers alternating in red and white, whereas mine, well, it's a hot mess. There is no pattern to it at all and there's a mix of purple, magenta, fuchsia, and one giant yellow flower right at the front. I was never good at crafting.

When Lucy shows up the three of us take silly pictures in my kitchen together with our crowns on. One by one the other girls arrive. Kristen from down the street who I met, embarrassingly enough, when she worked as a manager at the liquor store in my neighborhood. She has a soft spoken-ness about her that's rare for me in my friendships. She's observant and kind and an amazing listener. Dark raven hair frames her face, and she often smiles with her mouth closed. It reminds me of Tese when she does this, like she knows everything but will say nothing.

The next to arrive is C.J., who is a professional trainer, former fitness competitor, and one of the most stunning humans alive. A million feet tall, long blonde hair and a never-ending trail of Instagram followers. That's actually sort of how I met her. I had this old wagon wheel light from my nana's house that I wanted installed in my kitchen. I reached out to an electrician who followed me on social media. He was such a sweet man with a kind smile and gentleness about him. He offhandedly mentioned his wife was a fan of mine. "Oh, that's nice," I had said, trying to brush it off, because at the peak of my career I hated discussing my career.

"Yeah, I think you follow her too. C.J. Fit."

I slam my coffee down and fan girl.

"Your wife is C.J. Fit? Oh my god you have to introduce me!" I was on the road a lot that summer for work so it took a few months to coordinate, but once we met we formed a fast bond. I respected most about her that much like me while she lived her life in the public eye, she longed deeply for privacy and dogs and the comforts of home. Turns out she also literally lives around the corner from me. We've spent many hours together since at the gym or cuddled on her couch during winter watching horrible made for T.V. Christmas movies. She is selective with her company and it makes me feel special that she lets me be part of her life.

There's also Lisa, who is a close friend of Lucy's and by proxy a close friend of mine. She's a beautiful petite little thing with a wide smile and super expressive eyes that add humor to every story she tells or comment she makes. So there is the six of us, and Meesh will be joining later. A six-person party? I know, I keep the circle small, but

I tell you it's way better to have six people who you feel 100 percent comfortable with than sixteen who you just kinda know.

It escalates quickly in terms of how hard and how fast Lucy and I are drinking. We're racing each other to oblivion and she's winning, which is rare. We make burgers and C.J. and Kristen have to supervise me because I'm kind of drunk and not very good at using the barbecue. I'm also paranoid and drunkenly trying to be super careful and respectful because the barbecue itself belongs to Wes, he just hasn't picked it up yet. The conversations jump all over the place, the drinks flow, the music plays, and the dogs run up and down the porch stairs, laughter mixes in with it all. I'm just starting to wonder if I should slow down my drinking when Meesh shows up . . .

"Tequila!" she proclaims, holding up a really nice bottle. "Might not be the answer but it's worth a shot!"

And shot, after shot, after shot. Lucy holds a mini lime for after each shot and three times in a row I drunkenly, accidentally knock it out of her hand. I can't stop laughing and she's killing herself too. Night-time moves in and we set up the laser. Honestly, it works even better than I thought it would. The effect is breathtaking and combined with the solar lights, my back deck now slightly resembles something one might find on Pinterest. All of us girls gather round under the willow tree and Meesh pours a shot for everyone.

"Hold up, hold up, hold up!" I yell to them. "We gotta do the good cheers, the one me and Lucy and Fox did the last time my life blew up. Come in close." They circle in next to me. "It is: 'There are good ships, and wood ships, and ships that sail the sea, but the best ships are friendships, and may they always be.' Cheers." We all scream cheers over and over loudly and obnoxiously. We are "those" girls. My one hand holds my camera to record the moment and so Fox puts the lime in my mouth for me. Meesh hands her more and she tries to stuff another one in but it falls from my mouth to the ground and I stumble into the group. I look at Lucy, "Did I knock the lime out of your hand again?"

"No, no, I did it!"

"You did it!" we all scream at her.

C.J. has to train a client early in the morning, Lisa already jetted for another engagement and now Lucy is fading fast. "You!" I point at her. "Don't quit on me!" I throw on one of her favourite songs and to my surprise she starts talking openly about her marital situation to the remaining girls. I think this is a good thing; these girls are super trustworthy secret keepers and won't say a word. Sometimes you just need a group of women to bitch to and to get fired up on your behalf. Which they effectively do. Fox and I are hitting the point where dancing needs to happen. She comes out with more shots, trying to entice Lucy, who is starting to seem very very done.

"OK fine, fine," Fox tells her. And comes back with a little bit of bread and some water for her.

"Shoot this water then."

Even the water seems like it's too much for Lucy, who excuses herself and crawls into my bed apologizing.

"You're good, you're good," I tell her. "Get after that bed, no worries."

Kristen, Fox, me and Meesh, we dance our asses off. My neighbors are going to hate me. Kristen heads out, but Meesh and I do more and more shots. Tequila is my new best friend.

Foxes phone rings. "K, I'll be right out," she says to whoever it is. "Shit that's the designated driver service. They said they'd be 45 minutes but that was like 10." I honestly didn't even see her call them the first time, so I can't say if her sense of time is off or if they were super fast.

"I'm going to catch a ride with you," Meesh says. "Here." she hands me the tequila bottle, which is now essentially empty. "You need to keep this."

I hug them both goodbye and they leave. This was a good night, I think to myself as I sink back into a patio chair and light a final cigarette before bed. I turn the music off and assess the damage silently. The solar lights are glowing and the laser casts a beautiful hue over everything but the cleanup is going to be awful. There are cans and plastic shot glasses everywhere, limes strewn on every surface, but I don't care. I'm mesmerized by the laser lights twinkling on the willow branches. When I finish my smoke, I crawl into bed next to Lucy. I haven't slept next to anyone since Wes left, and her presence is more comfort than she knows. I close my eyes, blissfully happy. Happy right up until 4 a.m. when I barf all the tequila back up.

## July 22

Lucy is gone when I wake up. She hasthe kids and her husband to get home to so I'm sure after sleeping it off she jetted the second she was able. I shoot her a text just to make sure.

She tells me she's home fine and offers to come over again later and help me clean, which I decline. I drive myself to the local greasy spoon, sip coffee, and have bacon and eggs. I feel like shit but thank goodness it's not the headache kind of hangover. I can take feeling sick and tired; it's when my head pounds that I'm the worst. I'm oddly comfortable eating alone at this diner as the majority of the patrons are seventy-five plus. I ask the waitress for a refill on water so many times it becomes absurd.

After finishing my meal, I head home and once again survey the damage on the deck. Nope. I crawl back into bed. I spend the rest of the morning and the majority of the early afternoon alternating between sleeping and watching TV. Around 1:30 I force myself to get up and start cleaning. James will be passing by today to visit the dogs, and I don't want him to think I let them live in squalor. The cleaning goes faster than I think. It's mostly just gathering up recycling and garbage, loading the dishwasher, sweeping, and tidying. I leave a few of the decorations out on the porch because they make me smile. I gather all the remaining flower crowns into a pile and tuck them away.

Wes calls to see how the party was, and I give him a brief rundown. He tells me about his daughter's birthday party too, and I listen but try to numb myself to the emotions his words well up inside of me. I'm surprised he's even called me after seeing what a gross shitshow I was at the cosmetics store yesterday. It was nice so to hear about his daughter's party, and it was sweet and thoughtful of him to ask about mine. I have this strange thing about voices, which is super unfair because my voice is raspy and annoying; however, I find Ipay more attention to them than most. I often find myself commenting, "Did you hear her voice, it was so nice," or "How can you talk to that guy, his voice is like instant pain in my earholes." Wes, he has a wonderful voice; there's something about the timbre of it that just . . . ughhh. Got to stop thinking about it.

By the time James arrives I'm much less hung-over and I'm starving. We let the dogs out for a play in the backyard and then decide to go for dinner at the pub down the street. I haven't gone out for a sit down meal with James in...God it's been years. We take his vehicle to the pub.

"That waitresses here are going to think I'm a huge whore, I'm always here with a different guy."

"Well, unless you're giving out blowjobs at the table I doubt they've even noticed." Ahhh James' wit. Fox will back me up on this: he is one of the funniest people I've ever met. He's not particularly silly the way he was when we were younger, but he has a subtle, flat, sarcastic delivery to his jokes that always seem to make them even funnier. It's like he never knows how funny what he's said is. He often claims I attribute more funny comments to him than he deserves. We sit on the patio at a corner table and the waitress takes far too long to bring us waters and take our orders.

"Ya know," I sigh, "I thought I'd done better this time. I don't know if I've ever said this to you so explicitly, but I know there were a lot of ways in which I wasn't a good wife. I was too focused on my career; I didn't take enough interest in things that were important to you. I was more of a homebody when you wanted to go out. There were so many things I did that contributed to the distance between us and the way it all went down. So this time with Wes, right, I was like, different **everything**. If he wanted to do it, I did it, even if it was epically outside my comfort zone. You think I wanted to go to Vegas? That's like my worst fucking nightmare, but I did it because it was important to him, and we had a blast! I never did that for you and I failed you in that way bigtime. Dinners out, drinks, people over at the house, being more social. He made my world so much bigger. Anything he wanted to do I tried my hardest to do it so that I was .

. . not making the same mistakes, you know. And we're talking, I'm doing this in addition to having fallen madly in love with those kids and changing my priorities to try and be the best person for them that I could. Like, fucking overhaul. So how, then, when I did everything different . . . and this pisses me off because Wes once told me we were supposed to do things different together and then it just ended up being the same, which for me was soooooooooo not true. I did everything different, every little fucking thing that I could, and I still got left. So I guess it **was** the same. And I still disappointed someone . . . someones," I emphasize, nodding to him. "I just truly, not a sympathy evoker but really honestly believe, there isn't someone out there who's ever going to stay. Just stay with me, and just keep choosing me, even when it's awful or I'm awful. And I'll tell ya this much, I feel like a prize asshole because I never would have broken up with him, probably to my detriment, but I just . . . I just never would have. I thought we had picked each other. For the fights and the shit and bullshit and the good times, like everything. So why, even when I try so hard to do it different . . ." My voice breaks and catches. I'm pleading now. "James, why will no one pick me?"

He looks at me in that long silent way you can only do when you've known someone so long. "Oh, Roo," He says finally, his face reading such deep sympathy and sorrow. "You didn't get it wrong. It sounds like you did so much right this time and worked so hard to be better than you thought you could be, and more selfless than you were before." He takes a sip of water and places the glass down, leaning in. "Don't discredit everything you've learned and how hard you've tried. You take way too much responsibility for how this all happened. He was just the wrong person. That's all it is. Really. You don't ever give yourself enough credit for how wonderful and rare and special you are. Someone is going to choose you. Someone is going to stay. This is a huge loss for him, even if he doesn't see it. I guarantee down the line he will regret losing you." I'm thinking about how I wish I believed him when he somberly adds, "I would know."

I ask him lots of questions about his girlfriend and her kids, about their lives and how they interact. The commuting is killing him with her living out of town. He tells me several ways he's trying to do that relationship differently than we did our marriage, and all his strategies make sense. He's being more forthcoming about communication and his needs.

"I'm proud of you," I tell him. "Seems like you're doing it differently too and I'm really glad it's working."

"So, tell me about this Greyson living situation."

I explain in great detail the story of how I originally met Greyson, how he resurfaced in my life again via Wes, and how Wes had been the one to suggest that he move in. I tell him about some of the looks I've been getting when I've told people he's moved in, and about the expressions on people's faces they don't have to verbalize for me to hear when I mention camping.

"Close friends too, it's not like I'm wandering around providing this information to strangers," I explain. "So flat out . . . do you think letting Wes's best friend move in downstairs and continuing to be friends with him is a bad idea? Like, is the nature of all the connections a little too incestuous?"

"Ummm . . . well, I live in my ex-wife's best friend's basement suite, and I am dating the sister of my twin brother's fiancé . . . so . . . nope." I laugh so hard, and he laughs too. I've never flat-out heard him put it like that. "If he's going to be a good tenant, pay his rent on time, you enjoy his company and you guys wanna hang out, then fuck everyone else. It's your choice and if you're happy, I'm happy."

We finish our meals and talk lots more about our siblings and other family members. It's such a wonderful conversation. We take a photo of ourselves to send to my mom and dad; they love James and will be over the moon to know we had dinner together.

When the bills comes, I reach for it. James covered some of my dog's medical expenses for an emergency while Wes and I were in

Vegas and he never asked me for a dime back, so it seems right. He sees me putting the card into the machine the waitress has handed me.

"You're just doing half, right?" he asks

"No, I got this."

The waitress is still standing there.

"You," he says flatly, "you're just trying to get a second date with me." I burst out laughing, the absurdity of his comment, the idea of a second date with my ex-husband, the flatness with which he said it, the fact that the waitress doesn't know he's joking. I can't breathe I'm laughing so hard and I'm mortified in front of the waitress, who laughs at what she perceives as being a great joke on his part at the end of a good first date. She's laughing, and I'm laughing, and James starts laughing at me, and never before were there three people standing so close together laughing at entirely different facets of one singular comment.

On the drive home his joke still lingers in my mind and I'm reminded of two specific incidents for some reason. In the first I am dropping him off at the airport. We've only recently started dating, we're young, and being apart even for a few days seems like the end of the world. I'm pulled over and we're kissing goodbye. The moment is serious and sensual and passionate. We finally break away from kissing and he leans down to say something to me that I think will be "I love you" or "I'm going to miss you." Instead he whispers, "The couple behind us is breaking up." I look back, and sure enough behind us is the anti-version of us, and I lose it laughing. The juxtaposition was hilarious at the time. The second instance was years later, after we'd been married for quite some time. We were at his mother's and father's house, and his dad was wearing a dress shirt, the breast pocket filled to the brim with highlighters. James looked at him and said with feigned enthusiasm, "Ready to do some highlighting, Dad?"It was such a dumb off-handed comment but something in his delivery was priceless. His dad didn't clue in either which made it seem extra comical. James drops me off in the driveway and I give him the biggest hug.

"Thanks, dude, just for everything. I appreciate you so so so much."

"You're welcome, it's no problem."

In bed I think again of that moment at the airport saying goodbye to James, which brings my mind to Wes. I got to pick him up from the airport once when he was returning from a business trip, and I remember that heart-fluttering feeling of anticipation I had waiting to see him. Remember? Hell, I feel it still now when he calls or texts me. I feel it now if I let myself think of him too much. I swear to God, what the thought or the sight or the presence of him does to me, it's some fucked-up hormone brain chemical thing because I come undone. It's never worn off. Those butterflies that come with a person whose very presence just makes your heart soar. The person whose voice lifts your spirits. The person whose body makes you ache for theirs. The person who just feels like home. Like the world makes sense when they're nearby. On one of mine and Lucy's trips back from California, the roles had been reversed and Wes had come to pick us up. It was the best. Simply put that's just it, there was no better feeling than knowing someone was waiting for me, someone I couldn't wait to get home to. I'm lying there thinking about him when he texts me. It's a link to a new album from a band we both love that we heard had broken up. I listen to the whole album in bed, thinking only of him.

I have a nightmare. Wes has come to the house and we're talking, we're talking and we're laughing. I say something funny and he leans back to look at me and says, "Fuck, I love you," just like he used to when we first started dating. I am just about to say it back when someone calls my name, it's a construction worker and he's started something on my house without my permission. I tell Wes, "I'm so sorry. I'll be right back, I promise." As I run to the worker everything changes, I'm in a series of tunnels of underground construction below my house and it's like Vegas, I can't find the exit. There's restaurants and bars and fast food establishments, and every time I think I'm outside I realize it's just a fake street designed to look like outside. I know Wes is waiting but I can't find my way out to get back to him. There's an elevator and I get in, but my hand gets caught just like it did in real life, and I'm screaming and screaming and there's no one around. It finally opens and releases me but even though I've taken it all the way to the top I'm still somehow not home. Fox is there and then Greyson.

"Wes," I pant breathlessly. "Have you seen Wes?"

Greyson's face saddens.

"Sorry he left, he got tired of waiting."

Fox stares at me, adding, "He was pissed."

I wake up covered in sweat, my heart racing like I've just run a marathon.

"Fuuuuck," I growl out loud. I pull my pillow over my head and it takes hours for me to fall back asleep.

## July 23

I can't even get my eyes to stay open. After falling back asleep I had a second nightmare, this one less clear in my memory but I know it involved being locked in a burning house. I let the dogs out to pee and fumble around for gym clothes. In the mirror I see the huge bags under my eyes, which are refusing to fully open. It is July 23, and this, this is the day Tese died. I hate this day.

My workout is ineffective at best; at worst and probably the most accurate assessment, it's a complete waste of time. I do more staring off into space and wandering than actual lifting. I couldn't even tell you how long I'm there before I leave. I have errands I should be doing. There's been some error with my property taxes. They were paid well before the deadline, but for some reason I've been sent a final notice to pay and an additional late fee. I'm behind on garbage because I've either been out of town or absent-minded on the actual day it's picked up. I grab all the papers I need for city hall and take a couple bags of garbage and some recycling to the waste transfer station. When my errands are done I'm just not feeling well. I don't know if it's a sadness thing thinking about Tese, or a sick thing. I actually feel like maybe I'm getting the flu. I fuck around on my cell phone for lack of anything better to do or the energy to do it. I write a post about Tese and include some pictures. I always like her family to know she is never forgotten by me, that I carry her still. I write about telling people you love them and vulnerability, because I wish today, and every day, I had told her more of what she meant to me. I shove thoughts of the day she died out of my mind, trying not to allow my brain to replay the moment when I understood she was dead. *Don't*, I tell myself every time the memory rushes up. It's knocking at my door and pulling at my hair and whispering in my ear for me to pay attention to it but I fight it.

My mother used to be a coroner and while she kept any details of her cases 100 percent confidential, we did have a discussion once when I was a teenager about different types of crying. For the life of me I couldn't tell you how or why we had gotten on the topic. I do remember though her explanation of how often upon hearing the news of the death of a loved one people would, and this was the exact term she used, "fold in on themselves." She described to me how this primal sound would be released, not a cry but a guttural call that welled up from their soul and then they would fold right in half crumpling themselves into two pieces. I never understood the description until the day Tese died. I had dropped the phone, yelled something that sounded like "No" and "Oh god" combined but it came out like "Naaaaagaaaaaawhd" and then I folded. I folded right in half. I've spent the last eight years trying to smooth that fold back out, but like a piece of paper I know everyone who knew me before and after can always see that line where I was bent in two. *Stop, stop thinking about that moment.* The elevator accident happened shortly after and it was then that I was diagnosed with acute PTSD. I underwent years of therapy trying to get back to normal again. I never fully came around, I don't think. I used to be social, the life of the party, everyone come to Roo's. I retreated inward, I had panic attacks, I was scared of undergrounds and elevators and, hell, my own shadow some days. I constantly had this sense that something terrible was about to happen or that I was going to die. My panic attacks became debilitating after James left, but I hid them really well. Poor James, I used to be so fun and so lively and social. It cannot have been easy falling for someone whose personality completely changed. When I met Wes the panic attacks stopped. I'd had just one the entire time I was with him and it was when we were changing which room the kids would sleep in, trying to make the house more functional for all of them. I'm sure to this day he thinks it was some subliminal weirdness or aversion I had toward the kids. It was the exact opposite. When we started struggling we'd exhausted every option of how to make the house work for us. He was even considering moving out. The room change-up was a last-ditch effort to integrate our lives in a way that made sense. That day when I panicked it wasn't because I was unhappy or the kids made me unhappy; it was because I loved them so much and was putting so much pressure on myself for this to be the solution. I remember thinking over and over again, "please please please let this work. Please let this make them be able to stay with me." It was not at all what was happening that triggered it; it was the fear of what would happen if the solution wasn't viable. That's the thing with anxiety and PTSD; it's rarely about what's happening in the moment and is more so the fear of a thing that could come. Tens of thousands of dollars' worth of therapy hadn't seemed to have eased my panic attacks the way Wes did, and I've always wondered what it is about him that has that effect on me. He makes the world make sense to me; he makes me feel like I belong . . . although I couldn't tell you how or why. He makes me feel safe. I look at pictures of Tese and me, pictures of her smiling, laughing, dancing, and remember her how she was as best I can. OK, I seriously must have the flu. I feel fucking exhausted and terrible, so I crawl into bed and fall asleep immediately.

When I wake back up an hour later I feel a million times better. Maybe it was just sleep deprivation from the nightmares. The sun is shining, and it's calling me to come outside. The garden beds could use weeding, the roses need pruning, and everything needs watering. I make a pot of coffee, throw some tunes on, grab my pruners and head out front. I've read a whole bunch of studies that say getting your hands in soil is actually really good for you, and every time I garden I think of this, because it does just feel relaxing and good. I mow the front lawn and then carefully weed around the roses. I pull weeds in the garden boxes and clean up my succulent bed. I prune back the rose bushes. It's starting to look much better. I cook myself dinner and watch old videos of myself and Tese. I video-chat my parents and they both shake their heads in disbelief when I tell them it's been eight years. They were with me at the funeral, as was James. I remember everyone was crying, just crying so hard, and I kept looking at my mom's and dad's faces and at James's face, and just thinking over and over again, "This is not real." Ten minutes after the funeral you could have asked me to describe it to you and I would not have been able to call to mind a single detail. The brain, or maybe the heart, catches more than we think though.

Three years later I was in a native art gallery with James and I had a full-on panic attack, flying out of the store clinging to a lamppost on the busy street, heaving, crying and gulping for air.

"What, Roo, what's wrong?"

"The box!" I yell. "Did you see the box in there?"

"No?"

"It was a cedar box, like the one they carried Tese's ashes in at funeral."

I knew then that should we learn to get too good at burying painful memories, life will find a way to force you to face them.

## July 24

I spend the day on a lengthy hike with the dogs and then come home and clean. Wes is coming over in a bit and I'm trying to get the growing pile of things I keep finding that belong to him together in some totes so he can take them. I grabbed the paperwork earlier today that's required for the sale of The Beast, so when he comes he'll sign those and take the boxes. I'm nervous because there is something else I really want to talk to him about and I want to do it in person. I want to tell him that all our "fresh start" talk and "nothing's off the table" chats should be considered off the table. I have no desire right now to date or to get into a new relationship, but I just don't want it looming over my head lest I find myself inadvertently waiting for him to come back. My fear is that in a few weeks when he meets a woman he really likes he will essentially have to "break up" with me a second time by having the "things are now coming off the table chat." That would be humiliating. I also just truly care about his happiness, and there's not a single part of me that wants him to feel beholden to me in some way. I just don't like anyone feeling like they owe me anything, financially or emotionally. So it's time to make it clear that he is free in every sense of the word. I have no clue why I'm nervous to say this. He's the one who broke up with me, so I'm sure he'll be relieved.

He looks great when he arrives; his beard is a crazy sexy mess that drives me wild. I pull out the paperwork right away and we go over it together and discuss pricing details for The Beast. He signs his half. We make our way to my spare room, where I've gathered three boxes of his belongings to take. One box in particular is hard for me to watch go. It's got the special speaker in it. He also offered to let me keep the sound bar for the television, but I've included it in his stuff anyway and he doesn't seem to notice. He's grabbing for the last box now and if I don't say it soon I'm worried I'm going to lose my nerve.

I stare at the floor and start: "There is something else I wanted to talk to you about."

"OK," he says, smiling at me.

"You know all our conversations about nothing being off the table? Well, I was kinda thinking that it's probably in both our best interest if it is. Like, my fear is you meeting someone and having to come back and tell me that, which would suck for both of us, and it's really not fair to you. I think at this point it should be implied if not assumed that we're both going to date or sleep with other people."

I surprise myself when I say sleep with because I literally have zero intention of sleeping with anyone right now, but I guess maybe the word came out because I wanted him to know he doesn't owe me anything, and that he's truly free to be with whomever he wants in whatever way he wants. I'm sure he has already been with other people. I'm not an idiot. I can't read his expression at all because he turns his face somewhat away from mine. Is it pain? Is it sadness? Is it relief but not wanting that to show? I do notice he crosses one arm over himself and holds his own elbow first, then rubs his own bicep with his crossed arm. I have never seen him stand that way before. I search his face, and he looks entirely differently to me suddenly, which makes my heart so sad.

"For sure," he says to me. "That makes sense, if everything's still on the table it's always there like some elephant in the room, whereas if we just take everything off, it could come back on again down the road if that was what we decided, but for now yeah, that makes sense."

I have no clue how to interpret his mention of putting things back on the table later. Again, I suspect the majority of what he says comes from a place of trying to hurt me the least amount possible, and maybe he feels I need the hope still to be OK? Weeks ago I did, but now I do not. This is the last phase of letting go for me. We discuss a little bit more why the removal of any type of hope is for the best, and I make sure to explain probably far too repeatedly that all I want is for him to be happy. He most certainly wants the same for me. We take the last box out and then stand on the porch chatting before we both head out.

On the drive to Fox's place I feel good about my conversation with him, I feel lighter and relieved, and I hope he does too. It will be hard to see him with someone else when that happens, and honestly each day I question more and more if he and I ever really will be able to be friends, but if one day I see a photo of him smiling and laughing, embracing a woman who looks equally happy, I will feel immense pain, but find peace so long as he is OK.

I broke up with a guy once. It was only a several month thing, but afterward he sent me a meme that read "true love is when you want what's best for someone, even when it can't include you." I think of this now. When I arrive at Fox's I'm informed they're making steak and lobster for dinner. Holy shit, apparently I picked a good night to drop by. She's in a bikini lounging in the courtyard and Clive is barbecuing the most delicious-looking steaks. I tell her all about my conversation with Wes, and she's really happy that I seem to be starting to let go, and ya know what, I think I am too.

"I don't think a few weeks ago either of us would have guessed you'd be saying that to him."

"No. I know, right?"

"It's really good, Roo. That was the right thing."

The dinner is fantastic and I overeat by a long shot, drenching each delicious bite of lobster in excessive amounts of butter.

"I should get going to Lucy's," I tell her after I clear the plates. "I wanna check in on her and make sure she's doing OK."

Her kids are already in bed when I get there, so we quietly make our way to her back deck.

"You wanna beer?" she asks me.

"You know what, I totally do."

We smoke cigarettes and I tell her about seeing Wes. I watched a documentary once about a family who runs a funeral home, three generations of them all working together. Their insights on death and grieving were perhaps some of the most poignant and insightful I've ever heard. I recall the middle generation, the father, probably in his fifties, describing how when family members come in to the funeral home they are always compelled to tell the story of how they came to know their loved one had died. He spoke about how the story, and the retelling of it, becomes as much a part of the process of grief as the actual actions required to deal with a death. Here, retelling Lucy that which I've just told Fox, I'm reminded of this. The telling of this story, hell the writing of this book, this is grieving. Lucy is equally shocked but pleasantly surprised about it. "Bet he didn't see that coming from you."

And she's right. It's really an inconsequential conversation in the grand scheme of things, in that he had already ended the relationship. But those who are closest to me, they understand how unlike me it is to . . . give up. To essentially admit defeat and attempt to let go for real. More than anything, I think they see that's not what I want at all, but simply that it's right. My being able to admit that, and think that, and say that, that's new. I am a waiter, a hoper, a believer by my very nature, to my very core. Perhaps the saddest part of what all of this had done to me, is changed that. When it comes to him, I am, for the first time, hopeless. I was hopelessly in love, and now I am hopelessly sure that love will never be returned. You would think it would make me sad, and it does, but it's glossed with an appreciation for the changes in me that now allow me to admit this.

We talk underneath the stars, sipping our beers slowly.

I get a text from James

"Are you at my house?" He must have seen my vehicle out front.

"Yes, stalking you. JK, hanging with Lucy" I write back.

Who could have ever imagined this would be my life, so strange, so layered, so not what I expected. Here on the deck ten feet above my ex-husband's suite seated next to my best friend I think, "its OK, this is just how it is."

## July 25

I need to start packing for camping as I'm leaving tomorrow, but I have a training session this morning with Hendrik. I walk the dogs around the block first to try and quell some of their antsy-ness so they don't destroy anything while I'm working out. The sun is shining, and where it hits my shoulders it feels good and warm. The ride to training is riddled with traffic and I drink my pre-workout way before I've arrived which means it kicks in and I'm jittery and eager to get there. No sooner have I started rowing than Hendrix hits me with a comical arm raise and the words, "Ummm . . . I have questions."

I laugh.

"OK, hit me."

"James?" he raises a brow at me. He must have seen the photo I posted of myself and James after our dinner.

"Ahhh yes, I know, right? So here's the thing, he's been super helpful since Wes and I broke up. I stayed at his place all those times when it first happened and when moving day came and stuff. He's just been really—I dunno how to explain it. It's like after everything that's happened between us he just leveled up his friend game and came flying in to help. It's been really amazing, actually."

"Cool . . . next question, camping with Greyson and he's moving into your basement suite?"

"Weird on paper, I know, but you know me and my propensity for complex borderline incestual situations. Wes was the one who suggested it, the move in I mean, and then the camping was just like, a thing he was going to do and it was this national park I've always wanted to see. He's got a dog and all our dogs are buddies and so it might be good for me. Change of scenery, lots of hiking, already discussed making it not a drinking weekend, which is good for my fitness goals and stuff. We'll see how it goes. If the whole living with my ex-boyfriend's best friend thing blows up in my face then, like everything else, it'll be my own disaster."

Hendrik likes that. "My own disaster," he laughs back to me.

I tell him all about the garden goddess party and how much fun I had with the girls. I lament over facing the world of dating again and how or when that even becomes a thing.

"It's tough out there," he says with empathy and humor. That one I like, a lot, and I laugh and say so. He has this way of making simple phrases significant to me, years' worth of stupid one-liners that become the embodiment of my state of mind; half apply to fitness, half apply to life, and all are ridiculous. When we're all done we crawl to the floor and take a photo together. I hug him before I leave: "I'll check in when I'm back from camping and see what your schedule is like for next week."

I drive rapidly back from town to meet Seamus for coffee at the shop by my house. I arrive before him. The woman behind the counter knows me from my days in radio and from the podcast.

"Why no more shows?" she asks me.

Ughhhh this is the part I hate, but I've done it to myself. "My own disaster," I think.

"Well . . ." I shift from one leg to the other and drop my bag at my feet.

"Wes and I broke up a few weeks ago, so it's on hold for now. We're still going to try and do it, I think, but just sort of waiting to see and getting the studio set back up or whatever."

As I'm telling her this Seamus arrives. She launches into a story about a podcast she likes these days dealing with weird 911 calls, not realizing Seamus is a cop. I enjoy the awkwardness of it.

We get our coffees and head outside to a small table. Seamus is off. He, like many law enforcement officers, suffers from PTSD, it's actually one of the first things we bonded over. When his anxiety is piqued the smallest thing will grind against him, making it impossible to focus. PTSD is like having kindling inside you and wandering around the world with piles of matches. His ignition source today is two men seated behind us who are clearly drunk, and one appears to be waiting for someone. It's most likely a drug deal.

"We have to move." His eyes are flared and wild.

I follow him back inside.

"Sorry," he tells me, cracking his neck. A nervous habit of his when his anxiety is piqued. "That guy was just, ugh, just driving the fuck out of me, I couldn't concentrate."

"It's OK. I get it." Today he seems like a pot of water right on the edge of a boil.

I get to talking about my upcoming camping trip and his mood lightens. He tells me a few stories of what he's been up to. I love hearing about how his wife and kids are doing. It's a quick visit because he has to get back to the office like always.

"Same time next week?" I ask

"You betcha."

I grocery shop for camping supplies, some hot dogs, salads, yogurt, steaks. I don't buy a ton, just enough for a few days. I'm honestly not sure how well my cooler will work, because I've only ever used it for beers in the shed, and I don't want things to spoil. I gather up Fox's tent, my air mattresses, and the dog's supplies. In the morning I'll just need to pack my clothes and then I should be good to go. I message Greyson to see how far he's made it on his trip and where he will stay tonight. He's en route but has another five hours to go.

"I'm feeling 'adventurey,'" I message him back. "What if I start driving too and we meet in the middle? I can go past where I was originally supposed to meet you tomorrow."

He says to give him a few minutes and see what he can come up with. He eventually texts back with a location of a campground four-and-a-half hours from me.

"Perfect! I'll pack the last bit of my stuff and be on the road in half an hour."

I don't pay much attention to what clothes I'm packing, really I'm only concerned with making sure I have the supplies I need to manage the dogs. I text my parents, Lucy, Fox, and James to let them all know I'm leaving one night earlier than planned. It feels weird to be able to do something like this. My radio life had me so locked into a schedule. When I wasn't working, sleep, gym, and dogs were always my priority. Any trips I took needed to be planned months in advance and permission granted for time off. Spontaneity is not a quality my life has ever been structured to allow me to have. This gives me a charge. I haven't seen Greyson in a week either, and I'm looking forward to hearing all about his trip and how the wedding he attended was.

The drive is long, and, sadly, I really only have a few playlists on my phone, two of which were made by Wes. I listen to the same songs over and over but it actually doesn't bother me too much, he does have exceptional taste in music. I stop every so often to let the dogs out to pee, or to pee myself or get gas. By the time I'm forty minutes out I'm getting really tired. I hit the campsite before Greyson and check in at the office to get directions to our site. Of course, once I'm there I realize my flashlights batteries are dead so I have to point the Jammer's headlights into the spot to begin laying out the tent. The dogs bark every time there's any little noise, and the site is surrounded by RV's. This must be the result of Greyson having to find some place on short notice, because I can tell you right now this place will not suit his style.

I'm relieved when he pulls up. I race to his car and give him a huge hug. Thank goodness he has all the appropriate flashlights. He quickly helps me set up Fox's tent and seems to comprehend without having done it before how to do it, which is funny because I've done it many times and I'm basically useless. He puts his up like a pro, making it look easier than I think it actually is. Greyson makes smokies and tells me all about the wedding and his time away. He shows me a hilarious picture of himself asleep on the couch the day after still wearing his tuxedo. We go to bed relatively quickly after eating because it's close to 1 a.m. and we're both exhausted from driving. The site is hilarious because it's located next to the highway and train tracks, so every few minutes a train goes by or the railway crossings starts dinging.

"This is lovely," I say to him sarcastically through my tent.

"So peaceful," he says back.

More industrial sounds.

"Are we near an airport?" I call to him and there's more laughing.

We end up bantering through the tent walls, which I'm sure all the neighbours love. My dogs bark and huff constantly. My air mattress has not seemed to fully inflate and there's a rock digging into my shoulder. Tiredness overtakes me, and I eventually drift off.

## July 26

I awake to the sound of the god damn train again. When I unzip my tent to get up and pee, the dogs both clamber out, raising holy hell. Thank goodness Greyson is up already and wrangles them onto their long lines.

"Coffee is needed," he tells me. "But I kind of want to just pack up and get out of this site."

"Yeah, me too. Let's just roll and find a good place to go. But coffee at the first gas station we see."

We pack our things up and I notice he's very organized about the whole process. I on the other hand jam things haphazardly into wherever they will fit.

"My car looks like I've been on the road for a week," I tell him as I survey the damage.

"Mine too, but I actually have been." He truly has, and his car is still only a fraction as bad as mine.

We head out, stopping at a nearby gas station for coffee and then on to the visitor information center for the national park we'll be going to hike in, about an hour away. The woman at the counter gives Greyson some details about nearby rec sites. I follow up through the small town and eventually along a gravel road to a middle-of-nowhere site. It's perfect. There are two sites right down by a beautiful lake literally on the water, and there's no one else around. We park one vehicle in each of the sites and get our stuff set up. All three dogs happily run around and chase one another. Seeing my dogs happy and feeling like I'm giving them a life they enjoy always gives me this weird Zen. Once the tents are done we start pulling out stuff we'll need for hiking. I forgot my backpack, so lucky Greyson gets to carry all the supplies. Bug spray, snacks, toilet paper, bear spray, dog-poo bags, water for us and the dogs, and a water dish for the dogs too. I feel bad I forgot my bag.

The first walk we do is to a smaller waterfall with several tiers. It looks like icing dripping down a layered cake. Greyson makes me nervous because while he inches closer and closer, I tell him I'm going to hang back. He goes way farther than I ever would have, eventually standing on a log just before the falls.

"Be careful," I whisper to myself, watching him scamper around. I take a few pictures of him crossing it and smiling back at me. The second walk is to a much larger waterfall with boardwalks above it and viewpoints all over. Tourists line the walkways and fences, all trying to get the perfect shot of it. We're no different. Prior to leaving I read a lot about this national park and there's a beautiful meadow hike that's supposed to be astounding and filled with wildflowers. The drive to the trailhead takes about forty minutes, but we make our way there.

Right from the onslaught, it's not what I expected. The bugs and flies are horrific and I don't mind so much for myself, although it is kind of gross, but the poor dogs. All three of them are covered in flies and mosquitoes and god knows what. On top of this, I'm not kidding, the forest has this disgusting smell.

"Do you think it's the flowers?" I ask Greyson.

"I don't know, it's like skunk cabbage or something."

"Well, between your choice for a campsite yesterday and my disgusting smelly flower walk, we're really nailing this."

We're about an hour into the trail when I tell him I can't stand it anymore. I feel way too bad for the dogs, and it's gross and not as pretty as I thought it would be. In addition my blistered feet have held up OK but they're starting to get sore now.

"Sorry to be a Debbie downer, I'm just like, I think I need off this trail now."

He's super nice about it and doesn't seem to mind, as I know the bugs are getting on his nerves too. Back at the car I drink epic amounts of water and demolish most of the various trail mix snacks we had.

The dirt road down is really dusty and I'm caught eating the dust of a car in front of me.

"I'm just gonna pull over and let this guy get ahead." I say.

Greyson has a book with insane amounts of information about the hike and various sites you can see at certain mile markers. While we sit and let traffic pass, he reads out loud about an infamous murder that took place in this park. Eerily enough the family that was killed was from our town and it explains why so many things in the area are named after them.

We follow the book's navigation to a set of beautiful rapids underneath a trestle bridge. Again, Greyson makes me nervous when he climbs rocks right under the bridge to get a view no one else can and snag some impressive photos. We finish the hike with one last waterfall. At this point I'm exhausted but when we finally get there, it's the most stunning thing. Just completely overpowering. Truly the real thing the word "awesome" was intended for, and I don't think I've ever seen anything like it. The mist creates a rainbow-like effect. For a long time, I lean against the rails just staring at it, letting it make me feel insignificant and temporary. Greyson comes up beside me.

"Amazing, hey?"

"Yeah. I feel so small." We don't talk much while we stand there, but by the time we hike back to the car I can't shut up.

"When I worked, ya know, I'd say stuff to myself like, camping, who the hell has time for camping, and it's because I wanted it to not be important so I could justify the fact I didn't have time to do it anymore. Then I stand there and have that "I'm so small" feeling and it makes you realize just how important nature is and how cathartic and healing it is."

"Yeah, I mean, that's all I did when my ex and I split up; I just tried to be outside and in the mountains as much as possible."

We stop at a random store to pick up a few things we're missing. Camping coffee mugs, I need a towel, a hairbrush. I really didn't pack very well. Up near the till I see Greyson throw a couple of packets onto the counter. They're some powder you throw on a campfire that will make the flames glow different colours.

"Cool!" I exclaim.

The woman behind the till furrows her brow.

"Just be really sure," she warns us, "to wait until it's really dark before you put those on the fire. We get a lot of tourists coming back in to return them saying they didn't work, but it just wasn't dark enough to see it."

For whatever reason my towel displays on the till as "Deluxe Ass" when she rings it through and I can't stop laughing. I swat at Greyson with all the maturity of a 14-year-old boy.

"Look," I nudge him.

He laughs too and snags a picture. Even the woman behind the till laughs a bit.

When we get back in the car, Greyson turns to me.

"Who . . ." he holds up one of the fire packets, "drives all the way back to the store to return an item that cost a dollar fifty?" I hadn't even caught that and now I'm giggling like crazy. We wind our way back to the rec site and see we're not alone anymore. A burgundy camper van is parked in the remaining campsite slightly up the hill from us.

"We should go introduce ourselves," Greyson tells me. "It's rec site camp etiquette, every time I've been at one of these people came over to shake hands."

"OK."

Introducing myself to new people is one of my least favourite things, but we park and I follow him up the hill to the van. A young, petite woman with overalls and a beautiful mess of curls is now standing outside it, back to us, taking photographs of the van. She seems startled when we approach.

"Oh hey, you caught me taking van-porn shots."

"Its super cool," I say to her.

"Thanks. I live in it." She introduces herself as Alicia and spends some time explaining to us about her various solar panels and generators and how she manages to live off the grid in this beast she calls Kirby. She was in the area tree-planting, had engine trouble today, and has to stay the night waiting for the mechanic to order a part he will install tomorrow."

Both Greyson and I are super intrigued and can't ask enough questions about how she's doing it. We both have a mild obsession with tiny homes and minimalism.

"Well, when you're settled in if you want to come down and join us for a fire we'll be here," he tells her. We make dinner and have a beer. We take a swim in the lake that's right in front of the campsite. Loons call out and every now and again a fish jumps. We don't talk a ton, but we sit in two camp chairs right at the water's edge staring toward the slowly setting sun.

When Alicia makes her way down, Greyson starts a fire. She regales us with tales of running into a wolf, bear attacks and tree-planting life in general. She tells us about the origins of Kirby and how she fought the university she was attending to keep it parked on their property. During the battle she became an inadvertent local celebrity. She essentially decided apartments and roommates were too much trouble and committed to living off the grid and sustainably for an entire year. She's really cool, and very funny, and I like how herself she is. We throw the packets onto the fire and the flames dance wild and unnatural colours. It's beautiful. A ban on fires is coming into effect in this area tomorrow so I let my eyes soak it in trying to appreciate every second of the multi-coloured flames. I'm the first to excuse myself to crash and the dogs follow me into the tent.

## Week Six
## July 27

Greyson is up again before me and I can hear him rummaging around in his car, so I unzip the tent and release the hounds, who are flying around the campsite full of energy after a night cooped up. I give them a minute and then leash them up.

"I'm making coffee, and then breakfast," Greyson tells me.

"I want both of those things."

Nothing boils slower than water for coffee while you're camping. When it's finally ready I take a huge sip, only to spill down my face. I adjust the lid and try again, and it still happens.

"These mugs we got suck," I tell him, laughing. I remove the lid altogether, and it still somehow drips down my face.

"How is that even possible?" He laughs at me.

He makes eggs and bacon with garlic oil and some flavoured cream cheese; it's delicious.

We don't rush at all and leisurely eat and drink more coffee while we form a plan of where to hike today.

Alicia wanders down. "Mechanic has the part so I'm off now."

"It was so nice to meet you." I stand up and give her a hug. "Hold on." I run to my vehicle and find a receipt I can write on to give her my contact info.

"If you're ever out our way you're more than welcome to come park in my driveway and hang, we'd love to see you again."

"That would be awesome, oh and I brought this for you." She hands me a small tube. It's an all-natural insect repellent. I had been getting eaten alive last night by mosquitoes.

"Thanks."

Greyson gives her a hug too and she heads out. We slowly rearrange the hiking bag, making sure we have everything we need for a day out with the dogs.

We passed a hike to a fall yesterday that was overrun by tourists and Greyson's hoping if we go back today it will be less busy. On the road he reads me the book and points out various sites and their aligned mile markers. When we reach the parking lot of our hike it's packed but we manage to find a spot. In the beginning the hike is easy; the only problem is it's incredibly hot. The further we go, though, the steeper and more challenging the terrain becomes. It's busy too and my dogs aren't exactly great with all people, so passing them on narrow, steep, angled trails makes me nervous.

"Why don't you take her?" Greyson says and motions to his dog, who is much better behaved than my two. "I'll take them."

"Are you sure?" I ask?

"Yup."

I'm glad for his offer because I honestly don't know if I could have made it down the trail managing my two. My mother often says to me of herself, "I am not sure-footed," and in this moment I question if that is an inherited trait. I'm uneasy as we make the descent to the base of the falls, but holy god is it worth it once we're down. Again, I've never seen anything like this. It has a huge basin that pools at the bottom and a fine mist glows up from it. The sun creates multiple mini rainbows as far as the eye can see. We get the dogs some water at the bottom and then Greyson points to a trail that circles directly underneath and behind the waterfall.

"Let's go there."

I could throw up, the thought makes me so nervous. There's no one over on that side and the trail looks narrow. He can sense my unease.

"It's safe, there's an actual trail. I'll take your dogs again. You just manage her." He doesn't give me time to really think about it or protest, which is probably for the best.

We wind our way to the trail and reach the last part, where we will be able to walk side by side or really hear one another over the sound of the falls.

"It's slippery." he points down to the path, which is muddy from the mist exploding off the falls. "I'm gonna move quick. See you on the other side" and then he's off like a rocket running with my dogs up and behind the falls. He seems to disappear and then emerges from the opposite side waving to me.

*Holy fuck.* I asses what would happen if I fell in. Unlike some of the other falls we have seen, this one is not particularly high and we're at the base of it, not the top. I stare down into the pool, which is not overcome with rapids, and asses that if I slide off the trail and fall in it will hurt but I will definitely survive. I point my eyes down and stare only at the trail and don't allow myself to look more than two steps ahead of my feet. I try to make myself move quickly but the closer I move toward it, the louder the falls are and the thicker the mist that hits me until it stings my eyes. My heart is kicking me in my ribcage and my stomach. My adrenaline spikes so high I feel dizzy. I don't look, I just go, and I keep telling myself "Move forward, move forward." Finally I emerge on the other side, where Greyson is waiting.

"Oh my god, that was so scary."

"Well you had a smile on your face the whole time."

"Did I? I didn't feel like I did! Fuck, I'm like having a heart attack over here. I feel so panicky."

"Look at this," Greyson points. Hidden behind the waterfall is a beautiful crevice filled with cool stones and coloured rocks. We stay on that side for quite some time, taking pictures and clamoring around over rocks. When we're finally ready to cross back over I feel foolish as I've now seen several small children make their way across the trail that seems so intense to me, but I'm still nervous about it. For some reason going back is scarier, maybe because now I know what to expect about how my body is going to react, but I manage to make it.

The hike back up is even more challenging than the way down; I have to grab at roots and trees to pull myself up some of the steeper parts. Greyson finds an offshoot trail and wants to follow it, which leads us to a bridge crossing about the water. There's signage saying "Not national park property use at your own risk." Before I can tell him not to he hands me his dog and wanders across it. I look at him wondering what it would be like to be someone who's so fearless. Not really a quality I have, and in fact I would most likely be described by those closest to me as a nervous person. It strikes me as odd then how many chances I took with Wes, and I'm not sure if this was growth or stupidity on my part. Was I being brave or being an idiot? Probably both.

We meander our way back toward the small town nearest our campsite, stopping at several viewpoints along the way. There's a BBQ joint just on the edge of town that Greyson wanted to try, but I'm nervous about how to manage the dogs. Way too hot to leave them in the vehicle but the establishment has a patio and he figures we can have them on leash close to us while we eat. It's 4pm now and they don't open until 5, so we sit in the vehicle with the AC cranked. I can barely keep my eyes open I'm so tired from the heat and the hike and the wear-off of all the adrenaline. I fold my sweater into a pillow and close my eyes in the front seat. Just before they open, Greyson calls to check about the dogs and they let us know it's fine to bring them by so long as they're not on the actual patio.

"I'm just worried Atticus is going to scream, he doesn't like being tied up and having me walk away, but worst case if it's brutal we just won't stay, I guess?"

"Yeah, for sure," Greyson reassures me.

When we round the patio we see a row of trees covered by shade and decide it's a good spot to leash them up. All three dogs get attached to a tree and we put a water bowl out for them.

To my complete and utter surprise, neither of my dogs makes a peep when we walk away to the table, and I stare in astonishment when they both lie down and go to sleep. Not just lie down on their side and relax, but straight up take a nap.

"I gotta send a picture of this to James," I say, snagging photo after photo of the three sleepy dogs. "There's no way he will believe it."

Greyson and I look at the menu and decide to order a giant two-person sample platter that comes with a little bit of every type of barbecued meat they offer. It's expensive, but the thought of getting to try everything is just too tempting and splitting it makes sense. They blast country music and I sing along to every single word of every single song under my breath, professional hazard.

When the platter comes it looks amazing. It's filled with pulled pork and brisket and chicken and beans and coleslaw.

I take my first bite and it's really bland, but I don't say anything.

After a couple bites Greyson hold up his meat-laden fork and says to me, "I thought it would be more flavourful."

"Me too," I laugh. "I thought maybe it was just the chicken."

"No, none of it really has any flavour. They don't believe in seasoning in this town."

"Apparently not."

"It's the town that salt forgot. I betcha this place is so popular for locals, they don't really need to be good, they just have to be . . . open."

I laugh again. Blandness aside I still stuff myself, ravenously hungry from the hiking.

When we're done I'm so full I could die, or throw up, or both. We head back to the campsite to try and form a plan for the morning. There's another road we can take the follows along opposite of the national park and we should be able to get some really great views along a beautiful river. We can't have a fire now because the ban has come into effect, so we call it an early night.

## July 28

It's weird how after only two days something can feel like a routine, but I enjoy the fact that the morning unfolds in a similar fashion to yesterday. Greyson makes breakfast and coffee and we move about in a lackadaisical manner setting aside the items we will need for the hiking bag. We read through his book and find that at the end of the road we were considering driving, there is a sizeable hike that ends in a beautiful cascading falls. Unlike the others we've seen, this one is wide. The photo shows it to be an expansive, beautiful work of nature, and I want to see it.

"About an hour and a half in, so we could chill at one end, eat some snacks, and then come back, would eat up most of the afternoon for sure." I agree this sounds awesome and we get rolling.

Greyson drives and about two minutes into the ride he says to me, "Do you ever feel like maybe this thing needs new brakes?"

"Nope". I laugh this off. "I don't ever feel like that. I haven't heard squealers or anything."

"Well, sometimes you don't hear them, it just feels a bit crunchy when you break."

"It's just the road," I assure him. We are in 4 wheel-drive and we're dodging some pretty massive potholes.

He doesn't push it further. As we wind along the narrow gravel road, we follow a beautiful river dotted with crazy rapids that are well known for the water rafting. We pull over several times to take photographs. As a group of river rafters approaches we wave to them and they all wave and holler back up to the bank at us.

"You couldn't pay me enough."

"Yeah, not my thing either," Greyson agrees.

"I met this really nice guy, barely knew him, but this dude I had met through my work once or twice, and he passed away just a bit before his wedding doing that."

"Yeah, I know who you mean," Greyson said. A mutual friend of his knew his widow. He was a very beloved man in our town.

"That was so sad." I pause for a long time staring out at the river.

Meanwhile Greyson stands so close to the edge on several of our photo stops it takes everything I have not to ask him to back up. For a guy who doesn't like the idea of a carnival ride, he sure seems to have a fearlessness about him that unnerves me every time we come close to a ledge. We stop at a beautiful beachy spot on the river and let the dogs out for a quick swim.

"On the way back, we could stop here again and bring some chairs down," he tells me.

"Yeah, that would be great."

As we get further and further down the road, it narrows and narrows.

"See how the grass is growing in the middle of the road?" Greyson points out to me.

"You can tell hardly anyone comes down here. That's what I like; the places that aren't tourist traps and you know very few people have actually gotten to see." He talks a lot about the copious amount of time he spent in the woods after he and his wife were no longer together. He's a much more seasoned hiker and camper than I am or will probably ever be, but it's really cool and nice to be seeing some stuff I otherwise never would have. Had I come alone, which first of all I never would've, but I would have stayed at some highly populated area and hit all the standard places, the ones with parking lots and warning signs and crowds of people. At home I hike the same route in my neighborhood again and again unless I have company to try something new. I'm a creature of habit, but to see Greyson's ability to immerse himself in whatever environment he's in is truly inspiring, the fact that he does stuff like this alone with great frequency, awe inspiring. When we reach the very end of the road, we set out on the hike. At first it's OK, but about twenty minutes into it the ground turns somewhat marshy and the trail is replaced by old wooden trestle paths. The problem is the trestles are old, and unstable, and the gaps between the boards are really wide. I'm super worried about my dogs hurting their feet or breaking an ankle. Those two idiots get so amped, unlike his dog. They don't watch where they're going and they don't have a "slow" speed. The quick pace they're using to try and rush across the boards is a recipe for disaster, and Ducky falls off the side into the mud several times, seemingly unaware of how to follow the path.

"Looks like someone built the trail and then basically never came back to maintain it," Greyson tells me.

"Totally, I'm getting worried about the dogs, this just seems like someone is going to get hurt."

"If it doesn't get better up ahead we can totally turn around." I'm super relieved when he tells me this. My worry and nervousness factor has a tendency to turn me into a bit of a killjoy sometimes, and I'm always really self-conscious about ruining a good time for anyone else. It's nice that he has the ability to accommodate in such a way that doesn't make me feel bad.

"Yeah, let's keep going and if it doesn't get better in a bit we might have to call it."

We carefully navigate several more platforms, and there's no end in sight. Eventually we reach a section where I can't even find the trail anymore.

"Sorry, I just feel like one out us five souls is gonna get hurt somehow."

"Yeah, it's pretty janky. If we head back we can take those chairs down to the river and just chill there for a bit." I agree this is a good plan and we make the drive back to the river spot.

The dogs are playing in the water when the bus pulls up. It goes from silent to a flurry of activity in a heartbeat. We clamber around one another and the camping chairs trying to get the dogs tied to a log. It's a group of tourist whitewater rafters, and apparently this is their departure spot. My dogs bark and cry and the sound stresses me out and agitates the hell out of me.

"We'll be gone in ten minutes," one of the rafters, who seems to be the head instructor, tells us.

They pull down three rafts and the dogs are losing it the entire time. Each noise they make drives me through the roof and as they tug and tug against their leashes I'm worried the log is going to break.

"Ughhh, I hate those sounds," I say to Greyson. "When they're stressed it just stresses me out so bad too."

"Yeah," he agrees. "I thought this would be a quiet spot, but there are literally boatloads of people." I can't stop myself from laughing.

"Fuck, right?" When the boats finally depart and I think the dogs will calm down, a woman and a man walk down the path from the road with their two dogs, which sets mine into a second round of frenzy.

"Are they friendly?" the woman calls out to me.

"No!" I snap back at her. Shit, I'm full on how I get now.

As she struggles to move her dogs away from ours another bus arrives.

"OK, I'm so sorry. I'm the worst, but I can't handle this, I gotta get outta here, it's stressing me out really bad." I hardly even wait for his reply and instead just grab the dogs and with concerning speed head to the vehicle.

"I'll be behind you in a second" he says to me, but I'm already loading them into the vehicle.

I crank the A/C and sit inside. It's so frustrating having these two dogs who are so challenging. Within the confines of the life that James and I shared they worked perfectly for us. We had opposite shifts, so they were rarely left alone for more than a few hours at a time. We weren't hugely social in terms of having people at the house, so we were able to limit their interactions to just a few friends who are used to them, and we didn't really go away a ton. While I know

I am exceptionally lucky to have been the one to keep them after the divorce, it is a gift I sometimes resent. Two dogs like this were not built for a single person's lifestyle and I would be lying if I didn't admit that on some days I feel burdened by them, or I resent James for the fact that I am the one whose activities are inhibited by them. These dogs were a huge issue and stressor in my relationship with Wes. They were a factor in why it wasn't working, nervous rescue dogs and small children. It was just so much. It's hard not to wrap them into the way I see myself. Someone with baggage, someone with problems, someone who no one is going to want. But then I think of them, and the way the cuddle me, and how they make me laugh multiple times a day every day. How safe I feel sleeping alone between then. I know that I would never for a second consider not having them. Would I adopt two crazy rescues in the future, probably not, but these are the dogs I have and they will be my responsibility until the day they both pass. I think it's a real asshole move to get a dog and then get rid of it because they no longer fit neatly into what you thought your life would be. Nope, these two little weirdos will be my problem forever, like it or not.

Several minutes pass and Greyson climbs into the passenger's seat after having hauled up the camping chairs and bags and snacks I abandoned him with. On the way back home we stop for more food and snack supplies and get all prepped for our last night at the site. I feel like I could actually drink tonight and I tell Greyson this, so we hit the liquor store and grab Bud Light Lime, which in my mind is like adult ginger ale. The day has felt really long even though the hike went sideways and the beach time didn't work out. That's probably why it's felt long; when I get stressed I just sort of become kind of unbearable and short-tempered. On the gravel road back to the campsite I come around the corner and a woman flying down the road the other way just about collides with me. We both slam on our brakes. I wave an apologetic "sorry" at her as I think we were both driving a little naively around the blind corner, but instead of reciprocating she gives me a dirty look and mutters to herself.

"I love the muttering," Greyson says. "I see people do that all the time, just totally at fault but talking so bad about you right now." I burst out laughing.

"Yeah I mean, it's a blind corner on a camp road so I should have been going slower, but I was definitely going slower than her and that would have been both our faults for sure."

We climb the hill up into the rec site, and on the descent toward our tents there are two more vehicles at the bottom.

"Fuckin' bumpin' here today," I tell him.

The vehicles are blocking Greyson's car in his site and the spot where I need to pull my vehicle into mine.

"I'll go talk to them," he tells me and hops out.

Something feels very odd about where they're parked and just the look of the vehicles and the one woman I can see. You know when you instantly see someone and think, "You sketchy as fuck"? That's what this whole thing screams to me. I'm watching closely and notice Greyson has bear spray hanging from his pocket. Well, hope he doesn't have to use it. The interaction drags on for far too long for what I assume would have just been, "Hey, could you please move your vehicle so she can park." Eventually both cars take off past me, leaving room clear for me to pull in.

"What was all that about?" I ask him.

"Sketchy as fuck, the guy gave me weed though." He holds up several little green balls.

"Oh, he gave you some marijuana, did he?" I say sarcastically.

"Seriously it was so weird, the guy who I was talking to was bleeding from his head."

"What?"

"Yeah, just blood pouring from some head wound he was not acknowledging, looked like he hadn't even tried to clean it or anything, and both guys and the woman seemed drunk. He said he was showing a buddy some fishing around this area or something. Whole thing was super weird. Then he pulls out this giant bag of weed, like a big satchel and gave me this."

"Like a drive through," I laugh. "I would like one drug, please." The whole scenario is too strange to be believed. I almost wish I had seen the guy with the bloody face so I could describe it myself in first-person detail, but, sadly, I have only Greyson's account to rely on. The day is still hot even though the sun is starting to set, and we swim in the lake. My two dogs happily do circles around me. Greyson almost steps on an adorable little frog as he approaches the water but manages to avoid it. I try and snag pictures, but the little guy is too quick. For the first time, I think about the fact that it's been several days since I have written. I'm excited to go home and sleep in my own bed, but I know as soon as I pass that "welcome" sign in my hometown all the feelings of sadness will come rushing back to me. The emptiness of the life I'm returning to looms inside my head. When, when will my life feel full again the way it did with Wes? The way it used to with James. Or hell maybe even the way it had before I met Wes and was alone but doing really well with it. Can I make peace with being by myself again? I know that I can, it just takes times. I'm so sick of spending time healing. I'm bored with my own problems. I am looking forward to getting back to training though, and video-chatting with my folks to tell them about the trip. Greyson and I agree being hung over for the drive home tomorrow would be less than ideal, so we call it an hour or so after the sun has completely set and the sites go dark.

## July 29

I'm up before Greyson today to pee and the dogs fly out of the tent with me excitedly ripping around and frolicking in the water. When I come back from the outhouse, Greyson and his dog are up.

"I could make breakfast," he says, or we could just hit some place on the way out?"

"Yeah, maybe today we just pack up and go, less dishes and shit, and I gotta get gas and we can get coffee in town or whatever."

I'm motivated by the need for coffee and suspect he is too. We manage to tear down and pack up in about forty minutes. Again, his pack job is neat and tidy and his vehicle appears unscathed. My car, on the other hand, looks like it's been ransacked and I'm already dreading the idea of having to unpack it and deal with all the shit inside when I get home. We convoy for gas and coffee and then hit the road. We stop twice on the way back, once so I can get gas and another time to let the dogs out for a quick pee and play and run around. When we finally make it home, I am exhausted. Greyson sets about unpacking his car right away.

"I'm beat," I tell him. "Gonna make that . . ." I motion to my vehicle "a later me problem. Could barely keep my eyes open that last stretch. I'm gonna go nap."

"OK," he says.

"Hey, thanks for a super fun trip, that was awesome." I give him the biggest hug.

"Yeah I had fun," he tells me.

"Catcha later." Inside I shower and then crawl right into bed and pass out.

I text Fox when I'm awake and tell her I'm coming over to catch up. I throw on a cute little sundress and I hear miniscule sounds hitting the floor as I unfold it. Cuba sand. Fuck. I've washed it three times since that trip, that should not even be possible. My vehicle handles weird on the way over. Every time I turn it feels crunchy. I know something is wrong. S*hit. Going to have to deal with that tomorrow.*

I let myself into her house and wander through to the patio, where she and Clive are sipping drinks in the fading sun lake-watching.

"Well, aren't you adorable," she says to me.

"Thanks," I say, crawling onto the cement patio step at the foot of her Adirondack chair.

I motion to my very unladylike splayed legs.

"I do have shorts on underneath, in case you're thinking I'm being a little free-spirited in front of your husband." They both laugh.

"Beer?" she asks me.

"Nah, I shouldn't."

"Coffee?"

"A world of yes."

I ask them all about the music festival they were at over the weekend, and they give me the rundown on the various shenanigans of high people they witnessed.

I tell them all about the camping trip and show them pictures of each of the beautiful falls we saw, as well as several of the dogs living their best dog life. Clive tells me if his ex went camping with his best friend he'd be pissed. I get it, seems to be the running sentiment.

"Yeah, I don't know . . . for me that was just like, a them problem . . . I honestly don't think there was, though; those two seem to get each other." Clive is oddly eager to chat relationships tonight. It's very out of character as he's normally more stoic. He gives lots of opinions on why men behave the way they do after a breakup. I tear up talking to him about Wes's kids.

"I think you're doing everything right," he says. "You're gonna be a hot ticket, I promise. Guys will be lining up for you."

I must really seem more down than I think, because it's not in his nature to ego pad and I wonder if he feels I need a boost, although he seems sincere. Clive wanders into the kitchen.

"Check out Mr. Relationship over here." Fox motions back toward him in the kitchen.

"I know, hey? He's super insightful tonight."

"You staying for dinner, Foo?" he yells to me from inside. Since I've known him he's called me Foo Relps, which Fox says for him is a term of endearment.

"I don't wanna bogart your dinner, I should roll."

"I'm making a brie bake," he entices me.

"What's in that?"

"Brie, mushrooms . . ." he lists off a whole bunch of things that sound amazing.

"OK, well, when ya put it like that . . . yeah, I'll stay."

"Now beer?" Fox asks me.

"Now beer," I agree.

We eat and we laugh and tell stories as the sun disappears. Clive obsesses over a man on a paddle board who he is convinced takes pictures of people's homes and reports their goings-on to the city, which makes Fox and I laugh. I tell them I need to get a for sale ad posted for The Beast. Somehow this morphs into a lot of joking about writing a spoof ad. Clive throws around hilarious lines like "emotional baggage towing capacity." It's such a stupidly funny way of handling something I've been dreading that I think I might actually do it. Impervious to the time I all of a sudden realize it's getting late and I should head home, I have training tomorrow with Hendrik. I hug them both and thank them for a lovely night.

## July 30

I train with Hendrik in the morning and we have a good catch-up. I explain to him that I'm finally ready to start taking my goals to the next level, and could we up the number of training sessions I'm doing per week? He's really excited about it, which makes me happy and excited too. On the drive home James calls.

"Are you driving right now?"

"Yeah, just coming from training. What's up, everything OK?" We never ask each other "are you driving" unless we're about to give information you wouldn't want to be behind the wheel for. I take an immediate exit, pull over, and put the Jammer into park. My first worry is that something has happened to his elderly dad.

"I quit my job today."

"What!" I exclaim. I'm hard-pressed to ever imagine James getting riled up enough to get mad and just quit.

"What happened?"

"I got a job down on the coast. I'm moving august 24."

I go to say congratulations but before the word is even out I am sobbing. I am so caught off guard by my emotional reaction to this. It comes out "Congratu—-sob—-lations. I'm so —heavy breathing— happy for you." I can't catch my breath. Why am I reacting so strongly to this? "I'm sorry, I'm so sorry" I tell him. "I really am happy for you, I'm just really going to miss you."

I am furious with myself for not being better able to express to him how happy I am. He's wanted to move to the coast for a long time; his twin brother lives down there. He's got people he loves who are going to be so happy to see him nearer at hand.

"I . . . I . . . I'm so surprised how strongly I'm reacting. I'm sorry. I'm not trying to ruin your moment."

James was the reason we moved here. James and I have lived in the same city since I was twenty-one years old. What do I do if I have an emergency and he's three hours away? James is still my emergency contact with the doctor and the hospital. What happens when the dogs get old and I need someone with me for those final stages? What if I get sick, or he gets sick, or one of our parents gets sick. All these thoughts rapid-fire at me. *You're being so selfish right now.*

"It's OK." he sounds tearful now too. "I just wanted to tell you myself."

"Well thanks for calling, can we hang out some more before you go?"

"Yeah, of course. Do me a favour though, can you not tell Lucy yet? I'd like to speak with her first and give her proper notice that I'll be moving out of her suite and everything."

She was going to be my next call.

"Of course, won't say a word. But can you let me know when you've told her so I know when it's OK to talk about it with her?"

"For sure."

The worst part is I'm supposed to have coffee with Lucy in just a few hours and I'm not sure I'm going to be able to hide how upset I am. It's unfair to James, though, to not allow him the opportunity to handle his own business, and she has such an honest face I'm sure if I tell her first James will be able to tell.

The Jammer still feels really weird. I like how I left it a day as if it might somehow fix itself.

I text Jer and get the name of a mechanic who lives up the street from me that he uses.

I take The Beast to meet Lucy for coffee, which sucks because we normally sit in mine and smoke but we can't do that in The Beast, or at least we shouldn't because I'm going to post the ad and I don't want to damage it by making it smell like cigarettes. I throw some towels down in the box and we sit on the back sipping our drinks, sweating like crazy. It's disgustingly hot, and most of our conversation revolves around how gross we feel in the heat. It actually gets so gross we decide to wander some of the stores in the area just to get into the air conditioning. I'm less chatty than normal because I'm sad about James but also being careful not to accidentally say anything to her. She tells me she ran into Wes at the water park recently and his daughter was with him. I'm so jealous that she saw her.

"Is she as adorable as ever? Did she look bigger?" I take tidbits for boulders when it comes to information about the kids as I'm still not sure where the line on asking Wes about them is.

We part ways and I head home. I get a text from Wes. I haven't had any communication with him in several days. I was out of service while I was camping and we hadn't talked a ton before then. He wants to know how my camping trip was. We exchange a few messages about the hikes and waterfalls and how the dogs behaved. I admit they stressed me out a bit. I know he had an event to MC the first night I was gone, so I ask him how that went. He plays it off like it wasn't a big deal. The last message I send to him reads: "I have no doubt you were amazing

: ) "

I drop my truck off at the mechanic's that night, and he tells me I need new brakes.

I write to Greyson.

"Remember the time you asked me if I ever feel like I need new brakes and I said no I never feel like that? Well guess what...I need new brakes. And rotors. FML."

"Well...2nd opinion confirmed" comes his reply.

## July 31

I hit the gym first thing in the morning, still in a fog from the emotion of the day before. I put my stuff down and grab some kettlebells. I'm bent over rowing them when I notice someone approaching me. Holy actual fuck; it's Wes. I didn't even know he went to this gym anymore.

"What, you don't say hi to me?"

"Sorry I didn't see you!"

"So camping was good then?" he asks.

We chat a bit more about the trip and I flush out some of what we did more than I had in my texts yesterday. I'm jumpy when I talk to him, like I can't find the normal rhythm of how a conversation flows. I keep stepping on his words or waiting too long to reply. Eventually we politely excuse ourselves to continue our workouts. I keep the movements going, but my mind is 100 percent on him. I also notice a guy who Wes and I used to make fun of together that we like to call Chatty Kathy because of his propensity for unnecessary gym chatter. He was new when Wes bought his membership here but now he's bulked up a bit, shaved his head, and walks with a strut, probably why I hadn't recognized either him or Wes when I first came in. A text from Wes across the room.

"Did you see Chatty Kathy chatting me up?"

"Hahaha yeah and he's gotten so intense lately, hey? Shaved his head and walking around like he owns the joint . . ."

"Haha yep."

"The gym culture has hit him hard."

I superset some rows and pull downs and on my last round Wes comes over to say goodbye.

We talk about trying to podcast together tomorrow evening and he says he'll see if he can get things set up to make it work.

“It was really good to see you,” I tell him before he goes.

At home I mount up the courage to tackle the alcove. It’s a weird little jutty off my house, not a garage because there’s no room for a car, but much larger than a shed and attached to the actual house. I dread the alcove. When James first moved out I didn’t step foot in it for seven months. We cleaned it out together one day. Then I did a round of renos to my home, all new windows siding and doors, and it became the dumping ground for the construction crews. I cleaned it out again. Wes moved in, we rearranged it again, and so on and so forth. After each stupid life change I’ve undergone, it seems the alcove is the last thing to get dealt with, and now Greyson would like some room in there for his tools. Year over year I throw away more things from that area, and by the next time I go to clean it out, I’m amazed at how much stuff still seems to remain. The thought is daunting, but it needs to be done. It takes me the majority of the day. I sort through boxes, radio memorabilia, Christmas decorations, keepsakes. I swear this is where junk comes to procreate so that every time I come back it seems to have multiplied. I have tax papers dating back way more years than is necessary to keep. I even find one filo-fax that contains my high schools boyfriend’s taxes from 2003. I bag up so many things for the garbage with the intent of taking a load to the dump on Friday. My dad did a great job of sorting all the hand tools when he was last here, but there are still paint cans and odds and ends all over the place. Eventually I get it into some semblance of order, and at least there’s enough room to walk around, and hopefully Greyson will feel the room I’ve made is sufficient for his tools. I message him to get him to come and take a look. As he’s on his way up to meet me I get a call about The Beast.

The man on the line aggressively pelts me with questions about it that I don’t know how to answer, so I just keep telling him the model information was in the ad and he’s welcome to come and see it and test-drive it.

"I'm sorry, I really don't know a whole lot about vehicles, but it's a great truck."

I hang up the phone, missing Wes and wishing we didn't even have to sell it.

"Wow, you got lots done," Greyson says, eyeing the room I've made.

"Yeah, will this be enough space for you?"

"Totally."

He goes back inside to work.

My phone rings again. So help me god if I'm about to get inundated with truck questions.

The voice on the line says, "Hey, we just wanted to let you know that the speaker you ordered is in. You can come pick it up anytime in the next two weeks."

"I'll be right there."

Yes! It's weird how excited I am to have this speaker back. I had re-ordered the exact same one only in a different colour. I rip over to the store to grab it, come home, and immediately set it up. Opening the box, and carefully removing the speaker, I remember doing this exact same thing with the original. Same room, same item, only totally different. The excitement I had wanes . . . this was so much better with Wes. When I get it positioned and hooked up it sounds amazing, but something just feels different. The room and house are emptier, so the sound bounces in weird ways it never used to. The coffee bar Wes and I had ours on has now become my table, so the speaker is positioned on a wooden electrical spool much lower to the ground. Maybe how close it is to the ground is affecting the sound? There are also some knobs for bass and treble that I'm not sure what the old one was set to. Wes would know how to make it sound right in here. I repeat over and over again to myself that it's the exact same speaker and that any difference in sound I'm hearing has to be in my head. I throw music on and listen, and it's good, but I swear, I swear to god, not as good as the other one.

I get a text from the mechanic I took the Jammer to just up the street. He wants to know if I can walk up to his house to speak with him. Minutes later I'm peering into his garage where he has my vehicle up on the lift.

"I'm gonna go out on a limb and guess you didn't invite me here to tell me this was your easiest and cheapest job ever."

"I wish. I wanted to show you this in person so you know I'm not taking advantage." He shines a light into the wheel well and uses words like caliper and rotor and seized and replace.

"Listen, you're a buddy of Jer's so I trust ya. Whatever you think I need, just do what you'd do if it was your wife's car. Heads me up if the bill is getting to be over 1200 though, OK?"

I head back home and FaceTime my dad and explain the instructions I gave to the mechanic.

"You should have asked him how much he loves his wife." I laugh super hard.

While cleaning out my closets I come across a ridiculous dress. I write Greyson: "Find any weird old clothes during your move that you wouldn't be caught dead in?"

"Does a suit that's three sizes to big count?"

"Yes! Don't donate it yet, before you do we have to get dress up in some weird clothes that make no sense and go out somewhere."

"Love it. I'm down."

I lie in bed and read, struggling to focus on the book in my hands. Normally an avid reader, I'm ashamed to admit I have not finished a single book since Wes and I broke up, whereas I would normally consume at least two a week. I try reading until I fall asleep, not even having completed a chapter.

## August 1

I'm really excited because today is the day that Wes and I are going to try and podcast. It's basically my favourite activity in the whole world and I'm dying to get back at it, but I haven't wanted to rush him because he has so much going on. I spring out of bed dance-y and twitchy and ready to hit the gym. I crush my workout, and I feel strong and good. I FaceTime my mom and dad when I get home.

My mom asks, "So, have you seen the kids at all?"

"Nope. I won't tonight either when we podcast because they're at their moms, but even just being invited over is a start I think."

"That's such a shame, about the kids."

"I know, but maybe he truly doesn't want me around them after my microwave antics. That'd be a super valid thing I guess. Maybe he thinks I'm a danger to them or something? I mean, in all reality there's probably a case to be made for that based off of that one incident. I think there's waaaaaaaaay more evidence that I'm not, but the fact I'm even having to think about if that's a potential reason why he hasn't invited me to see them yet . . . or who knows, maybe he fucking thinks I don't want to for some reason."

"Possible," my mom says.

"I've asked about them as much as I think I can without being invasive."

"It's all too bad," she says.

"Yup . . . just not having a good time. BUT tonight will hopefully be the start of something better, just getting together with him and trying to friend and podcast or whatever should be super good, I hope, but I'm weirdly nervous. Nervous energy. Was good at the gym though, I slayed."

After wrapping up with my folks, I work on the deck for several hours while the dogs play.

Greyson pops up and it's a good break from being nose-down in a laptop for the majority of the day. We talk about good interruptions from work vs. bad ones, and he explains about his office.

"They designed it open concept, but then no one could get any work done because it's distracting. So my boss bought everyone noise cancelling headphones, and that was supposed to be the sign, if your headphones were on you were occupied. But then people just come and tap you on the shoulder. So he's looking into this new traffic light system. Where you have a thing on your desk with indicator lights of your availability, green yellow and red."

"That's ludicrous," I laugh. "If the headphones didn't work, that won't either! Offices are so weird, I never fit into office culture. I always was being told I could improve on my 'hallway etiquette,' which honestly for me is like code for 'waste more fucking time with these people' so they like you better. I was always just being as efficient as I can, doing my fucking work, and then going home. The worst, though, is e-mails. I'd get so mad when someone would wander into my office and say, 'Hey, I just sent you an email about . . . whatever the fuck.' Like, Christ, give me two seconds to read it before you come in here and reiterate it to me. Why'd you even write it if you were just going to walk over and then use your face to tell me the same thing you just did with your keyboard?" We get each other laughing pretty hard joking about all the ways neither of us was really 'designed' to work in an office. When he leaves to go to his office, though, I admit to myself I'm mildly jealous. Purpose, that's what an office provides. Stability too. Structure. All things I don't really have.

I pack my work up and head inside. I have some mail from California I should have sent to my parents ages ago and a parcel I also need to return. At the post office I run into my contractor, Jimmy. His company did all the exterior renovations on my house; it was a huge project. He's a hell of a nice guy and he and my dad got on really well. I had reached out to him when Wes and I were designing a new deck for my property and were considering layouts to best accommodate the hot tub. He repeatedly suggested we didn't sink it into the deck lest we break up and he were to remove the hot tub. It would affect the whole design and require more work. I had scoffed at him, 'Nah, that's won't happen with this one.' We had gone with a cheaper company, and I hadn't seen him in six months.

"Roo!" he grins at me.

"Jimmy! It's been ages." I give him a hug.

"So when that guy broke up with you did you wind up with a hole in your deck?"

"How the fuck did you know he broke up with me?"

"Saw it coming a mile away; you're just like my daughter."

I laugh, but I'm mortified.

"Nope, we put it up top, so now that, yes, he did in fact dump me, and will in fact be moving the hot tub, the deck should remain intact." I'm giggling about it, but I'm honestly really embarrassed. Was it that apparent to everyone around us that we were so wrong for each other?

Leaving the store, I see Wes's name pop up on my phone. YES! Today is podcast day—he probably wants to arrange a time. That's not it. He's missing some of the equipment we need to be able to record, and he wants to shoot for next week instead. Damnit. I'm mad at myself for how disappointed I am.

"Sounds good," I write back. "Didja still wanna try and just hang or ya wanna hold off and rendezvous next week?"

"What are you feeling? I may be getting off late from work so it may be a bit later if that's cool. Then I was hoping to try and find all the stuff for the studio, etc., and I gotta throw some coating on the deck."

This doesn't sound to me like someone who's really that jacked to have company tonight. I feel dumb for being so excited to see him. My disappointment is more than it should be, and it makes me mad at myself. I also don't want him to feel obligated to hang out with me or anything so I write back: "Sounds like ya got lots on the go....we can catch up another time."

"LOL ya it's a bit hectic. Maybe text ya later."

"Roger that."

I call James and ask if he'd like to see the dogs. I could bring them into town for a hike. I think he can sense I'm feeling low and agrees to meet me. He's just wrapped up a volleyball practice when I arrive, and he needs to hit the shower so I bring the dogs inside leaving my phone in the car. When he's changed and ready we head out, I grab poo bags from the Jammer and see I've missed a call from Wes. I text him to let him know I'm sorry I missed him, but I headed into town for a hike. He doesn't reply.

James and I leave Lucy's and wander just up the street through the same trail I've now hiked over and over these last few weeks, along a creek.

On the walk I ask him lots about his plans for life down on the coast. He's getting his own place first before he moves in with his girlfriend and her kids when her lease is up. He will be attempting to essentially become a blended family. He tells me his concerns about starting a new job.

"But do you remember your first day at your job now?" I ask him. I fully remember you telling me you were going to go in, and sit down at your desk, and not be 100 percent sure exactly what you were supposed to be doing. You were freaked right the fuck out, but now you're like the top dog or whatever. This'll be the same thing. That initial learning curve and settling in period, and then you'll kill it. I was the same way with my work when we came here. Starting a new job is always really scary, but you'll make it work."

"Yeah, I'll just have to," he tells me.

"And worst case, if it's not the right job you'll find something else down there. What about the Richardson's you used to work for? Do they still have their property?" Before we moved here he had maintained a property for a family near where he will be moving back to.

"Yeah, I reached out to him, actually, and all he said was, 'I dreamed one day about getting it started up again' and then really nothing else. I was like OK, Joseph, enough with the dreams, just tell me straight up what your plan is." I burst out singing a line from Joseph and the Amazing Technicolor Dreamcoat soundtrack, a long-standing joke between us.

"I meant the other Joseph." He's referring to Joseph Smith, the Mormon prophet who famously dreamed the church into fruition. James was raised Mormon. I laugh so loud, a few people we pass on the trail eye me. When we make our way back to his place, I come inside with him to get the dogs some water.

"So . . . want some stuff? Since I'm moving?"

"Whatcha got?"

"Well, I was gonna sell the bed but if you want it for your spare room, you can have it."

It would be really nice to have a spare bed again. Wes and I had tossed mine to make room for the podcast studio, often remarking that between our two king size beds and the kids beds we would always have room for guests. Now I just have mine and literally nowhere for company to sleep.

"What size is it?"

"Queen."

It would take up my entire spare room.

"Lemme think on it."

"Antlers?" he motions to the white antlers on the wall, joking. James had never lived alone when he first moved out, and he promised himself he was going to try and furnish the place in a style of his choosing. These white decorative antlers were the one purchase he had made, and he's never seemed to like them very much.

"I'm good."

"Sound system?"

The sound system was a wedding present from my dad's best friend.

"Yeah, that would work, actually. Wes offered to let me keep the Marshall and the sound bar, but I gave them both back, so it would be cool."

"I can come by one day before I go and set it up."

I earmark several other items for the taking. When I'm getting ready to leave, I see he is teary but not about me, it's the dogs. He's bent down to them.

"Gonna miss you guys when I leave."

"You can have them for a sleepover before you go. Whenever you want, just tell me the day."

I hug him goodbye and drive home and to bed.

## August 2

After quickly hitting the gym in the morning, I spend the entire day writing. I am in that zone of proximal development again where emotions and ideas seem to make sense to me. By the time 3 p.m. rolls around, I realize I haven't eaten breakfast or lunch and the bank is closing in an hour. I need to go get a certified cheque for the mechanic in case he gets my brakes done today. I do a quick bit of running around and then catch Greyson in the backyard at home, where we make plans for dinner and some beers.

"A beer is going to taste soooooo good right now."

He barbecues while I wrap up my work. Good thing I got the cheque done, because the mechanic does in fact have the vehicle ready.

"Back in 5, I'm going on a retrieval mission," I text Greyson.I pay and thank Jer's friend—he did a great job and by all accounts has given me a ridiculous deal that my friends surmise was essentially just parts and hardly any labor charges.

At home I tell Greyson: "I paid him extra because how rad is it to have a mechanic a block away? Want to stay on that guys good side." The afternoon turns to evening and then the sun, slowly setting, gets me super excited.

"Just wait until you see this laser the girls and I used for the garden goddess party, it's so fucking cool. Just has to get dark enough."

The dogs play and wrestle, and the beers give me a warm buzz. When it's dark enough I turn the laser onto the maple tree, certain I've now over-hyped it to talk.

He's silent for a second and then: "wow...that's sooooo cool."

He's even more excited about it than I thought he would be, which makes me really happy.

"It looks like it'd 3D or something."

I find the remote and we fuck around with the setting. I squeal with delight at the twinkles and cry out "ahhh" at one that lights the tree up with hundreds of solely red dots.

"That one's creepy," he says.

"Yeah, it looks like millions of little eyes . . . would be good for at Halloween."

We put it back to the pretty setting and listen to music and drink beers. I'm super content, I could stare at that laser all night. Greyson calls it first because he has to work in the morning. After he leaves I smoke one more cigarette lost in the laser lights and then, tipsy, I crawl into bed.

## Week Seven
## August 3

I open the record player and throw on a Neil Diamond album my mother used to play when she was cleaning the house when I was little. I dance my way across the kitchen to make a pot of coffee. The dump is finally open today, which is much needed. I missed garbage day when I was camping, so now between that and the alcove I have bags and bags waiting to be taken. I also have loads of boxes ready for donation, clothes, curtains, towels—things I just simply have too much of. I have dinner plans tonight at my friends Tim and Sherry's house and so I want to be really productive today before I head over there.

Tim and Sherry have two children, a son who was a teenager when we met seven years ago but is now into his early twenties, and a daughter who's just starting university. When I left my job and Wes and I got together, I sort of ghosted on them during that transitional time. I'd reached out to her a few days ago via text with an apology and a request to hang out soon. Like I knew she would, be she was forgiving and understanding of my absence and happily invited me over to their house for dinner. It takes hours and hours to load everything into The Beast for the dump, as well as multiple trips and then the donation center too. After all the bags and boxes have been dealt with, when I walk through the front door the whole house has a different vibe. It feels airy in here and lighter. I throw on all my diffusers and vacuum. I head to the liquor store and purchase a bottle that James has told me Sherry will like.

Walking through their front door feels a bit like coming home. I haven't been inside since Christmas, and it's welcoming, familiar and comfortable.

I throw my arms around Sherry.

"It is soooooooo good to see you." I squeeze her just a little more than I normally would.

We make our way up to the kitchen, where Tim is seated, and I embrace him equally as hard while he hands me a beer.

"So who's gonna go first? What's been going on?" I ask. They exchange looks with one another.

"You go, our news isn't that great," she encourages.

I laugh. "Mine isn't either, and it's long and complicated to explain."

"Well, ours can be summed up pretty easily."

"Hit me." I wave my hands toward myself like 'bring it.'

"Tim's been diagnosed. With MS."

This is not at all what I was expecting. I want to be very careful not to say the wrong thing as I can already imagine a million people saying a million stupid things to him like, "Oh my god I know someone with that who . . ." or "At least it's not cancer." I put my beer down and walk around the island to hug him again.

"That's wild . . . I'm so sorry. Tell me everything, how did you find out?"

We make our way out to the deck and they explain it all to me, starting with a day at the office when Tim's leg felt like it was falling asleep, right up to where we are today with his diagnosis. I love watching the two of them interact. They take turns telling the story, and there are lots of exchanges between them throughout. Lots of laughing and encouraging and joking.

"I can't do crowds anymore," Tim explains. "And the heat really messes with me. A walk across the parking lot to go into my office when it's hot out now just totally exhausts me. I don't know what it's going to be like today."

He explains how the medication he's on should bring him to a new baseline and that the progression will likely be as such: new baseline established another flare-up, medication to calm it down, and then new baseline again, but each time the baseline resets they won't know for how long.

"So, maybe retirement earlier than I thought, and vacations someplace cold," he jokes with me.

"Well, being that you're a banker I'm hoping you've got the retirement thing figured out." We laugh.

The meal is amazing, steaks and baked potatoes. We talk about their son and their daughter, how they've handled Tim's diagnosis and what they've been up to. We talk about people's reactions to his diagnosis and exactly as I thought they've experienced pretty much the gamut of stupid things people can say. Not only that, but people seem really hung up on wanting to pinpoint how this happened or what caused it.

"Ugh, yeah," I tell them. "I feel like people do that because it's too scary to admit you can't know. Makes people feel vulnerable to think there isn't a direct thing they can attribute it to, because if you don't know what caused it how can they avoid it, and then it makes them feel vulnerable too."

"My parents," Tim laughs "have blamed it on everything from weightlifting to all the beers I drank in my twenties." We chuckle.

They tell me about his special chair and walking poles and their diet now. I'm so incredibly proud in this moment to be their friend and to see the humor-laden and graceful way in which they are handling what life has dealt them.

"So. You," Sherry asks. "What has been going on?"

I fill her in on my writing, and Wes, the kids and the breakup, James's impending move, Greyson's move in, my California trip and my camping.

"So I'm just trying to life away over here" I summarize at the end.

Sherry and I get deep into it.

"It sounds like you just need to learn to love yourself again."

"Yeah, I think I'm getting there, the fog is finally lifting a bit."

I could linger all night with these two, but I don't want to overstay my welcome and the dogs are at home and will need out soon, so I excuse myself to hit the road and we all promise not to let it be so long next time. On the drive home I'm wired from the news of Tim's diagnosis. I don't know if I want to fuck someone or fight someone, but there's no in between. If I had an airplane to jump out of right now I'd go skydiving in a heartbeat. Life, it's just so fucking short, and you get these breaks in between where you can pretend it isn't and forget for just a second how precious the time is, but it's coming for you and the only thing stopping you from living in perpetual fear of that is the mundane distractions of bullshit that makes up our work days and our desks and our offices. OR, if you're very very lucky, it's love. It's that peaceful feeling you get when you lie in the arms of someone you know you would do anything for, and you think, "Having this, having known this, I've gotten all I ever wanted out of life."

Wes made me unafraid to die, because I finally had what I think life is meant to be about. More importantly, though, he truly made me unafraid to live. I had let my life become paperwork, phone calls, voicemails and emails, because I was truly terrified of the world. It was only when he showed up that I lifted my head to see the laughing faces of children, kitchen dance parties, rivers in Arizona, fishing rods in the back of a truck, the ocean in Cuba, fires in our backyard, the lights of Vegas and the comfort, not annoyance, of a wet towel on the edge of our bed. He opened the door to the world for me, and now I have to walk through it alone. Yes, one day I'll get caught back up in deadlines and shift schedules and pay stubs, I know it's inevitable, but I will never see life the same way again because of him. I used to think I was lamenting that I maybe didn't mean as much to him as he did to me. Now I don't care about that. Some days I just wish he could see what he has done for me, so he could understand why this has done what it has to me. I hope that whatever he's doing right now, he's happy.

## August 4

I have agreed to go to a housewarming/ birthday party for Lisa, a friend of Lucy's, mainly because I thought she would also be attending, but now she's away camping and I won't know anyone other than the host. She's a lovely woman who I really like, but parties with people I don't know are not a thing for me. I stress about it the majority of the morning.

Greyson wanders up onto the deck and I tell him about my "skydive" vibe last night and what incited it.

"Well, we should do something tonight then."

"Yeah, I'm down for anything. I just wanna go live some life and feel like I'm doing something."

He tells me they're going to use The Beast today to move Wes's barbecue and smoker to his new place while I'm at this party, which works for me.

I promise myself I'm not going to bail, although my mind tells me over and over again, "Just text her and say you can't make it." That's so rude, though, and she's attended several gatherings on my behalf so that would be a dick move. I do really like her; I just don't feel like people-ing with strangers today. I think Lucy will be proud of me if I do go, and that thought makes me happy.

A text comes from Wes telling me I won't recognize him when I see him next at the gym, he's cut his hair. I'm just about to write him back and tell him: "Don't send me a picture I want to be surprised," when a photo comes through. *Too late. Fuck. My. Life. He looks amazing. AHHHHHH!* The picture makes me so sad, although I know that wasn't his intention. It's just like this giant glaring reminder of what I don't get to have. I hate that I want him still so badly. I debate writing something very flirty and sexual back. Instead I write:

“wow...Wes. You look really really great. But for the record I’ll always recognize you at the gym as guy who chatty Kathy is chatting to.” I get an LOL back.

I head to the party and I’m a little relieved when I discover am the very first to arrive. It means that I can spend some time chatting with her and then not feel bad sneaking out when more people show up. Her new home is lovely, and her toddler daughter is one of the cutest kids I have ever seen. She seems genuinely surprised I showed up, and it makes me glad I did. I wait until three other people have arrived and then slip away after about forty-five minutes, exhausted with the human interaction but happy with myself for doing it. At home the empty space on the deck where the barbecue was is a weird relief. I can’t wait until the hot tubs goes too. I don’t want to keep looking at things that mean nothing to me without him.

Greyson has a ridiculous plan for the evening, which he details to me in a message. A friend of his whom he used to date is going on a first date, and in case it goes sideways she is wondering if we’d like to hang out in the same restaurant. Basically date watching.

“What? That’s insane! I’m in!”

The restaurant we are going to is not an establishment either he or I would normally choose, so I struggle with what to wear. In addition, I have a slight shoulder injury from weight-lifting and I have neon muscle tape lining my collarbone and my shoulder cap. Rather than try and hide it I go full tank top and just run with it.

“Hope you don’t mind me looking even weirder than normal,” I send him a message explaining.

“Bring it and I’ll wear some too.” I very much enjoy Greyson’s similar ability to mine in regard to giving zero fucks about how people perceive him. On the car ride into town I place two long strips of muscle tape on him, one down each forearm.

I can't remember exactly when, but some time ago Greyson pointed out to me that when you're paying your bill, the waitress will always say something to the effect of, "So, you guys have plans later?" It must be a trick to attempt to build some rapport or seem interested right at the critical moment when you're about to decide how much to tip them. We're both very taken aback when this evening the hostess asks us that before we've even been seated at our table.

"Wow," he whispers to me, "that was early in the game, they do things different around here."

"No doubt, I've never had anyone ask me that off the hop."

We are seated with only one table between us and his friend who is on the date.

"This is amazing," I tell him. "Date-watching should be a sport."

Greyson does way better than me at not looking; I basically stare the whole time and give him a running play-by-play.

He and I are a little too loud with our laughing, but it doesn't seem to draw their attention. At one point she drops her knife, it clangs loudly on the patio cement, and we both dissolve into laughter we can't keep muffled.

"I just thought of something." He leans in. "What if this goes really well, and then she brings him by the house later and he recognizes us. We're not exactly discreet with this." He motions to the body tape.

"Fuck, I didn't even think of that." Another round of laughter.

We're super annoying and there's no way it's not distracting. My laugh is frequent and loud, and Greyson jams his straw over and over again into the drinks against the ice emphatically and much too loudly sending ringing ice cube noises throughout the patio. We keep laughing.

They seem to be laughing a fair amount too, which hopefully is a good sign.

Greyson leans over.

"What if when the waitress comes with our bill I say something really weird about what we're doing tonight . . . when she asks."

"Oh my god, do it, say something super fucked up . . . but really straight faced."

Greyson's friend and her date leave. He holds the door for her on the way out.

"She'll love that," he speculates.

When she comes with our bill she sets the machine down in front of me and says, "So, what did you guys get up to today?"

"Dammit," he says when we've paid. "She threw me because I was ready for the reverse. Wonder if it's some weird intentional thing with their corporate culture to do things different than everywhere else."

We drive to a Mexican restaurant. It's packed when we walk in and there's no seating on the patio, which would be fine but the inside is sweltering. We order beers. The brand has some survey on the bottle you can do online so we fill it out with ridiculous answers while we wait for our food to come. We do tequila shots. We laugh tons.

"OK so this time," I tell him, "you have to say something ridiculous at the end when she asks."

We eat way too much food and drink a lot of beer and do another round of shots. When the waitress comes she sets the machine down in front of him.

"What else are you guys up to this evening?" she perfectly sets him up.

"Well," he starts. "Have you seen Harry Potter?"

She looks completely perplexed.

"Uh, yeah?"

"That." He says nothing else but raises a brow to her like it should be self-explanatory. I fucking die laughing. When we stumble out we are both still killing ourselves. We make our way down the street to a brewery with some pool tables.

"Do you play?" he asks me.

"Not well, but I like to."

He beats me over and over again.

"Eight ball, corner pocket, jump shot over the fourteen."

"Yeah fucking right," I snarl back at him.

He makes the shot perfectly, the cue ball hopping right over and sinking the 8 as intended.

"Holy fuck, I've never seen anyone do that, let alone call it first. You son of a bitch! That was incredible."

We drink more tequila and we switch to pea pool, which is like a secret weird version not a lot of people are familiar with, but it's a game my dad and I used to play. I sink my own ball a couple of times by accident. Other people are waiting to play so we saddle up to the bar and get more beers and more shots.

Greyson leaves to use the restroom and an extremely attractive man who's been flirting with every waitress all night turns to me.

"Motorcycle accident?" he asks.

"What?" I'm confused. He points to the tape on my collarbone and shoulder.

"Oh no no, just a weightlifting thing." He asks boring questions trying to keep the conversation alive.

When Greyson comes back he goes silent suddenly and then leaves.

"He made his move while you were gone, although no amount of your absence could make up for the fact I've been watching him hit on every chick in here for the last half an hour. I see guys like that and I think, 'Fuck, I've met you before,' not you, but you ya know? Every music festival, every bar, every douchebag artist that came through that thinks he can have whatever he wants, I've just met that guy so many times."

He nods. He knows what I mean, and I am certain there are a lot of men out there who have continually encountered "that girl" as well.

We catch a cab back to the house and I pull out the remnants of the bottle of tequila Meesh and I tried to kill at the flower party. It's just enough for two perfect shots, which he pours, and then I promptly knock them over onto the table and floor. I am wasted.

"Sorry!" I laugh. He doesn't seem annoyed, which makes me happy.

He saved most of one large one and we split what's left and then agree it's time to crash. In my bed, every time the dogs move it feels like I'm on a waterbed. I have to turn my bedside lamp on to stay oriented in the spins until I pass out.

## August 5

I am dying. What is with me thinking I can drink tequila? I was supposed to be slowing my drinking down and this weekend it's come completely off the rails. I lay in bed with the dogs thinking about it, and realize it was a conscious choice I made after Friday to go a little nuts this weekend. Tuesday, I think. I'll get back on track Tuesday.

"Greasy breakfast then vehicle retrieval mission for your car?" I message this to Greyson.

"Yeah, meet you out front in five."

We go to the greasy spoon diner, and I eat more food than any human should consume in a day let alone one sitting. Tuesday, I tell myself again, I'll get back on track Tuesday. I think of Hendrik and I know I'm gonna have to be honest about this one. This gluttony is a problem, but I make it a later me problem.

On the ride into town to get his car, my phone dings and I ask Greyson to read me the message.

"It's Van girl!" he says."Alicia wants to know if she can park here soon."

"Sweet, let's invite her to the concert tonight!"

We grab his car and then head back home.

I honestly don't even know what time it was when I went to bed last night, but if I'm going to survive this evening I'll need some sleep. I spend pretty much the entire day in bed watching TV shows and napping, only really getting up to let the dogs out for play and pee breaks. By dinner I'm starving again, which shouldn't be possible seeing as I've eaten my daily calories twice over already. Such is the nature of eating food that isn't food, and doing it all in one sitting to boot.

Greyson barbecues for us on the deck before we leave and I text with Alicia making plans to meet up.

“She’s supposed to work tomorrow but I think she’s going to straight up quit her job to come . . . which is pretty amazing.”

“Yeah, that sounds about right,” he laughs.

The guys in the band are friends of Greyson’s, and are all very pleasant and welcoming—one of them sits and chats with us at the bar. I start drinking again, this isn’t my type of music really so I’ve come more for the night-out vibe. The bartender gives the band shots, and since we’re in his company we get some too. This is going to be a problem again. Greyson and the guy from the band talk about festival and road life, something I’m all too familiar with. He laments not having much of a chance to see or experience many of the places he actually visits.

“Roo knows about that,” Greyson invites me into the conversation.

“Yeah, I get it. So many places I just flew in, got there super late at night, do the festival, and then fly right out without seeing any of it.”

“Well,” the band guy says with a stunned look on his face, “you’re doing better than us if you’re being flown in and out.”

It hadn’t occurred to me my comment might come off as snobby or out of touch, and I’m embarrassed but really don’t know how to backpedal. What am I supposed to say: “It wasn’t first class?” So I don’t say anything, but I’m not put off or upset. I’m happy just people watching and listening to the two of them banter. I text Alicia lots to make sure she gets clear instructions before I get drunk and can’t provide properly. It’s getting loud in here, and the buzz is getting stronger. I’m super excited for her to arrive. One of the guys in the band introduces me to his girlfriend, Sasha, and she’s super fucking awesome. Short black hair that comes to a longer point swept off to one side of her face, she’s stunning really. Drunken fleeting thoughts of wanting to cut all my hair off strike me. Meesh would kill me. More shots, more beers. The in-house music gets louder and I get drunker and the band gets closer to playing. I check my phone and see several missed texts from Wes, which I struggle to read in my current state.

One is about being sorry he missed me when he was picking up the barbecue because he would have liked to have seen me, the other is about having the studio ready, and then a third one that says to have fun at the concert. I want so badly to write him back and tell him I'm sorry I didn't see him on the weekend too, that I'm excited and appreciative that he has set up the podcast stuff, and that I wish he were with us tonight. I'm so drunk now though, that's not what I'm going to write. I know if I go to respond I'm gonna say, "Wish you were here xoxo," or something equally emotional and stupid. I'm going to throw something out there that makes him take a step back and go, "Yup, that's why I can't be with her, just too much." I don't know how to half it with him and haven't yet mastered the art of exchanging casual pleasantries. He's my Achilles heel, even seeing those messages from him just takes me out of where I am. Wondering what he's doing. I try unsuccessfully, multiple times, to unlock my phone to respond and eventually it puts me in a thirty-second holding pattern because of all the incorrect attempts. I tuck it back in my purse. I sneak outside for a cigarette when the place starts getting a little too packed for my liking to see if I can sober my mind enough to respond, but Sasha follows me out. I am just explaining to her about how I'm waiting on Van girl when Alicia arrives. I throw my arms around her, happier to see her than I thought I would be for someone I've only just met once. Introductions are made just as the band takes the stage and Alicia gets a drink. I feel a hand on my shoulder; it's Greyson.

"I'm going to probably go up close, so I'll find you after, k?"

"Yeah yeah have fun," I wave to him. "I'm good, I'll find you later."

We three girls sit on top of the bar, crowds of people at our feet. A small mosh pit starts out front. This is better than I thought it would be because I'm up higher than everyone so I feel a little less overwhelmed. Alicia hops on and off the bar stepping down every so often into a deep lunge and thrashing her wild mane of curls around. Sasha stands on the footrail sometimes to get an even higher vantage point to take footage of her boyfriend playing. The show passes surprisingly quickly, or maybe I've gotten myself so drunk my perception of time is totally off. When it's over, Greyson and Alicia and I do more shots. The three of us stumble around grabbing beer from Greyson's car in the parkade and calling a taxi to meet us at the van. Alicia wants to grab some overnight supplies before we head home.

The driver of the cab is cool and lets us pick the music, so we select a punk cover band and all sing along loudly at the top of our lungs. The night gets blurry. We sit on the deck and I show Alicia the laser in the tree. When has that become "my thing"? Such a weird obsession with it lately. We drink beers and watch the lights dance. I'm the first to call it bedtime, having definitely drunk too much . . . again.

## August 6

I wake up well before I actually get up and lie in bed for far longer than the dogs would like. I shoot a text to Wes to tell him the concert was fun and sorry I missed him, it was loud in there.

It's after 10, but that really doesn't mean anything to me because I have no clue what time I even went to bed at. I make coffee, I need coffee.

We make plans to go get the vehicles left in town last night, and then Alicia wants to buy supplies to make eggs benny for us. We're all really slow to get going and it takes at least a full hour for anyone to feel able to leave the house. After dropping them off at their respective vehicles it's another two hours or so by the time everyone does what they need to do and grabs what they wanted to grab for this breakfast.

Now early afternoon, we're all in the kitchen blasting music, singing along, and working away on the food. Greyson mans the hash browns, I chop onions, and Alicia does whatever one has to do to make bennies. It feels awesome having people in my kitchen for the morning, even though it's technically afternoon. I repeatedly take glances at the two of them head down in what they're working on, and just savour the fullness of the moment and the way my house feels with them in it doing this. The kitchen bar I have only seats two, so when the food is ready we all pile onto my tiny couch and eat shoulder to shoulder. I can't keep my eyes open after the meal and that's when I know I'm treating my body badly—when the food doesn't give me energy, it makes me tired. I'm super ready for bed and for quiet and for dog cuddles and alone time. This weekend has been way more socialization and stimulation than I'm used to, and I need to regroup.

When everyone is gone I crawl into bed and stay there until well after dinnertime. I promise myself I'll get my eating and not drinking back on track tomorrow. I've been saying that all weekend. Tired of my own promises and lack of action I force myself to go to the gym, where I guilt cardio myself to death. I sweat buckets and buckets out, and when I'm done on the treadmill I'm drenched. I come home, take a shower, and go to sleep promising myself this coming week Roo will be a more responsible human being.

## August 7

My alarm dings at 5:50 a.m. and I feed the dogs and throw on gym clothes. As I pull into the parking lot, I see Wes's truck and my heart skips a few beats. I hang my jean jacket on the hook, throw my purse up there too, and beeline for him. He looks incredible, the haircut and beard trim is even better in person, and, oddly enough, I see him the way I used to again. He looks just like he did when we met. I walk right up to him and he pulls out an earbud and says hi.

"Hi" I say, reaching for his head. I can't stop myself. I run my hand right down the closely buzzed side. "It's so short! It looks so good," I beam at him.

"Thanks, I actually went to someone to get it done. I was like 'this'"—he motions to his face—"fix all this."

"Well, they did awesome."

We chat for a bit about the concert and Alicia's van and her visit, then we both go back to our workouts. I do some dumbbell rows and some lunges and eventually make my way over to the bench press. I'm pushing only fifty-five pounds because without a spot it gets risky. Wes saunters over and sarcastically asks me if I want a spot. He knows I hate when random guys ask me that. He's said it in a kidding tone, but I know his offer is serious and he's the only person other than Hendrik I would ever let spot me for real. *Hell yes*. We load up a bit more weight and he stands directly behind the rack, fingertips below the bar, ready to catch it if I lose control. The first set goes great, so we add more and I go again. I like this, I like him standing behind me helping me, this feels like the good part of how it used to be. After the second set I sit up and spin around, straddling the bench to face him behind the rack. He reaches through and touches the bar.

"I'll curl," he says.

He grabs the bar back up and curls it—his biceps look amazing. The flexion in his arms accentuate his tattoos and veins, and as his muscles pull against the weight it tugs at all the very bad but "feels-very-good" parts of me.

"Now this I could watch all day," I grin at him. *Oh my god, am I flirting with him?* Between touching his hair when I first got here and saying that, I'm certain I am. "Stop it," I tell myself. This was your problem with him, you had no self-control.

On the third set it's starting to get heavy, and he leans down and counts them off for me, telling me "one more" just as I'm starting to fade and think I can't. I grind it out. He used to do this at the gym for me when we were together, and it brings me waves of joy to hear his voice so close.

When I've gone as heavy as I can go I say, "Thanks for that!"

"No problem," he smiles, "I'm going to go work triceps." I try and get refocused on my next set of exercises, but I keep watching him from the corner of my eye. Will my attraction to him ever fade? He's just this force to me that calls to both my mind and, especially in the gym, my body. When we lived together and worked out together, at the end I'd always ask him to do some pull ups for me. It was the biggest turn on. *So help me god, if he finishes with those it's game over.* Thankfully he doesn't, but he does wander by me at one point and, lightly, he brushes my hip with his hand as he sneaks past to grab something. Sparks everywhere. My heart is a horse kicking in my chest.

When I'm rowing he comes over, and I can tell he's getting ready to leave.

"Oh, I forgot to tell you, when I was by on the weekend using The Beast I just . . . I had forgotten how much I like that truck. There's this weird part of me that wants to keep it and just park it in my yard. Give you a couple grand for it and just have it still."

I nod. "I know, it's funny you should say that, I've thought the same thing, if I had the money I'd totally buy it from you. I just don't have any money to give you right now to get the hot tub moved. That truck makes me so ridiculously happy, but financially it just doesn't make sense. Guess we just keep it on the market for now and not be rush-y about it and if we can get a good chunk of money for it we will, if not we'll see."

"Yeah, I mean if someone wants to buy it it's the right thing, but it's nice to not have to rush to take a lower price."

"Exactly."

"I'll keep you posted on if any offers come in, and lemme know about the podcast when you'll have time."

"Yeah, what did you say your schedule was like this weekend, again?"

"Nothing solid so far but the closer it gets probably the more I'll have planned. If I'm doing stuff though it'll prolly be Fox and Lucy type things, so they're usually pretty flexible."

"OK, well, I'll let you know"

"Sounds good, and it was really nice to see you, it always makes me happy when I run into you."

"Me too, maybe I'll see you here tomorrow."

He heads out and I watch him longingly as he walks through the door to the parking lot.

I finish my workout and head home.

I text Fox to see if she's coming by for coffee today and she is, so I throw a pot on.

On the deck she gives me the rundown of the overwhelming long weekend she had with a house full of company. "Nothing was wrong, everyone was awesome, it was just a lot and I found I was like, just didn't feel right the whole time."

"Jesus you're turning into me."

"I know. I thought that too!"

We talk about Mexico plans at Christmas and how we could make that work for me to join her and her family. I tell her about my entire weekend, and all about seeing Wes this morning.

"He just looked so fucking good, and it's like, on my end that chemistry is still so there . . . I just wanna .....arghhh" I feign biting and grabbing motions at the air. "Did you see his haircut? He looks so fucking good."

"Yeah, I saw it on Instagram."

"I touched it when I walked up to him, like, what the fuck?! Why do I do these things."

"Well at least you know it's that chemistry attraction type stuff, and you're just telling me how hot he is and how the desire is still there. I'd be more concerned if you were saying he was the best boyfriend on the planet and you guys worked and were perfect for each other or something. That's not this though."

"No no, not at all. This is like that just electric, vibey, sexual, passionate attraction. Maybe if I didn't have that with someone else down the line I'd make better decisions?"

"No no," she disagrees. "You gotta have that, along with all the other stuff you guys were missing."

"I'm worried because I'm excited to see him, like, genuinely can't wait until I see him again, and that's a problem."

"Yeah, that's not good, but it is what it is, you can't change it. Today was probably just really hard because it was the first time since you broke up that it seems like you really enjoyed the interaction."

"Yeah, and let's be honest, I could totally be going to the gym at a different time of day, but I'm not. I want to run into him . . . obviously. I do prefer to make myself go to the gym first thing, it's just easier and out of the way and stuff, but in all reality I'm a moron and I still love seeing him."

We discuss our inability to choose partners for ourselves who match our emotional needs.

"Except for, you need someone who's opposite," she tells me. "Otherwise what would you do all day with that person, lay in a cuddle pile. Just cuddling and crying. It would basically be like if we were a couple." We laugh super hard.

"You and I are basically soul mates with the only problem being that we aren't lesbians."

"Think how many dogs we'd have . . ." she quips.

We talk about people we know who are in happy relationships, to the point where they come off as snide.

"When people tell me how happy they are now I kind of just . . ." she tilts her head comically to one side and makes a face like she's trying to hear something or squinting to see something. It's so funny.

"Totally," I laugh. "The curtain has been pulled back, and now I can't un-know it. I see someone happy and I think to myself, you're just standing on a train track foolishly thinking you're not gonna run into a train. My one solace is not being in a relationship so I'm off those tracks."

We're quiet for a second. "Except . . ." I start laughing. "Really, it's more like I'm at one of those switch stations on the tracks, this junction where I've got Wes one way, an ex-husband in there too . . . and I'm standing here like, 'I'm not gonna get hit.' But the funniest part is the last track is right behind me, and that's a locomotive of my own making, just whatever the hell I've done to myself like I always do. Just a train full of Roo's poor choices. That'll be the one that takes me out, but I'm not gonna turn around, though. Gonna act totally confused and surprised when my own train strikes me down."

We're killing ourselves laughing so hard we can barely talk.

"You know, I was looking through my phone the other day for something, and I came across all the messages from when I first started dating Wes, and the shit that he used to say to me . . ." I clutch at my heart dramatically. "All this stuff about clouds lifting and 2018 being our year and so much emojis and adorable-ness. Like, doesn't even seem like the same person I knew by the end, and we fucking did that to each other! There's a million ways in which I can guarantee he must feel I didn't turn out to be who I said I was either, but I was, and I am, and I can be, we just fucked each other up so bad that I couldn't be who I know I am. It got so confusing I wasn't even me anymore. Isn't that fucking awful?"

"Nah, that's just how it goes. Clive was like that too before we got married. One day I'll show you messages from him, you wouldn't even believe the way he used to talk to me. I swear to god I have one message where he says, 'good morning, princess.'" She makes an exaggerated sickened face.

"Fuck right off!" I exclaim. I cannot in a million years imagine her husband saying that, just not the type.

"Like, I feel like pulling it out and telling him, 'I wanna go on a date with THAT guy!' Granted, he didn't think he was going to marry me, so he probably never thought he would have to face the consequences of me dealing with who he really is down the line. I'm the first date that just refused to go home, basically."

I snort at that. "What's fucked now though is, I don't think Wes's a liar or a bad person or anything—I know he meant all that stuff at the time. So now whenever anyone else new comes into play I'm just going to have it in my head that they'll mean it when they say it, but that it's all ultimately like . . . meaningless? I guess, in the end."

"Yeah, here's the thing with Wes: I really do believe he loved you, and I think he loved you as hard as Wes was capable of loving. You just love different, and need different. Doesn't mean he didn't love you as hard as is possible for him."

"I hope you're right." I sigh. "I'm just not sure how real 'love' can be if it doesn't endure in some way. But . . . I believe it more and more, although I don't always feel it, that he probably did me a favour by breaking up with me because I never . . . ever ever would have broken up with him. Like ever." I throw my hands up, baffled. "No matter how bad it got I'd just keep choosing him and the kids, and that was it for me."

"I know," she tells me, and she leans in and pats my leg. "I gotta go adult now, believe it or not I do have a job."

"Get life-ing" I tell her.

I book my training with Hendrik for the week as well as a hike with his wife Roxy on Friday. It'll be so awesome to get some time with her. I always train with Hendrik, so she and I rarely get time just to catch up and chat. Her energy is infectious and I can't wait to soak it in. When Lucy gets off work, we meet in the middle for a coffee. If I could get paid to have coffee with people, I'd be rolling in the dough.

I am so happy when I see her as her five days away for camping felt like a long time to me. We sit in the Jammer and smoke cigarettes; I soak in every detail of her camping trip. She had a fight with her younger brother over the weekend, which truly baffles and amazes both her and me—they have never fought before in their lives. Lucy, the perpetual peacekeeper, has chalked it up to everyone's emotions running high. She ended up disclosing to her brother what's been going on in her marriage. I think it's really good she told him because those flare up with people are normally in direct correlation with a lack of understanding of someone's situation. When given the context, things start to make sense. I tell her all about seeing Wes at the gym and how hot he looked.

"I did see the haircut," she admits.

"Fuck, I know, right?" I tell her how sometimes I wonder if he still has feelings for me, but then I fight myself over the thought, poring over all the damage we did to each other and telling myself he can't feel that much because if he did he would be wanting to make it work, and he's repeatedly told me he doesn't want to.

"He hasn't made any move to tell me anything is different, so that should tell me everything I need to know," I say.

"For sure, you'd think he would say something if he ever felt like he made a mistake. What we need here is a completely random person to enter your scenario. Some person that no one sees coming and just shows up and changes everything."

"Ughh, that would be amazing."

She nervously confides in me a feeling she hasn't shared with anyone, and I basically laugh it off, assuring her I couldn't imagine her feeling any other way, and that it totally makes sense to me.

"See, I knew. I knew you'd be the person who would understand." She checks the time

"I gotta go get my kids."

"Cool, let's make plans soon, figure out a date to have another ridiculous party," I say.

Hopping out of the vehicle holding the door she says, "I'm always down for a reason to dress like an idiot."

"Sweet! Thanks for the coffee."

On the drive home I think about what she said about a completely random person showing up and changing everything. It stings me when I think to myself, *That's who Wes was.*

I kill the afternoon playing my banjo, which I'm selling to an online buyer tomorrow. When I get sick of that I switch to guitar. I walk the dogs around the block. My body is really taking a beating these days, but keeping myself moving is literally my strongest coping mechanism. I play more guitar, I make a batch of hard-boiled eggs for the week, I listen to music. My shoulder is just killing. On the deck, night is falling and I stare at the hot tub. Aside from when my folks were here I haven't set foot in it. I'm not sure if the chemicals are even OK to be in it. I open the lid and peer inside. The water looks totally clear and has no cloudiness to it. There's no debris inside either as the lid hasn't been opened in ages. I'm gonna do it.

I jump inside and throw on the soundtrack to "Ten Things I Hate About You," my favourite teen romantic comedy. I think of being in the seventh grade watching the movie and wondering what my love would be like when he showed up. "My love." One. Love. What a stupid thought. I had never known or perceived there would be three of them. My high-school boyfriend, James, and Wes. And that's just three so far. How many more times will I find my love, and then lose them again? It's a tiresome thought, the trying that will have to come down the line when I'm ready. When will I be ready? I think about the dating websites sometimes when I'm bored and lonely, and I wonder if I should create a profile. I never promised myself the eleven weeks wouldn't include dating, but it feels counter-intuitive to the healing I'm trying to accomplish. Plus, I know no matter how much letting go I've done, that Wes still has my heart in his hands. That my interactions with him are still the ones that make or break my days. That even the way I measure my progress still all circles back to him. Then I remind myself I sat in this very hot tub just a few months ago, totally naked across from him, but feeling like he was so far away.

Every book and article I've read says focusing on the differences, faults, and problems about or with a former partner will help you to move on, but to me that is the tactic I'm trying so hard to avoid. Most people cope like this. They convince themselves of their partners failings so they don't have to face their own. This method rewrites history and irrevocably changes the way you think of this person, not for the better. Focusing on someone else's flaws means you shift the responsibility of what went wrong to them. It means you don't have to fix yourself first. I promised myself at the onset of this that I would always hold him in the highest regard, and always remember Wes the way I wanted to. If that makes it more painful, if that makes it take longer, I don't care. I won't tell myself lies or diminish what I feel just to make this easy. He is worth that pain to me.

And so I sit in the hot tub doing the exact opposite of what should probably be done. I think of the things I went through that he was present for, truly some of the hardest moments of my life, and how he fought through them with me and for me. He will always be my **hero**. I think of yellow notes in coffee mugs set next to a timed coffee pot. I think of songs sent to me in the morning with a sweet text message. I think of thrift store records, baby gates, patio solar lights and a million other ways he showed me he loved me and was caring for me and our home. I think of being stirred from a bad dream and held close to soft whispers of, "Are you OK, Ruby?"

After showering off I throw on some pajamas and lie on my bed. I look at who's active online and see a friend of mine, Mitch, a comedian from New York who Wes and I had interviewed for the podcast. Fuck, I was supposed to video-chat him while I was in California and I totally didn't. Mitch is in his early fifties, thick New York accent, silver hair and a sharp nose. He has the attitude of Al Pacino but the handsomeness of Richard Gere. We made friends when I was a teenager working at a small radio station where I had become involved with the local stand-up comedy scene. He's known me for every major relationship of my life.

I roll over onto my tummy, turn the lamp on, and adjust the phone on the nightstand, calling him. I can hear him laughing before the video has even kicked on. The picture appears and he too is lying in bed.

"You!" he points at me. "What the fuck happened? One second you're gonna call me in California and then two weeks go by and I see pictures you're hanging with your ex-husband all of a sudden, what the fuck?"

"I know. I'm sorry, I got back and then I went camping and it's just been nuts. James is moving soon, so I've been trying to spend time with him, and like, it's all just crazy."

I give him a brief rundown of what's been happening and what I'm doing and where I've been.

"You went fucking crazy. Months before you met this guy you're telling me you don't want kids and you're alone, and then all of a sudden he and his kids have moved into your house and you're like, 'Oh Hi, Mitch, just changed my mind about everything.'"

"I know." We talk a lot about the kids and I get teary eyed. Mitch has a beautiful daughter in the fourth grade.

"You have bad judgment," he laughs, and then keeps laughing so hard he covers his own mouth like a little kid. "Next time you meet someone and you think it's a good idea, no, just do the opposite. Whatever you're going to do, don't do it because you're wrong. While you're at it write my address down, and then get an envelope and mail me every fucking spare key you have—no more boys moving in with you." He's got me in tears I'm laughing so hard.

I ask him when he'll be out this way next on tour.

"Probably October but I'm not sure yet, you'll be the first call when I get the date booked."

"OK, Fox and I are going to California in September and Mexico in December but if you make your way out here, your show date will be priority one."

"Oh Mexico, awesome. You'll come back with a new boyfriend named Juan and a heroin addiction, I'm sure." I almost spit my water out laughing.

"Alright, kid, I gotta go to sleep. You OK, though? You look sad, good, really good, but just . . . so . . . sad . . ."

"Yeah, I'm OK, the kids man, it's those kids it just feels like I'm not gonna get over it. I am really sad but it's getting better, I think. I just feel embarrassed and stupid."

"Why?"

"I'm just embarrassed it didn't work out again . . . and that no one wants to life with me," I confess.

"Don't be embarrassed about that, be embarrassed about trying to smash the microwave, and then feel stupid over the other stuff." He covers his mouth again laughing and I'm killing myself to the point where my tummy hurts.

"Only you could say this shit to me, you know."

"I know. I'll call you when I get the gig booked. I love you."

"Love you too."

The high from the laughter fades and I toss and turn; it is a mostly sleepless night.

## August 8

Ducky threw up peach pits in the middle of the night because she's been sneaking around back to the tree and eating the rotten ones that have fallen on the ground. Awesome. I'm exhausted but can't fall back asleep. I want to work out but can't really because I'm training at 9 and I don't want to push myself and then not be able to perform at max capacity for that. Fuck it, I'll go and just do some cardio. The gym is dead when I arrive and climb onto a Stairmaster. I actually kind of like it this early, when there's no one else around. After twenty minutes I climb down, and while I know it will fatigue me, I can't help but want to lift weights. I'll just go really light, I promise myself. I run through some things, more focused on treating these light weight movements as stretches than I am on really hammering myself.

Wes shows up and he looks really tired.

"Works just been crazy, I've been up since 4 a.m."

"That's brutal. Yeah, I been here for a while already, couldn't sleep. I'm just going really easy because I'm training at 9. Did some cardio . . ."

I want to talk to him longer but he looks almost mildly irritated. I know he probably just wants to get started.

"I'll leave ya to it," I tell him, and I busy myself with finishing my last few sets. When I'm done I stroll back over to him and tap him lightly on the shoulder.

"I'm heading out. Hope the rest of your day is less stressful."

"It probably won't be," he jokes, "but thanks."

On the drive home, I worry about him. I hope he's not burning himself out, but I know he is. Also, there's nothing I can do about it, or to help him. The urge to take care of someone is a hard one to fight. I remind myself of the smothering effects my love had on him. *Just leave him alone; he doesn't need your help*. It still unsettles me, though. What I wouldn't give to be who he could come home to, to give him massages like I used to, to be his respite and safe place from the rest of the world. *You weren't that, though,* I tell myself. *You were the biggest, easiest source of stress to eliminate.*

The lights aren't on in the gym when I arrive, but I fumble along the walls until I find the switches. Hendrik arrives shortly after me and I ask him about his recent trip to the coast. He throws me on the rower for ten minutes and gives me the rundown while I huff and puff.

"What about you?" he asks. "Tell me about your food?"

I tell him about my week nutritionally, and then my weekend socially, explaining that my eating and drinking got well away from me.

"OK, so tell me about that, where'd that come from?"

I explain about my friend's diagnosis and how it put me in a state of mind to just be gluttonous and carefree.

"I did it on purpose, as per usual. The problem isn't that I don't know what I should be doing to be healthy, I have the knowledge and the understanding, but I just sometimes straight up ignore it, and then I'm frustrated with myself." I'm a bit embarrassed to admit this to him, but I'd rather he know I have been listening all these years, I'm just still having trouble applying his wisdom. There is no judgment.

"Ahhh, now we're getting somewhere." He smiles at me. As I stand up and switch to the barbell he takes a seat on the rower and continues: "You know, in the morning, I can quit anything. I don't need any of it, fuck it. Cigarettes, drugs, alcohol, food, whatever it is for you . . . every morning, I quit it all." His face is lit up with optimism, and I swear his eyes are literally glistening with the hope of morning. He looks off at something I can't see, silent. I actually watch as his eyes transform from hopeful to pensive. The landscape of his mind has changed, and I wish desperately I could see what he is picturing. He runs a hand through his hair, staring down at his feet; such a large frame slumped into a small pile.

"But," he says, abruptly righting himself and shooting his eyes back to mine. I see they are dark and sad now. "Nighttime, when it gets dark . . . that's when it comes. And . . ." He says this last part very slowly, as if piecing it together for himself. "There is . . . no . . . tomorrow."

He rests his head in his hands, looking at me.

"Every morning you quit, and every night . . . that's when people go searching. From bulletproof to brittle in the blink of a circumstance."

I actually don't even know what to say. He's often funny, insightful, inspiring and thought-provoking, but this time he has truly left me speechless. How someone can so perfectly sum up such complex feelings in so few sentences amazes me. This is the gift that is Hendrik, this moment summarizes everything he means and has meant to me over the years. He sees the world in a way that I would be scared to live without. He might not always say a ton, but when he does you must stop what you're doing, and truly listen.

I felt sorry for some guy online who expressed interest in my banjo but couldn't afford both it and the case, so I told him he could just have the whole thing for free. I load it into the Jammer and drive to the coffee shop where I've arranged to meet him. He pulls up and he is gorgeous. Long shaggy hair tucked under a backwards cap, brown but lightened by the sun. Athletic although not particularly tall, but very muscular. I on the other hand look like a disgusting, sweaty disaster, having not yet changed from training. *Fuck of course*. He introduces himself as Matt, and we shake hands.

"Is this thing haunted or what? I don't understand why you'd give it away."

"No, not haunted, just getting rid of stuff that doesn't bring me joy anymore and it may as well go to someone who is going to use it."

He lingers for a long time asking me lots of questions about it. I cite him some resources he can use to learn to play.

"Well thanks, this is just the nicest thing anyone has ever done, doesn't even seem real. Can I give you a hug?"

I extend my arms and take it. "If you get good, you have my email now so send me a video of you playing it," I tell him. He grins.

"Maybe I could send you an email either way to take you out for dinner," he fumbles awkwardly. "As a thanks?"

"Yeah, I'd love that," I tell him.

"My name's Matt," he says again.

"Yeah, you already said that." I laugh. His nervousness is adorable.

"It's a stupid name I know, sometimes when I talk I mumble and people think I said Mark so I just let them call me that."

*Who is this ridiculously good-looking bumbling idiot*?

"Well, enjoy it," I say, and I flash him a smile before I get in my vehicle.

I get a call about a broadcasting job opportunity locally that's really peaked my interest. I want so badly to call Wes and tell him everything, but I force myself to hold off and not be invasive. *I can tell him whenever I see him next. Leave him alone.* It's crazy hot and smoky even as the sun is setting. It makes me feel lazy and tired. Greyson's in the same boat. We had discussed hiking, but I don't think either of us or the dogs are really up for it in this heat.

"What if we take some camping chairs and just go into the little hidden spot in the canyon, dogs can dog in the water and it'll be cooler down there?" Greyson suggests.

I'm totally on board with his idea. He's right; when we arrive in the hidden pooled area off the well-known trail it's shaded and much cooler. He sets up two camping chairs and we sit and watch the dogs play.

I tell him all about the guy with the banjo.

"Maybe I should be trying to date or something, I don't know. Maybe I need to go out and have some awkward dinners or someone to be excited about or something. I think about the dating websites, and it just feels like a distraction."

"Yeah, it's definitely a distraction tactic for sure. It just becomes a time filler."

I take lots of pictures of the dogs in the water and send them to James to show them they're happy and having a good time.

We talk about some of the girls Greyson is seeing, and about our marriages. I tell him I just don't think I'm ready to move on from Wes yet.

"I just feel like there's more there somehow still . . ." I know it's stupid and not accurate, but I can't help but express the sentiment. "The way I love him, man . . . that well runs deep."

Some time ago Greyson had a girlfriend; they dated a similar length of time to Wes and me, his first relationship since his marriage ended. They weren't able to be friends afterwards because she always wanted more. He never speaks of her unkindly, but my biggest fear is that the way he's come to think of her will be how Wes comes to think of me.

I'm lying in bed when I get a ding on my phone. The preview pops up and it says, "We're fucked," which catches my attention. It's from Wes. *Shit, what could this be?*

It's a link to a truck that's for sale with a much lower price than ours, but it's also much less nice and has way more problems. The messages go back and forth and we both lament having to even sell The Beast. I thank him for his patience with not rushing me on this. He seems to know how hard these types of things are for me, even if emotionally it doesn't have the same significance to him.

One of the things he and I were going to do together was learn some Spanish, inspired of course after our trip to Cuba. We never did. I turn on Google translate and find a phrase that means "It's very kind of you." I send him this message in Spanish. He doesn't reply. I close my eyes and rest my head on my pillow. This is why I didn't let myself text him the night of the concert when I was drunk. If I'm this stupid sober, think how bad that could have gone. My phone dings and I reached over, surprised to see a Spanish reply. I translate it: "For you, of course."

I pull the blanket around myself, smiling as I drift off.

## August 9

OK, self, you're gonna have to dial this shit down a bit because this is ridiculous. I can't pull my own workout pants up without wincing because my right hand is swollen and sore. What actually would have caused that? I didn't do push-ups yesterday or really anything I thought would be a weight bearing problem to my hand itself, but each time I grip my pants and pull up, fire shoots through my palm and down the external side of my wrist. Definitely a cardio day again. Fuck, I hate cardio. I've promised Hendrik I wouldn't lift weights today anyway, but I'm still annoyed.

Wes has beaten me to the gym today. I set my stuff down and head over to say hi. It's strange what you notice. He has a green shirt on that I've washed and folded so many times I can almost feel the fabric in my hands.

"Good morning," I say.

"Hey, how are you?"

"I'm OK, how's you?"

"I'm tired. Still so much going on at work." he explains what he's been dealing with and it sounds like a lot.

"Woh that's crazy, so busy! So . . . I have some news . . ." I tell him about the call regarding the potential job opportunity.

His face lights up. "That's so awesome!"

Man, I miss him being my person. It took everything I had not to call him first yesterday and let him know, but this reaction makes me realize that no one else's input or reaction was what I wanted.

"I gotta cardio it up today because I promised Hendrik I would."

"Yeah, you been going hard. Get your cardio on."

Sometime later Wes moves to the treadmill next to me and I take my earbuds out. When we're in the weight lifting section we normally exchange only a few words at a time, but now walking side by side it gives us a chance to catch up a little more.

He tells me about running into Lucy recently, and I tell him about James's move. He tells me about work and the kids, I tell him about taking the dogs to the canyon last night and watching Greyson's dog this weekend. It's the first time in a long time where talking like this feels . . . I don't know . . . easier somehow?

When we round the conversational corner to trying to figure out plans to podcast, that's the only time I get nervous. Attempting this feels like a huge undertaking now that we have delayed it for so long. I have a weird pressure inside me about it.

"Maybe you could come over and we could barbecue, and you could see the kids and stuff too. They could show you their rooms?"

My breath catches at the mention of seeing them.

"Yeah, so about that . . . like, what have you told them?"

He explains he presented it to them in an "exciting news, Dad bought his own place and wasn't it so nice of Roo to let us stay with her" kind of way. This makes my heart happy because I really hadn't even begun to guess what he had told them.

"I would really really love to see them." I try so hard to not tear up when I say this. Panic is overtaking me, though. What if I can't keep it together when I do see them? Is this a horrible idea? Am I going to upset them or him if I come undone? How could I finally get to hug and hold them and not fall apart? I don't think he has any idea what this will mean to me.

"I built them this cool hidden fort area over the weekend . . ." he tells me all about the project they did together. It sounds awesome. He's just such an engaged and fun dad. I love that about him.

"Yeah ,well just call me tomorrow and let me know what's better, Friday or Saturday. I think my schedule is a bit more flexible than yours, so we can work it out."

He shuts his treadmill down and wipes it off. I catch him out of the corner of my eye as he's leaving and wave and smile.

I fill the morning with errands and then at lunch I head to house the Fox owns. She and her husband bought the house but they never moved in, as their rental is right on the lake and it's too beautiful to leave unless circumstances would force them to. After a series of bad tenants, Fox discovered they could turn more of a profit by using this house as an Airbnb. It's doing really well, but she constantly has to clean it in preparation for new guests. I sneak in through her back door using the code.

"Are you upstairs or down?" I call out.

"Up!" I hear her call back to me.

It's five billion degrees in this house and she's wearing workout pants and a sports bra. I take my shirt off and my socks so I'm just down to shorts and a bra.

"Sit outside?" I ask.

"Yeah, be right there."

A cute patio in a shaded area out back proves to be only slightly cooler. Fox gives me the rundown of the insanity at her work right now in light of potential changes coming down the pipe. It's really stressful on her, but I think she's got it.

"So . . ." I tell her. "Wes invited me over for Saturday . . . so I'm going to see the kids this weekend."

Her face reads a mix of excitement for me and concern. "That's going to be really hard for you. But, I mean, it's hard for you not seeing them too, so you'll have to just see how it goes."

"Yeah, I don't know if it's a good idea or a bad idea, but I won't know unless I try. I just wanna—I'm nervous I'm gonna burst into tears or whatever, and I know that's not fair, so going to have to work hard to keep my shit together. I feel like he's trying to friend me really hard right now, you shoulda seen his face when I told him about the job thing, he like, was so happy for me. I miss him being my best friend, and I know everyone else around me saw the bad of it at the end, and how sad I was and stuff, but no one really saw all the ways he . . . he . . . I can't even put into words all the things he did for me those first few months. He changed my life completely. He was my best fucking friend, and today on the treadmill he did this silly face—it's dumb, but it's a thing he used to do, and I just thought, God, I miss him so much."

"I know. Well, just see how Saturday goes and then take it from there."

"Yeah, there's no reason why if things aren't good between us I can't just be one more person the kids have in their life. I'm not sure they ever really understood the scope of the relationship between Wes and me anyway, so maybe—I don't want to do it if he's going on dates or whatever, but maybe I could even get to babysit them down the line or something. Like if he had a work thing?"

"Yeah, that would be nice."

"I get the feeling . . ." I look right at her. "That I'm not done being stupid with him yet. I don't know how else to explain it, and I'm not going to do something dumb like sleep with him or anything, but I just, I get the feeling lately there's probably more going to happen somehow. I feel like he might still care about me . . . or even love me, and I know even if he does, it doesn't mean anything or change anything . . . but I can feel myself knowing I'm just . . . I'm still there. I mean let's be serious . . ."

She doesn't say anything, so I follow it up with a shaking of my head and a "Fuck, it must be hard to be my friend. I do these things, all the time, that people around me are just like, you should know better. But you love who you love right . . ."

"No no no," she dismisses my negative self-talk. "You're not hard. I get it." She yawns. "Also, I swear I'm not bored. I just have barely slept properly in three days." She's staring over my shoulder watching something, and she extends her full body down onto the outdoor love seat next to my patio chair. I think she's going to close her eyes, but she leans in closer to me to speak quietly: "That's sketchy as fuck."

I follow her eyes to where a very strung-out-looking man across the lane is using a broom handle to adjust the security camera in a yard that's riddled with shit.

"That house," she laughs. "They always have all this shit in their yard, clearly stolen. Obviously a drug house or whatever. New shit every day, different shit all the time . . . but I swear to fucking god . . ." she leans in right close to me and lowers her voice to a whisper. "One time the two guys that live there came home . . . on a bicycle built for two."

I fucking lose it. I'm laughing so hard, the two of us are in stitches. "I shit you not," I tell her, "at the condo in Palm Springs my mom and dad have a bicycle built for two. We are so getting on that thing in September and taking pictures of ourselves. Can you imagine how funny that would be, just a shot of us like "Oh heeeeeey."

"I'm totally in so long as you ride in the front."

At home I blast music and hand wash the dishes. I have a dishwasher, but there's something about doing it manually that I find relaxing. The hippie in me likes to believe it's probably less bad on water, but I doubt that's actually true. James texts and says he's on his way. He's bringing me the lamp, the sound system, and a few other things. Life comes full circle. I hear his car pull up and head outside, where he's backing in his SUV to reveal an open trunk of boxes. I walk over to help him load the stuff in.

"I feel like my entire fucking life these days is boxes moving into or out of this god damn house. I know you understand."

"Seven moves in five years," he agrees.

Will he and I ever find the stability again that our marriage provided us? I don't know. I thought I had.

"If I never see another fucking box come or go . . ." I let my sentence trail off. We pull all the boxes inside and then sit on the deck to watch the dogs play. I ask if his new girlfriend likes dogs.

"Yeah, I mean she wants to get a golden retriever, but I don't think I could. These guys are my dogs," he says, playfully swatting with our two monsters.

"You can still take them for a sleepover before you go. Just let me know what night you'd like to."

His phone keeps dinging with people from websites wanting to come and look at the remaining items he has for sale.

"Before you go, could you actually set the sound system up?"

"Oh right, shit." He hops up, quickly realizing he will be tight-pressed to make it back in time for his buyers. He unpacks the system and gets it all connected. The tuner is working for the radio, so the speakers are on but we can't make it play the sound for what's on the television.

"Sorry, we must be missing something, I don't know if you have someone else who can help you . . ." Wes pops into my mind. He could wire this with his eyes closed.

"Yeah, I know a guy," I tell him. I wonder if Wes would do that for me or if it's weird if I ask.

## Week Eight
## August 10

The routine of the gym has become one of the few things that brings me comfort lately. It's a weird sensation being accountable to no one and I think it's important I hold myself to some sort of standard or routine. I sometimes wonder if anyone would notice if I died, not in the way where I plan on that happening, but really how long would it take? I have no job to show up for, so would anyone notice if I was missing? These are the things I think about as I pedal. I go slowly and easily, concerned with fatiguing myself. My hike with Roxy is going to be a total bitch as it's really steep and the skies are still smoky. Driving home it looks like October, not August, the smoke fog-like covering the whole town.

"It's so good to see you!" Roxy gives me a big hug.

"You too, it's been way too long since we actually caught up," I tell her. I see her in passing all the time on my way to train with Hendrik, but we never get a chance to talk.

I'm a little relieved when she tells me she is sore, because she's basically a superhero and I had been anxious about being able to keep pace, especially because I'm sore too. Between huffs and puffs on our way up the mountain, the conversation flows rapidly and easily. We hit all the major topics: love, family, nutrition, work, relationships. We talk about it all. I'm surprised to learn she had a serious boyfriend or two before Hendrik. I can't picture those two with anyone but each other.

"I had a few that were a few years at a time before I met him, wasn't a serial dater but there was two years here, a few years there."

It's interesting to think of her life without Hendrik in it, those two complement each other so well. There's an odd comfort in knowing there was a time when she didn't even know him yet, hadn't even found him in the world. Maybe there's a person out there for me and one day years later someone will think to themselves ,"I can't even picture Roo without him!" The thought is nice and I let it linger.

We laugh about the differences between small towns and big cities we've lived in.

"I remember feeling so old before I met Hendrik," she tells me. "Like I'm twenty-three, wow, when am I ever going to find someone."

"I know! When I got married in my twenties everyone in the city was like, 'You're too young,' and everyone at home who'd already been married for years and had three kids was like, 'finally Roo's getting hitched.'"

We daydream about second homes, vacation homes, cities we'd like to own properties in. I've hiked that same route countless times, probably hundreds, but with Roxy that was the fastest it's ever felt.

The training with Hendrik is an absolute grind. We spend a lot of the session discussing strategies for heading into the weekend so I don't "gutter ball," as he calls it, like I did this past one. Basically, yeah, have the beers, but don't let one bad meal turn into an entirely bad weekend. Go for the hung-over breakfast, but maybe have an egg and two slices of bacon versus all the food in the world. All the plans we make seem sensible to me and I hope I can keep myself accountable to them. I just need to actually be conscious of what I'm putting into my body and listen to what I already know. I'm the worst for ignoring myself in this regard. We also make plans to take some measurements of my body with those old-school pinchy caliper things so we have another method of tracking progress verses just the scale.

Between the gym, the hike, and the training session, I've done to myself exactly what I knew I was going to do, and I'm completely worn out. I busy myself with the dogs and with some bill-paying, but by early afternoon I'm really not feeling well. I've got a horrible headache, and I think I feel an earache starting. *Fuck.* I've been pushing myself really hard lately and my body is not having it. I can't remember the last time I took a rest day from the gym. My left eye has started twitching, which is ironic because just a few days ago, Greyson and I were having a talk about stress symptoms. He told me that when he's super stressed he can always tell because he can crack his neck. I'd explained that my left eye twitches when I'm stressed but that hasn't happened in years. And now, days later, it's happening. Maybe I'm more anxious about seeing Wes and the kids than I even want to admit to myself?

I message Greyson and tell him about my eye.

"Eat spinach it cures everything." he replies.

"If that's true that would be amazing!"

"Broken heart? Gone!"

"Now that...would be unreal."

I've got his dog in addition to mine for the weekend while he's away, so I send him lots of pictures of them. I spend a solid hour brushing his dog's long hair out and snag shots of her looking pretty. I get a text from Wes confirming we're still on for tomorrow, which makes me happy. I crawl into bed with all three dogs, barely any room for me, and I throw a heating bad on my earache. I down massive amounts of oil of oregano recalling how James used to tell me it made me smell like a delicious forno oven pizza. I sleep like the dead.

## August 11

I feel a million times better when I wake up, maybe all I needed was a really good sleep. There's no hint or trace of my earache. *Thank you, oregano.* I hit the gym, really lightly doing what I like to call an "active rest day." I move around and get limber, I get my heart rate up a bit, I lift but not heavy—basically, I'm just trying to wake my body up. I've been racking my brain trying to think of a housewarming gift to bring with me to Wes's. I remember a particular brand of coffee he really likes and search out where it is. It's literally nowhere near my house, but since it's the weekend and it's early, traffic shouldn't be bad, so I decide to do it. After getting the coffee, I find a cute box with a cassette tape design on the front and throw in a few other things I think he might like. I'm not sure if it's weird, my bringing him a gift, but I want him to know I'm excited for him and this new home, and that it does warrant celebratory status in my mind.

A text from him comes through: "Kids are pretty stoked to see ya."

"Omg I can't wait!" I reply.

At home I put the gift basket together and play with the dogs. I'm not sure how long I'll be over at his place, so I want to make sure they get a ton of exercise today. I think his house is quite close but I'm not sure, if it is I might even pop home in between to let them out again after dinner. I gather up all the things I'll need to take over there: some stuff of his I still have kicking around, my microphone, and things I'll need for the podcast. My heart races faster and faster each minute that passes, thinking about getting to see the kids.

I knock, but there's no answer. My guess is that Wes has music playing. I wait a bit and then ring the doorbell. I hear them before I see them and when the door opens I hug them both. It is hands down, one hundred percent, without a doubt, the happiest I have felt since the day he broke up with me. I promised myself I wouldn't hug them extra long or cry or be weird, so I get excited and ask them to show me everything! The house is amazing. It's a former rental so it needs some work, but I see it 100 percent through Wes's eyes and I know it will meet all his needs far better than my house ever did. The joy I have for him and the kids mattes the sheen of my hurt that I'm not going to be part of it. It takes the glare off of what I'm feeling and allows me to look right into what this house represents for him, for them. I know without a doubt that he is capable of making it everything he wants it to become.

He makes us dinner and I savor every second of watching him move around the kitchen like I used to. The kids are wired and silly and their laughter makes me laugh. We're sitting at the table Wes had bought for me, the same table where we all shared so many meals together, but I try not to let it bother me. The food is amazing; he truly is the best cook. I don't think I ever did a good enough job of showing him how much I appreciated that. After dinner the kids want us to all watch a movie together. I'm ecstatic when his daughter wants me to sit near her, and my heart swells when his son, who's constantly moving, sometimes snuggles right into me before busying himself again. On one of these snuggle-stops, he pushes his head against me and says: "I Love you, Roo."

"I love you too, buddy," I tell him. He touches each one of the rings on my finger and asks me who gave them to me, something he would do all the time when we lived together.

"My mom," I say, then, "I bought that one myself." And then finally the one furthest on my right hand. "Your daddy gave me that." Wes looks over from beside me on the couch, and I can't read his look.

We sit on an angle from one another. Everything about this is different than it used to be, I feel disoriented.

"So?" he asks me. "What's this look like?"

We try to discuss prior to recording if we're treating this like the last episode or a continuation after a break.

"Because the way I would handle it would be different, depending on what we're doing . . ."

"Yeah, the hard part is I don't know. I'm not sure if the rapport is still going to be there, I don't want to put out anything I'm not proud of. I mean we used to talk all week so we had so much to put in, but my life is really boring now," I admit.

"Your life was just as boring before," he jokes.

"I don't know, maybe we should just have this discussion during the show, and just be honest and record this part where we're trying to figure it out?"

"Well, let's just start and see."

We're choppy, and there are large lulls, and it feels awkward, but we laugh and share some stories I think could probably get posted. It's all the stuff surrounding the breakup that feels off. Wes explains that the original concept of the show, and essentially our relationship, was that we were going to do things different.

I chime in with, "Which proved to be an epic fail."

"I don't think it was an epic fail at all . . ."

"Oh, then how do you think of it? Wait, I think I know, it was a really great six months, seven months, whatever it was."

He disagrees and speaks very kindly of our time together, telling me he will never forget it. The bar on that sentiment seems so low to me. As if forgetting it were even an option? He's said this to me before and it irks me a little every time, but I remind myself his experience is not my own and that's OK. If not forgetting it is the best platitude he has to offer about our time together, I'll take what I can get.

We roll through as best we can but when we round the bend to the end it still just doesn't feel right.

"There's just other stuff I wanna say," he smiles at me shyly, "but I can't."

"What? Now you have to tell me!"

He proceeds to explain the kindest things and feelings about me, and says more than once that he still loves and cares for me but just needs to be alone. This is the first time since we broke up that he has expressed he still loves me, and it both builds me up and tears me down. He's said before that he still cares, or that I'm important, but never that he still loves me. This is a hard word for him, and while I know its use carries no commitment and he doesn't want to be with me at all, it still feels super powerful to hear. He talks about the day and me seeing the kids for the first time, and how challenging being alone is for him. I mumble something like, "Thanks for that, that's incredibly kind," which is totally an inadequate version of what I want to say, but anything else will result in my sobbing.

I explain we're on two opposite extremes there because going back to being alone is hard too, and how painful the whole thing has been.

When the mics go off, he's shifty.

"You're cute when you're nervous because you rarely ever are," I tell him. He laughs.

"I just really wanted you to know all that." He says.

"It means a lot," I say, and again my words don't even touch the surface of what it truly meant. Sitting across from me in his office chair I just want to fly at him, and kiss him, and rip his clothes off. I want to beg him to give us a chance to be different. I want to make a case for poor timing, lack of healing, the damage of rushing. I want to tell him every way in which I know it could be done differently. Instead I just smile at him and he suggests we go upstairs. We sit on the deck drinking beers and talking about mutual friends and music and laugh a lot.

"You know, everything else aside," I explain, "I really just, I know Roo emotions are a problem or whatever, but I miss you as my best friend. I miss this so much."

"Roo emotions aren't a problem, you've taught me so much about emotion, I just can't be where you are. I just couldn't keep disappointing you, and I can't do what you do, and I'm not where you're at. I don't have those types of emotions. There's shit going on in here that I probably won't deal with for ten or fifteen years, I just leave it and don't feel it."

"I wish I was like you in that regard, I'd give anything not to feel it."

"I miss you too, but I just don't feel like it's fair to say that because you do feel things so different than me. If I'd had it my way it woulda been like right after we broke up: 'oh, hey, what's up,' hanging out again. But I'm trying to give you your time to be OK, and your space, because I knew this was going to hurt you but I just didn't know how bad."

"And you know THAT is frustrating for me," I level with him. "Because how do you move in, when you knew, you knew what a big gap that was to shoot for me to ever do that again with someone. And bring your children into my life? And buy a truck with me? A joint bank account? And talk about building our own house one day, and everything we did . . . and then be surprised when it's painful for me? The audacity you have to be surprised that I thought we were going to be together for a really long time is super counterintuitive to every choice we made along the way to do that! This wasn't just a thing I made up in my head. Do you know there's days when it isn't even about you? Sometimes I'm with Fox . . . and I just cry about the kids."

"I genuinely . . . it was so much for you! You were finding it so hard and then all the stuff about how I wasn't available or 'present' when the kids were there, so I thought they were like, this obstacle to you." I can see how he would feel that way. It was a major challenge;

it was the hardest learning curve I've ever had. It did stress me out. It did freak me out. But I obviously didn't make it clear to him that every single second of it was worth it to me for those kids.

"I am sorry if I **ever** made you feel like they were an obstacle. Those kids are the best thing that ever happened to me."

The silence of the night fills the gap for a few minutes.

"Just so you know . . . my alone time hasn't been good," he says.

He confides in me the struggles he's been having, and I tear up. Selflessly I wish I could fix everything for him, but I can't and I don't know how, and this is work he has to do alone. Selfishly, I wonder what's wrong with me, that all that he's going through, all the pain and the sadness and the loneliness, still feels better to him than a life with me. That given the option between having a person who would love him no matter what, and experiencing the struggles he is now, struggling is more right for him than I am. I hate myself in this moment, because I must have made him so truly miserable for that to be true. I must have made him feel so poorly about himself. I must have made his life so unbearable by my needs that any suffering now pales in comparison. I won't forgive myself for that. I would do it all differently, so God damn different, but it means nothing now. There are some actions, some moments, some lives we never get a second chance at.

"I sometimes wonder what would have happened back in May if we had of just not broken up but you had of gotten your own place," I say.

"Me too. But we spent so long trying to figure that out and we made the choice and we just kept forcing it and forcing it."

I agree.

"I also wonder what would have happened if I had of moved slower in the beginning," he tells me. "But you just . . . you took me. You still do every time I see you."

You took me. I think the phrase back to myself. How had I possessed the power to "take" someone but not to keep them? Inches from him, with the kids asleep down the hall and his body so close to mine, everything I don't get to have surrounding me, I have never felt like more of a failure in my life.

The night cools off and so we head inside and sit on the couch listening to music and talking. We laugh a lot and tease each other. We cuddle and hold each other close. I relish in how good it feels to have his hands on me. He, like his son had earlier, touches my rings.

"I like that you're still wearing it," he says, running a finger over the ring he surprised me with in Cuba. I had admired it at the jewelry stand and then later he'd produced it from an envelope and placed in on my finger. "I didn't think you would anymore."

"Oh I'm glad, I was worried you'd think it was weird."

"No, I like it." He pulls my hands close to his face and kisses them. I think about kissing him, but he leans in and kisses me first. We wind up with him on top of me, making out like teenagers on the couch. Abruptly he excuses himself to the restroom.

"Sorry," he says when he comes back in. "I shouldn't have done that."

"No, it's Ok . . . I like it."

He comes back to the couch and we kiss more. All these thoughts are running through my head. How good he feels, how much I want him. *This doesn't mean the same thing to him that it does to you.* I repeat this over and over again. *He's doing this exact same thing with other girls. Don't do this to yourself, Roo. Don't do this to him.* Things get really heated and now we have a problem.

"I should get going, if we keep at it you know what's going to happen, and then tomorrow you'll have a Roo problem because I'll be feeling all the feelings."

"That's a later me problem."

"I know, but . . . it's a big problem. I know you want simple and this is just gonna be not that."

We kiss for a bit more.

"Will you at least tuck me in?" he grins at me. Fuck, how does he get at me so much? I've never wanted to do anything as much as I want this.

"Sure...but then I'm going."

As he gets ready for bed, I grab my bag and throw my jacket on, then follow him into the bedroom.

"You've got your jacket on," he notices. "You really are going?"

"Yeah, not unless there's something in between us having sex and me needing to leave."

"Probably not at the moment," he jokes.

I crawl onto the bed with him and we kiss more. His hand reaches for the places I won't be able to say no to.

"OK, OK, seriously, I gotta go."

"OK." He looks flustered.

"Are you mad?"

"No."

"Are you frustrated?"

"Yeah, but not at you, but I'm frustrated."

"Fuck," I say right in his face and then kiss him one more time. "I seriously gotta go."

He walks me to the door.

"Thanks again for everything, talk soon."

I walk out the door and don't look back. Physically I'm gone, but mentally I am still in that bed with him, doing all the things I know I'll never get to do with him again.

At home I toss and turn, too riled up to sleep. *You did him a favour,* I tell myself repeatedly. *You're saving him from all of the emotion that would have brought out in you. You know that doesn't mean the same thing to him. You know he has other women now.* None of the things I tell myself make me ache any less for the things we came so close to doing. I hope he understands there is nothing about that decision that was rejection. I hope he can see it's protection, self-preservation. He has me in every way that matters, but he doesn't want what I inherently am. If the bad of me is so much that he doesn't want to keep me, then I have to keep just some tiny shreds of the good in hopes that someone else will want them both. If he still has all of me, then what will be left to give to someone else?

## August 12

I roll over and feel a non-Ducky-or-Atty-like shape beside me, and for half a sleepy moment my heart glows thinking it's Wes. In a fog I roll over and see its Greyson's dog. *Someone has gotten used to sleeping in the bed.* I hit the gym with a fury fueled by my unsatisfied desires last night. I do everything hard and fast and heavy and attack the whole room. It doesn't abate my need. By the time I leave I look like I just stepped out of the shower. My hair is dripping wet and my clothes are soaking. I text Wes.

We exchange a few messages and he admits he was worried I'd be a bit mad this morning, he's sorry if he pushed things too far.

I explain I'm not mad at him at all, was just fighting myself against all the things I wanted to do and have done to me, but I think we both know it was the right decision I went home.

"Haven't decided if it was the right call or not. No, it was . . . I think."

I don't know what comes over me, but I write him back a dirty text message. His response says he would have liked that, but it's written in a very formal style.

"So polite," I tell him.

"Gentleman and a scholar."

"And the sexiest fucking beast too . . . not fair."

I get an LOL back, which means the conversation is done.

I ask my phone: "How many days until September ninth?"

"There are twenty-eight days until September ninth," it replies.

Shit. Twenty-eight days is four weeks. There are so many problems with this. First of all, four weeks from now I don't believe I'm going to be "over" Wes. Just flat out, don't believe it. Especially after last night. Also, I've basically defined myself by writing for the last two months. What if this has all been a waste of time? What if nothing comes of it? What if my delusions that sharing this type of personal story would have some appeal are exceptionally misguided, and when all is said and done I'll have wasted three months writing, money on an editor, however long on revisions, all so I could what . . . print myself a copy to sit in a drawer somewhere? Forget this being a waste of time, how will I fill my time when it's complete? Does everyone who takes a risk feel this way? Or is this a sign that I've out-stupided myself even harder than I ever thought I could? This writing, this processing, this has been my only plan. Who will I be when the next loss I suffer is the only sense of purpose I have? When the book is done . . . then what? Twenty-eight days. Fuck.

Lucy is coming over today; she has some stuff to do in my neighborhood for the charity she runs, so I head to the coffee shop to have our drinks ready for when she arrives. She's been interviewing potential tenants to rent out the suite James will be vacating, and I shit you not she interviewed a couple whose last names were Twitty and McDickers. When I get home I carefully write this on her cup with a Jiffy marker, laughing to myself.

She lets herself in, and I hand it to her.

"Look at it closely." I nod to her cup and she spots it, then bursts out laughing.

"Please tell me you had them do that at the coffee shop."

"Nah," I admit, "I did it myself."

"How'd it go with Wes and the kids?"

I rant and rave about the kids and how great the house he bought is for them, how happy I was to see them, the movie we watched, how adorable they are, some of the funny things they said.

"And Wes?" she asks.

My face spreads into a wide grin and hers starts to expand too, but I cut her off :"Don't worry, I didn't sleep with him . . . but it was fucking sooooooo hard not to."

The people she had a meeting with are coming from out of town and they run hours late, so we spend the entire afternoon sipping coffee and smoking and chatting.

"We should go to my mom's cabin in fall," she tells me. I've been hearing about this cabin for years but have never actually had the chance to go.

"All the yes," I tell her. "That would be unreal. What are you doing September eighth?"

"I'm gone . . . for my anniversary." She half rolls her eyes at the word. She's not in a celebrate her marriage kind of zone and I don't blame her.

"Ah ok, I think Fox and I are going to try and do something, because at midnight that night it'll be the ninth, and then . . . that's eleven weeks."

"Wow, that'll be crazy. Yeah, shit, I won't be here."

"OK, well we will work on picking a party weekend still . . . I keep not getting that done."

When Lucy heads out I meal prep for the week, cooking some basics and pre-chopping lots of vegetables. I'm excited to let Hendrik know tomorrow that there was no gutterballing. I crash early.

## August 13

I have training with Hendrik first thing, so I'm up and at 'em. I tell him about my food and my drinks, and we both agree I did better than last weekend. I tell him about seeing Wes and the kids and the meeting I have later today regarding a broadcasting gig. He more than puts me through the paces, which I need because it quiets my mind. We make plans to train again on Friday.

When I'm home I that see my old work cell phone has a text message from my dear friend Matthew. There is a sizeable age gap between us—he's much older than me and it doesn't matter now, but when we met through a charity event I was a teenager and so romance was never considered. Instead we formed a lifelong friendship that has spanned several decades, breakups, spouses, cities, years, the birth of his children, and a plethora of dogs. I have always had what could quite simply be described as a "crush" on him, but it's so much more than that. He's one of those people who brings me home, who when he's around I feel like I'm the same me I was at sixteen, before life got the best of me. I keep a great distance from his life, knowing the types of feelings I have toward him are totally inappropriate in relation to his marital status. Boundaries. Sometimes the most loving thing you can do for someone is stay out of their life. Matthew's wife is kind and wonderful, and has always made me feel welcome, but a guilt sinks in whenever I see him that I know I shouldn't ignore. There has **never** been a single inappropriate action, never a line crossed, never an improper word spoken . . . and we will keep it that way. And so it's been a yearly call at Christmas, a call after a divorce, the birth of a child, the loss of a loved one. These are the events in which we allow ourselves to reach out. We tread very lightly and respectfully. He's in town for a work meeting and wants to know if I'd like to have a coffee. I'm elated. I let him know I have a meeting but can get together right after.

My potential job thing goes well. I'm not going to lie, it boosts my confidence that I have options when the book is done if that's what I decide I want. I wish I could call Wes and tell him every last detail. How much of my life these days is trying to ignore my impulses, my urges? It feels like way more than ever before.

I arrive first and when he walks through the doors, it is the greatest comfort I've had in weeks. Before he even hugs me I feel it, home, familiarity, comfort, consistency, dependability. Time has been kind to him, his face still as friendly, handsome and young-eyed as ever. He wraps an arm around me.

"It's so good to see you, girl."

"You have no idea," I say and I fold myself into his arm over my shoulder, hugging him around the waist because he's so much taller than me. The look of concern on his face tells me he's seen it like everyone else does: something is wrong with me; I'm not quite the same.

Outside, we sit with our coffees and my heartache just pours out. I expect I'll edit or censor for the benefit of not appearing too pathetic, but I don't.

"Do you feel like you're through some of the worst of it though?" he asks.

"You know . . . there was this day . . . that I know was rock bottom." I haven't spoken about that day with anyone other than Fox.

"I was going to kill myself, Matthew." He bites his lip staring hard at me, through me. "You know the pier?"

He nods, he knows the one.

"I just, something broke, and everything came out, and it wasn't even about Wes, it was this snowball effect of everything that's happened since Tese died. I had this crazy thought that all life was going to hold for me was more pain and loss, and it seemed . . . so real. So certain. Like I'd be an idiot to think I'm ever going to get anything else." We are seated side by side staring off the same way, and he reaches a long arm out and grips my shoulder.

"What did you do?"

"I started making a list of everyone it would hurt, and everyone that keeps me here. I haven't even really told anyone else that because I'm so embarrassed that I considered it. I sat there forever, Matthew, like the longest time, and then I just got dressed and went to a wedding like life was normal." I can't believe I'm telling him this. His eyes redden with tears and he dabs at them.

"I wish you could see yourself how I see you, Roo."

We catch up on his life and work, his wife, the kids. Everyone is doing well. He has to leave to head to his next meeting. This whole exchange takes less than half an hour, and it's a testament to our bond that so much can be exchanged so quickly without any preamble. At my car he towers over me.

"Listen, I hope you don't ever have to do that again, but when you're making your list of people that tether you to this world . . . say my name too."

I hug him and get teary-eyed.

"I love you, Roo. You hold such a special place in my heart always."

"You too . . . always," I say, and then he's gone. We likely won't speak again for years.

Wes picks me up on his way home from work; we're going to see a ridiculous action movie in 3D about an oversized shark. At his house he makes us dinner and I tell him all about my meetings and a bit about seeing Matthew. I love going to the movies with Wes, it's probably one of my favourite things we used to do together. The film is super ridiculous and we laugh and make dumb comments and speculations and eat far too much popcorn. Old habits die hard, though, and part way through the movie I realize at some point during leaning in to speak to him I've placed my hand on his leg. I feel his body stiffen slightly and he doesn't move his hand toward mine at all. It sits there like a dead fish. *Fuck. I'm such an idiot.* I lift it to grab another mouthful of popcorn and act like it never happened. I'm glad the theatre is dark because my face is beet red with the shame of this small unreciprocated gesture. At the end of the movie we take goofy pictures in front of its poster.

At my house we linger in his truck in the driveway.

"Should we post that picture?" he asks me. There has been zero social media activity on our shared account for the podcast since we broke up.

"Yeah, I dunno, maybe we just put it up and say something like, 'Just because we broke up doesn't mean we can't go to the movies.'"

" . . . and podcast," he says.

"Yeah, I like that . . . should we say new episodes coming soon?"

"Yeah maybe a question mark though so it's open ended."

I write the post and he reads it over.

"Do it," he tells me. I hit the next button and it uploads.

"OK, well, thanks for that, that was really fun." I slide over to get out of the truck but he reaches for a hug first. I quickly hug him and hop out. I've forgotten to turn my porch light on, he pulls away before I'm inside.

## August 14

Perhaps it was seeing Matthew or maybe it's simply that I haven't cried over it in quite some time. It could also be some of the mean comments from internet trolls on the post we did yesterday, but today sucks. Every little thing feels difficult; I spill coffee everywhere, twice. I forget my proper gym shoes for my workout. At home I attempt to fix the roof of my shed and really hurt my wrist falling off the ladder. It's swollen and pulsing with pain. I ice it, wrap it, and then decide to just give up on today.

In bed, I think of Matthew's face when he saw me. I think of Mitch's reaction to me on video chat.

"You look good, sad, but good."

I know that my ability to feel deeply is both my greatest strength and my worst stumbling block. I hate my tender-heartedness today. I hate seeing people I love look at me in a way that tells me they're worried. I hate that I care so much. I cry, and I'm not really sure why I'm crying. I'm lonely and frustrated; I'm exhausted both physically and mentally. I'm sick of myself and my own sadness. Greyson messages me to ask if I'd like to have dinner with him. I feel like a jerk, but I decline. I want the company, but I just need to be alone today. He's so kind he even offers the food but not the company and I tell him that's OK. I spend the entire day in bed. Around 8 p.m. the dogs are antsy. I don't blame them, I've been a horrible dog mom today. I ask Greyson if his dog can come out and play with mine for a bit so they can burn some energy. He comes around to the back deck and we sit and let them run.

"Did you end up eating?" he asks me.

"No, did you end up cooking?"

"Nope."

"Well it appears we are both at a food impasse," I smile. "I've been craving a grilled cheese all day."

"I'm sure somewhere around here does one. You should call places and ask them to read you the menu," he jokes.

"I should call places and rather than have them read me the menu just ask if I can list things and have them say yes or no . . ." we laugh.

We decide on a nearby place to go get some food.

"I'm not going to drink," I tell him.

"No, me neither, my ears still bugging me."

He's been fighting a bad cold the last week or so and the smoky skies have only served to exacerbate his situation.

At dinner I try and explain why I've been feeling low today. I draw out loud the correlation that I had actually had coffee with Matthew on the day Tese died, and so seeing him often brings up a lot of emotion, but especially this time.

"I just wish I weren't so emotional, but I keep thinking, what is life if not emotion? It keeps getting pointed out to me by men that they don't think as deeply or as much about things as I do . . . and honestly," I lean in toward him,"I try to picture what it would be like to be wandering through life thinking about stuff, but not feeling it. What do you do all day? If you're not thinking about everything you're just . . . looking at stuff? Without having an emotional reaction to it? That sounds so boring, just looking at things all day."

He laughs. "Well I think people look at things and think about them, but just aren't feeling them."

"I know . . . that's the problem, that's fucked to me." I pause. "If you're not feeling everything, then when do **you** feel?"

"When I'm in nature." His answer doesn't surprise me.

"Yeah, I could see that."

"I just think feelings and interactions with people are what my life was meant to be about, that's when I'm most me, is when it's good with people. Which is weird because you know, on the whole, how much I despise people."

We chat about religion and I eat the closest thing the restaurant has to a grilled cheese, which appears to me to just basically be a burger with cheese on it. I crawl into bed a little too full and still feeling blue bad glad to have at least gotten out of the house.

## August 15

I'm later than normal to get rolling to the gym. Ever taken a sad day thinking all the rest would help you bounce back, and instead your body seems to go "Sleep, I remember that, let's do that all the time"? As a result of my slow start time, I have to rush like mad to meet Seamus for our weekly coffee.

"You look haggard," are the first words out of his mouth.

"Nice to see you too, jackwagon." I throw him a hug. "Everyone's been saying that to me lately."

"Sorry. You look good, just haggard."

"Yeah that seems to be the common theme."

"What's going on? Saw on social you and Wes were together?"

Under a patio umbrella I tell him about going to the movie and recording the podcast.

"Fuck that," he says. "Sorry, Roo, I know I don't know him at all, and I'm sure he's a great dude, he has to be if you care so much about him, but a guy shouldn't be telling a woman any feelings unless he's going to do something about it. Otherwise it's just kind of cruel. Dude needs to shit or get off the pot. Be with you or leave you the fuck alone."

"No no, it's not like that." I defend Wes. "He was really hesitant to tell me anything about how he feels because he does worry about how it will impact me."

"I'm really not trying to be a dick. I trust your judgment if you say he's amazing. I just hate seeing you doubt yourself. I hate what all of this seems to have done to you. You have so much to offer—hell, I think every guy ya know would take a go at you if they were single. I don't want to see you get hurt again or wind up feeling like there's something wrong with you. There's nothing wrong with you, you're amazing. Everyone who knows you knows you have this kind of …I don't know what you'd call it. You do a thing to people . . . you're just . . . there's something special about it, and you. You're more special than you think. That's my unsolicited advice so take it for what it's worth, and I'm not trying to tell you what to do because no matter what you do I'm always going to love you. You could be like, 'Seamus, it's 3 a.m. and I'm doing blow off a hooker's tits, and I'd be like, 'OK, where should I pick you up?' I just don't want you to get hurt; you deserve someone who can give you the world. You're like my sister."

"I know, buddy."

He leans down and pats my arm.

"I love you, Roo."

"I love you too."

I have a friend from my radio days coming into town for work this evening, and we're meeting for dinner. I've known Rick since I was a teenager; he worked with my family's business in my hometown for a brief bit, and since then our careers have followed similar shifts with us often having found ourselves in the same city or employed by the same company. With the smoky skies and tourist season, traffic has been an absolute bitch lately so I leave myself forty-five minutes to get downtown, which traditionally should be way more than enough time. It proves not to be. Even though it's the 5 p.m. rush and the majority of traffic should be coming out of town, it's swamped getting in, too. Wes Calls. He tells me a hilarious story about a new employee who ditched out on her orientation to go get a Tylenol and then never came back. I can't stop laughing.

"What are you doing?" he asks.

"Well . . . I'm currently on pace to be late for a dinner I'm supposed to be going to. Traffic is brutal. I'm trying to get into town."

"Yeah, hate to be the one to tell you this but I'm coming out of town trying to get home, and it doesn't look like it's moving your way, really. Who's your dinner with?" he asks.

I explain about Rick being in town for work. We talk for a while and then agree we should focus on getting where we are going. When I arrive in the restaurant, Rick is already there, seated in the back corner. I give him a huge hug.

"You look great!" I tell him. He really does; he's noticeably down in weight and he looks very healthy.

"You too!" he tells me.

The conversation flows super easily and, as I always am, I'm pleasantly surprised at the level of support I get on my current state of affairs. He and his wife met back in college and they have two beautiful children and over twenty years together under their respective belts.

"Did you have many serious girlfriends before Lily?" I ask, curious to know more about who he was before her.

"No, not at all, I wasn't even ready for a relationship when I met her but it just kind of changed and I got ready fast. We've had our ups and downs, but the good always outweigh the bad."

"Yeah, the ups and the downs are expected, it's the good I miss. I liked being married." I confess. When you're divorced people expect you to have a bitter attitude toward marriage itself but I could never really muster that up. It's not something I'm gunning to do again soon, but inherently I believe sharing a life with someone sounds amazing, regardless of what you call it. We have a beer and eat some food and we talk vinyl. We chat about mutual radio friends. We pontificate on the state of the industry. It's a great evening with a lot of laughs. I snag some selfies of us side by side and send them to his wife back home, who replies with a heart. At the end of our dinner I find myself doing what I've agreed to do with so many people over the last few months, and "not let it be so long until next time."

These bonds I'm getting to re-form with people, these conversations I'm getting to have, and the questions I now have the time to ask, they're meaningful to me. Listen, you don't write a book about your own life if you're not self-absorbed. I know it's one of my worst qualities. The focus on healing and being present for these moments, though, it's allowing me to be a better friend than I could have been before. When you strip away your career and your love life, what is left if not your friends and family? Do I give as much to all these amazing people as they have given to me? I certainly hope so.

When I make it back to my vehicle, I see I've missed a text from Wes. We exchange a few messages, and he tells me I can swing by if I'd like, although he's not really up to much other than unclogging the drain at his house. I let him know I've had a good night and I'm riding the "good time" wave. I head over.

"I didn't tell you about my friend's diagnosis, did I?" I say, sinking into the couch. He looks up from the TV, where he's fumbling with some cords trying to finish setting up his entertainment unit.

"No?"

I explain it all to him, ending with, "So now when I get that good-timey kind of feeling I sort of just roll with it, like, ride the high or whatever. That's how I tequila'd myself with Greyson on the long weekend and the night of the concert and stuff. It's not specifically about the drinking; it's just the embracing the good time . . . life's just too fucking short."

"Yeah, you definitely didn't tell me that," he says. I wonder if for him this explains something about how I've been acting. He tells me a story I'd never heard before about the day his father passed away, and he talks a fair amount about his dad, something he doesn't do a ton. He reflects on his desire to find the balance between being a present and engaging father, and still being a person with a life. When he's done with the entertainment unit we move upstairs and sit on his deck talking a lot about his work and his schedule and priorities. I like listening to him speak—he could read me a grocery list and I'd find it pleasant. I'm not sure if it's because we're talking about his work, or if I've overstayed my welcome, but abruptly he tells me I should go because he needs to work on scheduling. I haven't even finished my drink.

"OK," I say, slightly confused. "I'll hit the road."

On the drive home I think about how the old me would have perseverated for hours on if I'd done something wrong that made him bum-rush me out the door. I hear Seamus's voice in my head: "There's nothing wrong with you." I choose not to think about it, at all, and I go home and set up the laser on my deck and stare contentedly at the twinkling in the trees until bed.

## August 16

I hammer out my workout at the gym and get swept up in waves of motivation. I come home and write, clean, dance, sing and play with the dogs. I get in a really good productivity zone and before I know it, it's nearing dinnertime. Greyson is going to cook some steaks, so we meet on the deck where I'm still perched at my laptop.

"Weren't you here at like 7 a.m. today . . . have you moved at all?" he jokes.

The steaks he makes are really good. Partway through dinner he pulls his phone out.

"So, Wes is on his way home from work and wants to know what I'm doing for dinner. I do have an extra steak."

"Yeah, sure, tell him to come by."

I'm in booty pajama shorts and a tank top with glasses on my head and no makeup. I can't go and change before Wes gets here, though, because Greyson will notice and that's embarrassing, so I sit uncomfortably knowing I look like garbage hoping it comes off as cute and casual versus homeless. When Wes shows up the three of us laugh and joke around a lot. It's the first time since the one day when Wes joined us at the pub when I've really been around both of them at the same time. It feels like a good thing, hints of what life used to be. The guys fuck around with my stereo equipment trying to get the sound system James brought me to work.

When they're done with that they tackle my burned out brake light. Wes says he needs to get going, but I mention the new "Purge" movie we wanted to see.

"It's the last night it's on in theatres . . ." I sing at him.

"What, really? We should go then, right?"

"Totally!"

He needs to change out of his work clothes before the movie, so I follow him to his place just up the street. Pretty early on we realize we aren't going to make it to the theatre. I get so swept up in his company, I don't even care. There's actually another installment in between we haven't seen yet, so we agree we'll have a doubleheader night when it's available at home. He's so hard to get a read on these days, and I remind myself I won't be able to get a read on him because I don't think he's got a read on himself. He's riddled with the stress and worry of trying to find a balance in life, but he also admits he's not worried about pleasing anyone other than his children and is just doing whatever he wants. He touches my leg often when he talks, and apologizes often for it, but I tell him it's OK. He tells me he's riding the highs and weathering the lows, he has no desire to try and level them out.

"You know in audio editing . . ." he starts, and I know exactly what he's about to say.

"Compression, right?" I can see it in my mind, the peaks and valleys of a wave file having been run through a compressor now squished down into one clean level line. I think of me the other night feeling sad that he would chose this loneliness or struggle over me, and then the thought occurs that maybe this isn't sadness for him. This is freedom.

When the night gets cold we move inside to the couch. We talk about our marriages and it seems so clear to me he's still hurting. I wish I had known when I met him how not fully recovered he was from that. I lean my head against his shoulder from slightly behind him on the couch and wrap my arms around him.

"I'm sorry your heart is hurting," I say, squeezing him.

"Hurting?" He turns right around and looks at me, puzzled. "No, I'm not hurting. I'm pissed. I don't think I even have the ability to hurt anymore."

The comment falls into a weird sad cavern in my chest. If he can't see his anger for the hurt that it is, I feel sorry for him. How did I end up loving someone who says he has no capacity to hurt? The stakes were always so much higher for me, I just never knew it. This comment should tell me everything I need to know. *Go home. Someone who can't hurt will inevitably hurt you.* I stay. I stay because I'm an idiot; I stay because I want him. I stay because he's my best friend and no matter what he says or feels, what he doesn't say or doesn't feel, I love him. I suspect that just won't ever change. We move to the bedroom.

I stare at him sleeping next to me, softly snoring, so peaceful looking. I will pay the price for this decision, and he will continue to sleep soundly. I want more than anything to curl up into him, to be here in the morning to listen to music together over coffee. To feel him near me in those brief few minutes as you're waking when you're orienting yourself by the familiar landmark of the shape and feel of someone you love. I want it to feel like it used to, and I know that in the morning it will not. I tell myself he will likely be happier if I'm not here. I have to go. I dress silently and then lay back on the bed next to him. I lean down and kiss him.

"G'night Wes." He pulls me in closer for just a second, kissing me back in a sleepy haze, then rolls over and is dead asleep again. I leave.

I drown myself in shots of rum when I get home.

My phone rings. What the fuck, it's 2:17 a.m. It's Fox.

"Are you OK? I had this bad feeling; I woke up all panicked and can't fall back asleep."

I burst into tears.

"I made stupid choices and now I have all the sad."

"I knew it, I just had this feeling something was wrong, I woke up and I thought of you and how you're trying to heal and what you're trying to do, and the time you've been spending with him . . . it just doesn't feel like what this time was supposed to be."

"I don't know what I'm doing," I sniff.

"Well . . . to quote my good friend Roo Phelps . . ." I burst out laughing before she's even said anything. "I'm not done being stupid with him yet."

"Why am I so fucking dumb?" I'm laughing but I'm sobbing.

"This can be a good thing," she assures me. "You were getting feelings again, and it's a reminder that there's just pain there for you. Was it at least good?"

"It was amazing."

"Was it like, cold or detached?"

"No, it was like stomach kissing, neck kissing, intimate feeling perfect for Roo type shit. I'll give him this much: he knows exactly what I like."

"Fuck, hey?" she says. "So, what are you going to do now?"

"Well the last thing on the planet I can do is be weird about it, because if I make it a thing he won't even want to be friends with me anymore and I still want to be able to do the podcast and stuff. He's all about un-complicating shit and my shit is always emotionally complicated. We're supposed to podcast tomorrow or Saturday. Fuck, maybe I should just pretend to be sick for three days so I don't have to deal with it."

"And then what?" she says.

Over-exasperated and like her question is the most ludicrous thing in the world, I yell back at her at the top of my lungs: "I don't know!"

She bursts out laughing, and then I'm laughing too.

"Hadn't thought that far ahead, hey?" we laugh more. "Calling you tonight was the closest thing I've ever had to mother intuition," she jokes. "I sat up in bed and was like, 'Roo needs me . . . you gonna be OK?"

"Yeah, yeah, I'll be fine. I'm just . . . mad at myself. There's going to be nothing left of me for whoever else comes along."

"I'll call you tomorrow. I love you."

I tell her I love her too, I down a few more shots of rum, and I pass out.

## Week Nine
## August 17

I show up to training in the morning hung-over, sad, and visibly having recently been crying. My eyes are red and streaky.

"How are you?" Hendrik asks cautiously.

"Not good . . . I made stupid choices, and then I tried to drown those choices in rum."

"Ya threw some rum on it, did ya? And how'd that go?"

"Also not good," I admit. "I don't know what the fuck I'm doing."

"Join the club," he smiles. "Let's deadlift."

"I'm just really disappointed in myself today," I say between lifts.

"Well, normally when we're disappointed it's because our expectations don't match our outcomes. Did you do something that didn't go as planned?"

"Nope . . . I knew exactly what the outcome of my choices was going to be. Wes did zero of the anything wrong . . . this is 100 percent a me problem."

"All the best problems are," he smiles at me. "Ah, kid, it's tough out there."

"Yeah, and I'm not making it any easier on myself."

"Don't be too hard on yourself. There's always a lesson in the negative feedback we get from the choices we make."

At home I lie in bed. Greyson messages me to ask how my friending with Wes went last night.

"It went," I write back. "I'm not super up for talking about it if that's ok...nothing to do with you."

He replies, "No worries."

"Brains just trying to brain about my life right now, so sorta letting everything ruminate."

"Yeah that's alright, processing can take time."

"But I'm ok though." I add a smiley face so he won't be worried. "Just super inside my own head."

I spend the majority of the day in bed trying to catch up on the sleep rum stole from me. Just before 2 p.m., when I'm out running errands, Wes texts: "So….I'm tired."

"Me toooooooo" I write back. I've promised myself I won't put the weight of my bad decisions on him.

"You ok?" It makes me feel good he's asked. I honestly wasn't even sure he would think to.

"Yeah sorry I was just driving."

"Don't crash," he replies.

"Haha, no no I'm home now."

No other messages come.

At dinnertime Fox texts me and asks if I'd like to come over, Clive is making pork chops. I head into town and we sit at her house watching the sun fade behind the hills of the smoky skies.

"You were so funny last night," she tells me. "When you said the thing about pretending to be sick and I asked you what next, the way you said 'I don't know' was like the most exasperated I've ever heard from you in my life." We can't stop laughing.

"Fuck, I'm so dumb." I explain what Hendrik said about outcomes matching expectations.

"I've just gotta shift my mindset about it and not let it be a thing."

"Yeah, or if it is a thing, let it be a good thing. A good reminder of a bad idea."

"Totally."

Clive makes an amazing dinner; he cooks an entire onion in god knows what, but it's one of the best things I've ever eaten. The barbecue he does is unreal, and I feel the weight I've been putting on myself lifting.

"Did you give Roo her socks?" Clive asks Fox.

"Nope, not without you."

"Socks?" I ask.

"Clive got you a present."

He wanders away and comes back with a little package, which I open to reveal two socks that are designed to look exactly like dogs' feet. The effect is hilarious, especially in a photo; it literally looks like dog paws. We share a lot of laughs and I lament having to go home. The night feels good and I don't want to be anywhere but here with them.

"Stay!" Clive urges me.

"Can't . . . dogs."

"Oh, right . . . dogs."

At home Greyson has a friend over who I really like. Naturally I need to show her the laser.

We sit in the backyard for a good hour laughing and joking. She loves the laser, which makes me unnecessarily happy. She is currently back in the dating pool and while I like hearing about it from her, I dread going back to it. I give her advice where I can, careful not to overstep and also fully aware I'm the last person on the planet anyone should listen to. I call it after two beers and put myself to bed.

## August 18

I run at the gym, which is not enjoyable for me. I used to be a better runner but after a muscle injury to my foot I can only go so far before exacerbating it. I cardio myself as hard as I can. When I get home, I have a wicked headache and my right hand is really bothering me again. It's the one that was injured in the elevator accident, and after injuring my wrist on the ladder the other day it seems to just be achy and problematic at all times now. I ice it and crawl into bed.

Around lunchtime I head to Fox's. We sit with the lake in front of us and she does my fingernails and toenails with her cool UV gel machine. She tells me hilarious and weird stories about some of her distant family members I've never met. There's seriously a dude who proposed to his wife with a ring he made in prison. I can't stop laughing at the idea of a makeshift prison ring and what that might even look like. I haven't heard any more from Wes and I text him as I'm leaving her place to see if we are going to podcast. A series of messages comes through about the kind of day he's having and that he just needs to catch up on sleep. It seems a little weird to me that after what happened the other night he doesn't want to see me now. I'm hard pressed to believe the two aren't connected, but if he's avoiding me, fuck it. I'm not going to push someone for their time. I'm puzzled though because after bailing he continues to send a few other messages about random things of no consequence that make me feel he's trying to keep the conversation going.

I spend the afternoon baking, making chocolate chip cookies for a treat and a double batch of muffins for Greyson and Wes. I read and play guitar and then get an early sleep.

## August 19

I'm really feeling proud of myself this morning for my gym consistency. Even on the weekends now I wake up early and head there first thing. I have my black belt in wado kai karate, but I haven't been to a class or practiced in years. There is literally no one in the gym right now, so I stand in front of the mirror and start. The movements feel unnatural at first but then they come back to me, quickly and with speed and power. Every time I switch to a new move I think I don't know what I'm supposed to do next, but my body automatically shoots me there. These movements ease something inside of me. The fighter in me still exists. Around 8, I text Greyson. He had a woman over last night and I'm wondering if she's still there or if he might like to go for a walk with the dogs with me. He replies he's dropping her off soon and then wants to go so I'm excited to get the dogs out. Another full two hours pass before I realize he and I have different definitions of "soon" and that I should have clarified I have other stuff I need to do today and meant soon soon. We both step on each other apologizing for not being clearer.

Wes texts and apologizes for bailing last night. He admits he had a hard day and just wasn't in a good headspace. I tell him it's OK and mention the podcast is probably proving to be a little much for both of us right now, so I understand. I'm trying really hard to let that be a thing I'm OK to let go of, but it's challenging for me. It's something that brings me so much joy, but I suspect we're nearing the needing to let go of it altogether phase. The messages keep coming and I'm surprised when he asks if I'd like to try and do it today instead and come over for dinner as well.

I tell him I'll meet him at his place at 4:30.

His daughter's first to the door and wants to show me the rocks she's tumbled. I love the way she sees the world, her little gathering of rocks, each one so special and so beautiful to her, and handpicked for being lovely.

"Where's the boy?" I ask.

"Pouting in his room about something," Wes answers from the kitchen. In Wes's daughter's room I see him poke his little head around the corner.

"Roo!" he yells and runs at me with a hug. My heart explodes.

His daughter wanted to make us dinner tonight, which is off the charts adorable, so Wes helps her with each step. I love watching her squeal with horror and delight as she mashes ground pork through her fingers to make the meatballs.

"Can I put your hair in an elastic?" I ask her.

"Yes."

I gather her hair in my fingers and pull it behind her head. I'll never forget the first time she let me brush her hair out after the bath, always having only allowed Wes to do it. I had felt so special that she trusted me. God, she's growing so fast. The last two times I've seen her she seems so much older to me than even two months ago. She is such a wonderful brilliant funny kind little person, and every time I see her my heart aches with failure and regret. I would give anything to watch her continue to grow. I know my days of seeing these kids are numbered. Something will change. Wes gets another girlfriend or decides he doesn't want me around them anymore. It's only a matter of time until circumstances dictate that my presence in their life in any capacity no longer makes sense. I remember the heartache I felt when I thought I'd never get to see them again. I savour these moments with them as secretly and casually as I can so no one around me senses what they mean to me.

After dinner we watch a show with the kids and then Wes puts them to bed.

"Should we give this podcast a listen or what?"

"Yeah." We head downstairs.

Possibly the only thing more awkward than recording it will be listening back to it together. We give it about fifteen minutes.

"It's kind of lackluster," he tells me.

"Yeah."

"Maybe we'll just have to edit out some of the pauses and stuff."

"Yeah, I didn't like some of the stuff I did in there about people asking why we broke up and things, kinda disintegrated into pretty negative stuff." I admit.

"Yeah, same with all my shit about people who have three kids but aren't actually happy . . ." he laughs.

"Well, maybe I can take the laptop and edit it, and see if we can put it together in a way where it's just the funnier, lighter stuff," I suggest.

"Yeah, like put us joking about it being awkward at the beginning and then some of the good stuff, and we'll see how it sounds. I need the laptop for some video-editing stuff though."

"Ah shit yeah . . . well . . ."

"I could give you a key?"

This catches me off guard. The traditional significance of being given a key to someone's home clearly does not apply here, but it still feels . . . I don't know. Big. A show of trust and friendship.

"Sure, that would be awesome."

"Then you can just come by tomorrow and work on it."

"Cool."

"Want more water?"

"Yeah, that'd be good." I follow him up the stairs to the kitchen table. He fills both our glasses and then sits down next to me.

"So we're cool, right?" he asks me.

"Yeah . . . why?"

"I was worried you'd be mad at me after the other night."

"No no, I was mad at myself, but I'm cool. We're cool." We spend the next five minutes basically reassuring each other we're both cool before we get anywhere.

"Can I ask you a question?" I say to him. "Do you ever think like, maybe it would be better if we just went a couple of months, like a month or something without seeing each other?"

"I don't think it would be better for me, but if that's what you needed or wanted to do I would totally understand and do it and then at the end of the month I'd still be around."

"Yeah, it's just hard because not seeing you was terrible, but seeing you, and then we do stuff like that and . . . it's just hard. I dunno. Here's another question . . . are YOU finding this hard?"

He's quiet for a long time and mumbles the odd thing about wanting to choose his words carefully because he knows how much stock I put in them. "No," he starts, "and yeah. No because . . . in a lot of ways now I think we're having the kind of relationship I always wanted, or should have had with you from the beginning, with no expectation. Sometimes I even think I could be better for you now that I'm not worried about all the other stuff, but you gotta understand in all reality, I'm fucked. I don't think I even knew how fucked I was. I don't know what the plan is and so I'm just, I'm just settling into what the new normal will be, and I think the new normal for me is not having any normal, for a long time, six months, a year, I don't know. I just want to be selfish and figure out what I like. I honestly don't give a shit about anybody or anything, other than the kids . . . and you might not see this, but you're the only other person I don't want to hurt. That's why I know you hate it when I say it's up to you how this goes, but I just don't want to hurt you. So yeah, it's hard for me. But it's a different kind of hard . . . " He looks down and I can tell he's thinking a thing he doesn't know how to say. "Just to give you an idea of how fucked I am, and put a wall up here . . ." he draws an imaginary hard line with his hand. "A year from now I could ask you to marry me . . . or I could quit my job and move to Brazil. We could be engaged, or I could burn the house down . . . I don't know."

I laugh, and he laughs too. I knew he was confused, but honestly, I really don't think I understood the depths of it until hearing these two extremes. "I just don't want to settle for anything anymore, and I'm not calling you settling, but I've felt settled before in life and I don't want to be again. Even when you get into a relationship they call that settling down, and really that's just another term for 'settling' in general. That's what marriage seems like to me."

"Well, I always kind of just viewed it as your partner in crime, your best friend. It's that cliché, joys doubled and sorrow divided thing. I like having someone to just do life with."

"I just don't want to say anything one way or another because I don't want to disappoint anyone. I mean even listen to how fucked my views on marriage are right now. I wish it could be like, we just do our thing, and we don't have to think about what it means or is."

"I get that you need to do your thing, and the other night was . . . fuck, it was amazing." I grin at him. "But I just have to be careful because I'm walking on eggshells, not to not make you mad or anything but to try not to have any expectations of you. That's why I try and let you take the lead on when we hang out or whatever, because I don't ever want to put any of my disappointment on you if you can't . . . so I find I'm always trying to form some backup plan to , , , you. And sleeping with you is one of those things that's going to lead to me having feelings and wanting things you don't want. Slow, I could do forever . . . like, fuck, heaven help the poor person who dates me next. I'm gonna be like . . ." I slide my hand across the table at a snail's pace. "But I can't share. I know what sex means to you and you know what it means to me, and the two just don't . . ." I interlock my fingers. "And besides, if I was the kind of person who could do that and not have feelings, then I wouldn't be who I am."

"Exactly," he tells me. "It's part of all the other things I love about you."

We look at each other and he shifts. "Anyway, we don't need to beat a dead horse, probably not a good idea for that to happen often, or at all, I don't know, I just want to make sure you're OK. All I care about is not hurting you."

"I'm OK," I tell him, and I beam at him. I've appreciated his honesty. I scratch his shoulder playfully. "You make it hard, though."

"You make it hard," he smiles back at me.

"God damn your face, Wes,"I say, inches from him. Longing for him. Wanting to be the kind of person who can just let myself enjoy what he has to offer. "I should get going."

He walks me to the door. "Oh, the key!" he remembers and digs through a basket producing one and checking it in the lock.

"Thanks." I smile at him and I add it to my keychain.

I look up at his eyes and give him a hug; he wraps an arm around me loosely.

"Hug me like you mean it," I laugh to him and he squeezes me tighter.

I pull back and bring my lips up to his, kissing him.

"Don't you worry . . . we'll get it all sorted, it'll all work out," I tell him with a grin.

He smiles at me in the door frame.

"Goodnight," I call out as I walk to my vehicle.

## August 20

I feel good this morning. My chat with Wes yesterday has really opened my eyes; I'm not sure to what, though? It's weird when you get that epiphany turning point type feeling and can't attribute it to any exact moment of progress or thought change. Maybe it's coming. I feel on the edge of something big.

Hendrik and I watch his previous client leave and then he turns to me.

"How are you?"

"A lot better than the last time I saw you." I smile.

"Have you heard from him?"

"Yup . . . get this . . . he gave me a key to his house? It's for podcasting-editing or whatever, but that was not what I was expecting in response to the other night."

"Sideswipe! Me neither," He tells me.

I have to get some measurements done so he can track my progress, so I chat away about my talk with Wes last night while Hendrik pinches and measures my fat. He listens intently while I stand there in booty shorts and a sports bra getting poked and pulled.

Back out on the floor alone in the space I can tell he's brewing up a series of thoughts that are going to be good. I lift away while he thinks on it.

"You know," he starts, "the philosophical idea that sex means anything other than sex is the worst thing to have happened to society." Wow, OK, he's really going for it.

"You're such an untraditional thinker in so many other ways, and a feminist, so I'm surprised you adhere to such an antiquated school of thought."

"Yeah, I just get emotionally invested and then disappointed or hurt, right."

"Right." He nods. "But that just comes back to expectation versus outcome. You're expecting a particular outcome. If you didn't do that, and he was just somebody you just wanted to have beers with and hang out, podcast, have fun and bang, that sounds like a pretty good deal to me if you enjoy each other's company."

"Yeah, I don't know where all my ideas about this all come from. I'm worried if someone else comes along there just won't be anything . . . left of me to give them," I confide. "I've thought this over and over again."

"You're viewing it as him taking something from you," he explains. "When really it's you gettin' for yourself. The 'giving a piece of yourself to someone' is for teenagers and high schoolers when we haven't yet learned how that will emotionally affect us. Hate to break it to you, but you're thirty-three, you've been married, you've been divorced . . . that ship has fucking sailed." We both laugh.

"This ain't *Romeo and Juliet*. And what—" he gestures toward my lady parts "—are you saving it for?"

I keel over laughing, and he starts laughing again too.

"Seriously, you're saving it for what? For some fictitious person who isn't even here yet? I hope, I really hope that he shows up for you one day, but it could be ten minutes, ten months, ten years from now. And guess what. When you meet that guy, I can guarantee you he hasn't been saving it for you."

I can't stop laughing. Nothing he's saying is new to me by any means, but he's the first man who has nothing to gain by having this conversation with me. He's someone whose guidance has literally never steered me wrong. He's someone whose advice I've ignored (read: Wes moving in and us moving a million miles an hour) and then later wished I'd adhered to. He gains nothing by encouraging me to rethink this . . .

"I'm super surprised." I shrug at him, embarrassed. "You've never done or said anything to make me think this, but I guess I thought even by telling you I slept with him when I wasn't in a relationship with him, I thought . . . I thought you'd think less of me, like I was gross or had low standards or something." Hendrik and I have really never discussed sex.

"Not at all," he replies.

"I guess I just can't shoot the gap when it comes to other people, though. I told him last night that I could do slow all day, but I just can't share." I hit my deadlifts and put the bar down, turning to look at him.

"Share is an interesting word choice, Roo. You know it implies ownership, right. You don't share something you don't own . . ." I think this through.

"OK, but the self-conscious loser part of me thinks about—there's this other person in particular that I know he's involved with, and I do the whole, what if she's better, what if she's prettier, what if he likes her more. What if she's funnier or they have more fun or better talks together? What if he tells her things he couldn't tell me? What if she's his best friend?"

"Ugh, you're just like Roxy," he laughs. "Everything needs to be ranked by order of importance or which is my favourite. Which is the best. I tell ya this much, when you're eating ice cream cake it doesn't mean you don't still fucking love brownies. There's a reason he comes back for you and it's because you offer something, and it's not about where it ranks. Roxy and I joke about the attractiveness of other people now all the time. I don't need to be lied to anymore; I know I'm not that fucking special."

Huh. My mind is blowing up right now.

"That being said, it's gotta work for you. Fuck, get yours too. Date other people. Set it up however it works that you like."

"But what if he falls in love with some girl and then wants to stop that with me, then it's like getting dumped a second time or something? I don't think I could take that."

"What if you meet someone and you're the one who has to have that conversation with Wes?"

I honestly had **never** thought of that. "You have a lot more power than you think. Just remove expectation and everything else seems to make sense."

"I guess I never thought about how my need to relate sex to the seriousness of the relationship has this weird tendency to up the stakes right off the hop. It was supposed to be a self-preservation tactic, but it probably ends up expediting a process that should move a little slower and then I get hurt anyways. I don't know why I'm holding onto all these guilty feelings about sex."

"Yeah, guilt is a young person's game, when we're still in that phase where we're trying to 'keep our numbers low or our virginity intact.'"

"And you're right," I laugh, "that virginity ship has long since sailed. Maybe it all goes back to standards I had when I was young. I had girlfriends that had moms that bought them vibrators or took them to get the pill. That was not a thing in my house; sex was not really talked about like that. The expectation was just that I was not to be having it. I didn't lose my virginity until I was nineteen. It's weird to think I'm holding on to the exact same beliefs about it I had fifteen years ago."

"Yeah, you gotta let that shit go."

"I think I've always had a certain sense of responsibility because of the public nature of my job too . . ."

"It didn't stop Madonna, so I think you're good."

Now I'm really laughing.

"If you're safe about it, and smart about it, this day and age I really don't see a downside. And if you meet a guy down the line you want to be serious with and you're having the talk about that stuff, telling him you have a friend who you sleep with sometimes sounds a lot better to me than you've just been banging your way through random dudes you meet at the bar. But even if, even if you wanted to do that it still doesn't sound bad, and I still wouldn't judge you."

"It also probably sounds a lot less weird than a woman in her thirties who's been celibate the entire time waiting for this person. That's so much pressure for someone."

"Yeah, so I don't know Wes," he cautions. "I don't know him well enough to know if that's a good idea for you or a bad idea, or what kind of person he is, but all I'm saying is the idea makes sense in theory. You just make it work for you. Too hard to see the kids? Don't. Don't wanna stay the night. Don't. Whatever it is that keeps your expectation outcomes nonexistent."

When we're done training I sit on the rower next to him.

"What a chat," I say. "This whole conversation blew my mind. I've had other people tell me similar things, but it always came off as . . . like, cold or self-motivated or . . . I can't explain it, it just never really resonated. Wasn't the right time or the right person or the right way to say it to me. Just hearing thoughts like this from someone I respect, it's so different today for some reason. Wes has said a lot of similar things to me . . ."

"Yeah, well, and hearing it from someone who it serves to tell you that . . ."

"Yeah, exactly. But you get nothing from this conversation, so it makes it more believable."

"I am the red pill," he smiles. It's a reference to a line in "The Matrix" in which the red pill signifies the understanding of a previously unknown truth, which once consumed you can't un-know.

I am in my head all day about this discussion. These are big thoughts, big ideas to me. Big concepts. What seems simple to someone else seems like it could be a complete identity changer in my case. Maybe some people can operate this way with someone if that's how it begins, but to separate Wes out from his kids and what they all mean to me, after the fact? They're one and the same. They are a huge part of who he is, the most important thing in the world to him. I don't know how or where I would even draw the kind of lines I would need for this to "work for me." I can't seem to un-ring that bell. I drive to Wes's house and use my key to let myself in. It's weird to be here without him. I'm careful not to touch anything and I make my way directly to the workstation with the computers I need. I expect that the editing will be slow going as it's been a while since I've used the equipment, but it comes quickly and easily. It's amazing how the simple act of moving things around, touching them up, brings me disproportionate levels of joy. God, I love doing this show with him. I love how much fun we have recording it. I love that we make something silly and ridiculous together. It only gets hard when the content turns serious. For the most part I remove all the negativity from the show, but at the end I'm left with Wes's beautiful words. I'm left with a portion that's raw and hard to listen to, but I believe it to be extremely powerful. I listen back twice to what he says when he addresses the breakup. Little bits stick out to me, pieces my heart grabs hold of.

*"I still love you, I'm still in love with you . . . To be honest, sometimes I don't even know why we broke up . . ."* I tear up. I'm not sure how to edit this.

I send him a text. "I'm getting stuck. Not sure what to include haha I dunno how you feel about the end. I think it's really powerful but it might be more than you want to share." I'm hoping desperately he will say it's OK to use it, but I don't want to push too hard in that direction, because it feels unfair of me. I think it would allow people to see an often-overlooked side of Wes, a tender side, a caring side, a side that is totally counter-intuitive and almost irreconcilable with the good-time guy most people seem to know. I think people will see a colder side of me that simply says, "Thanks for that, that's very kind," because it's clear I've shut down a part of myself. They'll hear a woman who loved to be alone choke up when she speaks about having to do so, and a man who wanted to be alone scared to death when it's actually happening. It is, in my opinion, the most real thing that's even come close to making it in. I hope so hard he chooses to use it.

He calls me.

I tell him, "So, I've left two versions—there's a shorter one that's light and it's about twenty minutes, which is kinda too short for a normal episode but I mean first one back, it could just be what it is, but then there's all the other stuff at the end that could go in too. I think it's really good, but I've pushed it over. You'll have to take a listen and decide if you think it should go in or not."

"OK," he tells me. "I'll listen tonight. Thanks for editing all that."

"No problem, I actually had a really good time doing it, it was super fun."

"Cool, I'll call you tonight or tomorrow after I've listened."

I have a massage appointment in the afternoon, traffic is terrible getting home, and by the time I'm back I'm just wiped. I haven't caught up with Greyson in a while, so I'm excited to catch him on the deck for a few minutes before he heads out on a date.

"So you're dating it up tonight?" I ask.

"Yeah, but she lives out of town so . . ."

"So what . . ." I laugh. "You're never coming home? You'll be gone but I can have your dog so I'm like, 'well . . . I hope Greyson's OK, but I really like this dog, so . . ." we both laugh.

We catch up on how he's been feeling lately; he's still battling that wicked cold. I tell him all about my mind-blowing chat with Hendrik.

"So now I'm just doing that thing where, I don't think the thought requires any action at this moment, I'm not gonna change my behaviour right away or anything, but it's stuff that I need to really sit with and just think on more and more. I mean you have situations like that that you seem to make work."

"Yeah, for sure," he agrees. "But the casual thing gets really complicated too. Different expectations, hurt feelings, managing time even. You honestly end up having just as many different types of problems as you do in a real relationship, sometimes even more, they're just different problems."

"I hadn't thought of that. I guess it's like, I got the sex solved but now there's this, that, and the other thing."

"Yeah, it's not as simple as you'd think. It's still a ton of work. I mean, if you're doing it in a respectful honest way and trying to communicate expectations properly."

"All I know is the chat today made me feel better, like, less hard on myself. Again, I don't think I'm going to change any of my behaviour right now, but even what he said about me getting out there and doing my own thing too . . . it's all stuff I need to think about. I just fucking dread dating." I can't even guess how many times I've said, written, or thought this thought these last few weeks.

"Yeah, it sucks," he sympathizes.

"I don't think I'll ever be that person who can just sleep with someone and not care at all, or be sleeping with multiple people. But if that's over here and I'm over here . . . " I hold my hands wide apart from one another. I inch the hand that represents me a miniscule bit forward. "I think it just nudged me up from the wall I was clinging to on this side. No huge changes for right now . . . not moving to the other end of the spectrum or anything, but I think I've loosened my grip on this end a little. Which for me feels like a major change or mindset shift of some sort. And this is from one of the people I most respect in the whole world, who gets or gains nothing from giving me that kind of advice."

He heads out for his date. I lie in bed wondering what Wes has thought of the podcast edit; he never called to tell me. I fall asleep hoping he'll want to use all the portions I've selected.

## August 21

I wake up at 5 a.m. to a feeling of complete panic. My alarm is set for 5:50 and there's no reason for me to be up so early. Fox was travelling yesterday, and I shoot her some messages to make sure she and Clive arrived safely, which they did.

I head to the gym and draw my workout out, hoping to run into Wes, but he doesn't show. My worry turns to him. I take out my phone to send him a message and decide to leave him alone. *He doesn't need you doing that.* Don't check up on him. The feeling of worry doesn't leave me though. At 8 I take my phone out again and a second time force myself to put it away. At 10 after working from home for several hours I compose a message.

"Hey you, super weird and annoying I know but had this weird worried feeling about ya all morning. You OK?" I don't hit send.

At 11 he phones me. Thank God.

He has the flu so bad he's totally out of commission. On top of that he is having a very low day. James did international travel for work sometimes and when I'd have the flu and be alone, it was the worst. I relied solely on friends to bring me ginger ale or, in Meesh's case once, even drive me to the hospital. I have all the empathy ever for alone-flu times. I let him know I can bring him anything if he needs it, and he declines. I go back to my work and my phone rings a few minutes later, Wes again, admitting he would like me to come over.

I take him to the doctor, I cook him comfort food, we listen to music, and he lies on the couch drifting in and out of sleep. His house is a billion degrees and I lament not having brought shorts with me. After dinner I swing back to my house, check on the dogs, feed them, and grab a pair of shorts. I stop at a cheapo store on my way back and pick up some ridiculous masks that go hand in hand with the horror movie we decided we'd watch when I return. We cuddle up on the couch, two losers donning our dumbass masks. I rub his back and run my fingers through his hair. We are intertwined. I think about my chat with Hendrik. These moments are why the gap seems so big when it comes to Wes and the idea that it could ever be casual. There's nothing he can ever do that would make me not want to be the one he calls when he's sick or sad. A day with him when he's at his worst will still always be where I want to be.

## August 22

James will be leaving soon and so I'm trying to soak in every last bit of his friendship before he goes. After the gym I drive into town to meet him for a quick bite on his lunch break. There's a river and a bridge with a pull-out where we meet. I hop out of my car and into his.

"Every time we meet here I wonder if people think I'm a prostitute or that this is some drug deal," I laugh as I slide into his passenger seat.

"Your imagination . . ." he shakes his head at me.

We order our lunch and take it to go along with two coffees.

In his car back at the river we sit silently, both aware we're nearing the ending of the very long, intimate story that has been James and Roo.

"If I tell you something, do you promise not to be too judgmental and to not tell anyone?" he asks me.

"I'll try," I promise. "What is it?"

He produces his cell phone and I see the image of a beautiful home. "That's my new house," he says.

Every single thought and feeling I am met with, every single jealous tear that wants to come out, every single judgment and resentment I have, I do the opposite. I take a deep breath, plaster a huge smile on my face and excitedly proclaim, "Wow, James! It's amazing!" He deserves this now, to be happy and to move on, and to build a new life with someone. He and I have been paying the price of each other for far too long. There is no point in meeting this with any emotion other than extreme positivity, although it's exhausting not to let him see how hard this is for me. We split a giant piece of delicious carrot cake from the deli. The bottom is his favourite part and subconsciously, while he rambles about the house, I pull pieces of the bottom off mine and keep handing them to him since he's finished his.

Finally he points out what I've been doing.

"I feel like I'm a dog and you're feeding me treats," he laughs. "I'm 100 percent a good boy!"

I cry laughing. "I didn't even notice I was doing that. I just know you like the bottom."

We make plans to try and have dinner before he leaves for good. On the drive home I think about the carrot cake and my feeding him crumbs. I think about these small signs of love, these second nature actions that we do for someone without even thinking. Sitting right beside them, giving them little pieces of the best that we have to offer.

In the evening Wes calls. He's still not feeling well. I could use some company. I'm lonely. It feels like my small circle is dwindling. I tell him I'd like company too if he's up for watching a show or something. We settle onto his couch and watch a crime documentary. He makes comments throughout that make me laugh.

"I hate how in these shows they always explain things too much, like do they really need to delve so far into what the insanity defense is?" I ask.

"OK there, crime expert, not everyone is as well-versed as you in what pleading the 5th means."

"Pleading the 5th isn't the insanity defense, it's when you can't testify about something because you'll incriminate yourself, but you don't want to perjure yourself by lying on the stand."

"I rest my case," he says comically.

"I may or may not have read a crime book or two in my time," I joke back. When Wes and I first started dating he had bought me a true crime book at the thrift store knowing my love of both reading and criminology. He was so thoughtful, always going out of his way to remember things I liked. He had spoiled me so much.

"I should try and crash," he yawns. He's hoping to feel well enough to get back to work soon.

"Yeah, I'll jet."

When I get home I get a text from him. "Don't forget your garbage. Goodnight."

I would have totally forgotten garbage day tomorrow, and the goodnight part makes me smile. I gather it all up, take it to the curb, and crash.

## August 23

While grinding through my workout, I complain to Hendrik about being unsure of what I'm doing with my life and feeling called in too many directions. At the end we sit next to each other on the rower.

"What if I'm just wasting all this time, and I should have been doing something different? What if I've gotten it wrong somehow?"

"I don't think you can, Kid." He says. "Get it wrong, I mean. Really the only way would be to not do anything or try anything. Most people don't even try something new or risky . . ."

"I just have this constant worry that everything I'm doing or trying to do is a waste."

"It isn't," he assures me. I wish I had his belief. "Can I show you something?" He's flipping through his phone. "You know how I like photography . . ."

"Yeah, Roxy told me you were maybe going to get a website going or something."

He extends his phone for me to see. The image is breathtaking. "I call it Netflix and Chill." In what appears to be a king-size bed, he and Roxy are intertwined. It's black and white. She drapes herself across his body, eyes closed, head resting on his thigh. He's leaning back, casually resting his head against one arm. Neither of them seems to have any awareness of the camera, and the shot is candid and feels deeply intimate. It's sensual. They both look gorgeous but incredibly real.

"Wow," I say. "This is really . . . it's incredible. It's so good!"

"Thank you. I started a page but didn't launch it. Once you do that it tells everyone you're live and all of a sudden people start getting notifications it's there and everyone can see it."

"Well, it's really, really incredible." I say again.

"Most of the images are that kind, once you see them you can't unsee."

He extends another image to me, Roxy naked, leaning out over a balcony down toward the bright lights of a city. The curvature of her backside is beautiful.

"These are seriously so good," I tell him when I hug him goodbye. I leave hoping he'll decide to share them with the world.

James and I sit across from one another on the deck again. The heavy awareness that these days together are coming to an end hangs over us. He's on his way to visit his parents and has stopped by just to quickly see the dogs. He's been dealing with selling his stuff online all day.

"I've had no dice with selling The Beast," I tell him.

"Selling stuff online is such a pain in the ass. People are the worst, this person tonight brought no help and so I pretty much loaded everything for her. Did I ever tell you about the time I sold my paddle board?" He's laughing to himself already, which makes me laugh.

"No, tell me!"

"OK, so one of my places had this sort of solarium thing attached to the house, not heated, kind of like your alcove but all glass. It was the dead of winter, and that's where I was storing the board. I help the lady load it and secure it and everything. The truck was too small for it, so the board is half in and half out of the bed. It was a nightmare. Finally, when it's all done, she goes to leave and she's locked herself out of her truck. With her keys and her wallet to pay me and everything inside. So now I gotta let her use my phone to call the company to rescue her. I didn't want to leave her outside while she waited for them because it was so cold, but my apartment then was all one room and I really didn't want her in my like, bedroom slash living room. So I tell her she can wait in this solarium thing because at least it's a little bit warmer. Roo, to this day I don't know how I did it but with the series of all the connecting doors, I locked us both in the solarium together."

I'm crying laughing. He's laughing so hard he can barely tell me the rest of the story.

"I didn't want to be stuck in there with her! The solarium is ground level and my suite was half underground, so there was this window that connected them. I straight up laid down on my stomach, picture me like this . . ." he feigns a panicked version of himself lying on his stomach flailing like a fish and then diving. "I pried the window open and had to dive-bomb four feet down into my suite just to get away from her."

I'm laughing so hard, I can't breathe. "How have you never told me this before?"

"I don't know. I thought I had."

I'm going to miss having James to tell all my dumb stories to; I'm going to miss hearing his.

## Week Ten
## August 24

Greyson and I have morning coffee on the deck.

"I'm thinking of making a dating profile again," I admit. "It might just be time for me to fucking do it, because I've built it up so much in my head to be this massive thing, and it really isn't."

"Yeah, you just have to be super clear on what you're trying to accomplish there. If you just want to have coffee and meet interesting people, then say that."

"But the problem is . . . I hate most people." We both laugh. "I definitely don't want to make going for drinks a thing."

"Just say you're looking for friends, and then say that, maybe even list on your profile that you don't drink. Might help weed out some of the people. I went out with a woman a while ago, and we met for a drink, and it was fine, but now that's one of the things that becomes a foundation for what we do, going for drinks, if you don't want that to be part of it you have to set that expectation right away. I always always talk about expectations, whether it's friendship or relationships or business. Being clear about expectations is the biggest thing." He's right, but even I'm not certain what I'm hoping for anymore. When he heads back downstairs to his place I make my profile. I choose some pictures of me with Lucy and Fox because apparently people look more appealing in groups than they do in just selfies. I make sure to include one where I have no makeup on so I can never be accused of false advertising. I write my profile:

*Looking to make friends and meet interesting people. Not into drinks, would much prefer coffee and a chat. I have two poorly behaved ridiculous rescue dogs I love to death and a cat that brings my neighbours his dead mice, so I'm pretty sure he despises me.*

*I drink far more coffee than any human should be able to consume, love hiking, reading and staring into a fire. I'm super into weight lifting. Not interested in material things. Being silly is my favourite... just enjoy laughing and joking around.*

Messages come just minutes after I upload it. *Here we fucking go again.* I feel no excitement, no joy, and no anticipation. Just dread.

A hot plumber has come to work on the leaky faucet in my bathtub, and it quickly turns into a whole thing, as it always seems to when my house is involved. I'm supposed to be having a nice goodbye dinner with James tonight, but it doesn't appear as though I'll be getting out of here in time for that. He wraps up just as James arrives and we settle on ordering pizza, something I haven't let myself eat in months. We sit side by side on the couch, eyeing one another. This is it. When this meal is done he will get into his car and drive out of my life, forever. For real this time.

We don't really speak except to comment on how full we're both getting. When we're done we move to the deck and the dogs play all around him. I see tears in his eyes and I turn my gaze away from his and let my own tears fall.

"Are you going to be OK?" he asks me.

"Yeah, I'll be OK." Tears are streaming down both our faces. "I'm just really really gonna miss you. I dunno . . . I don't . . . I'm not sure what life will be without you around."

"This town…" he starts but doesn't finish.

"I know…" I agree. "Sometimes I think moving here ruined my life."

"I feel like I made you come here and now I'm just leaving you here alone."

"Yeah, but where else would I go?" I ask. "I'm not tied to anyone. There's nothing keeping me, but there's certainly not a reason to go anywhere else yet."

He stands up with purpose and comes straight at me, taking me in his arms.

"I'm so sorry, I'm so sorry for everything," he cries.

"I'm sorry too." I bury my face in his shirt.

"I wish I could be here for you. I hate leaving you alone when you're having such a hard time."

"I'm going to miss you so much. I love you so much," I tell him.

"I love you too."

We are both soaking each other in tears and shaking against one another. I keep squeezing him tighter and tighter trying to hold onto this moment, this second, trying to delay the real goodbye, trying to stall the moment when he starts his engine and goes. He squeezes tighter back and we are one, one messy pile squished together, clinging to each other. Clinging to something that's been gone for so long, but will never cease to exist to us.

"I'm going to leave too, go to the store or whatever," I tell him.

"Why?"

"Because I can't watch another person drive away from this house forever."

I let myself into Fox's house, where she and Clive are watching TV. *Thump*. My purse hits the ground. My shoes come off. I squish myself wordlessly in beside her, place my head in her lap, and weep.

"It was just so much harder than I thought it would be," I cry.

"I know." She pats my back. "That was the real goodbye."

When I'm home I call Wes, who had texted me earlier.

"I'm just havin' . . . a day," I tell him. "I don't mean to put all this on you, I know you have your own stuff, but I'm just really—it was a really hard day."

"If you want company you can come over."

"I really want company."

On the couch we sit close.

"I'm lonely," I admit. "Today just brought up a lot of stuff, James is moving to this amazing new place and I'm back at my house with my plumber problems dealing with shit alone. I miss like, the stuff of having someone to share problems with or even just cuddling or like, the comforts that come with that. I signed back up for the dating website too and I wonder what I'm even trying to accomplish there. I wish I had a situation like you have." I'm referencing one woman in particular I know he's involved with.

"What do you mean about her?"

I regret having said it instantly. Hard reverse.

"Ignore me; I'm speaking about things I don't know about. I just think it's comforting you have this person and you care, but you guys aren't emotionally invested in anyway."

"I think you think that's more than it is."

"Maybe," I agree. "But you've got somebody who wants to be close, or somebodies I should say, and those extracurricular can go a long way in alleviating the loneliness."

"Well, I'm putting in zero effort in that department. If I hear from someone, yeah, I might message them back if I'm bored, but I'm not trying. And she knows I will never want to be in a relationship with her, she's known that since . . . well . . . January first." He means when he and I started dating and he ended their previous arrangement. "I don't know how much of this you even want to hear, about other people or whatever. I can't relationship with anyone right now. But if you wanted *that* type of situation with me, I mean I'm happy to oblige. I just don't want to hurt you."

"I know. That's why I need a person like you have with her because I have too much the feelings for **you**. I need somebody like you have that I'm not at all worried about ending up with. I don't know . . . I don't know what I'm capable of or what I'm trying to accomplish these days, I'm just lost."

"Just a full-on existential crisis?"

"Yup, pretty much. Just a rough day."

"How about I give you a massage?"

"Really?" I'm surprised. I'm more surprised when he sets his bedroom up with a diffuser and spa music and melts my whole body with his hands. What I'm not surprised about at all is how amazing the sex is, and how this nonexistent, probably meaningless to him, isn't-going- anywhere-relationship we have, is one of the few things these days that makes me feel real.

## August 25

Greyson holds the door to the greasy spoon diner open for me, and I'm mid-sentence when I spot him. Jer. He's seated at a table with his dad and his two kids. Never. Never in the entire time I've known him have I felt like this, but it is awkward. I haven't seen him since before I left for California, and I'm really not certain why. I don't know if he's upset with me. I've asked, and he's said no. I don't know if he's just been busy with his new role at work. I don't know if us both being single for the first time since we've known each other has irrevocably shifted our dynamic. All I know is that for the first time I can remember, I don't know. I truly don't know what is going on with him, and the five feet between us feels like a massive void to me. How was it that two shorts months ago I collapsed into a pile in his arms—he was literally the first person I turned to in crisis—and now I feel awkward staring at him from the line forming in the entrance to the diner.

"Hey, you," I proclaim, crossing the chasm between us. I hug him with all my might, standing on tippy toes to get as much of him as I can in my arms. "It's so good to see you."

"Hey lady, you too."

I reintroduce him to Greyson and get some snuggles from his adorable son.

"Want our table? We're just heading out," Jer offers.

"Nah, that's OK."

Once he's in line to pay, though, Greyson points out it really is a better table so we move over. When Jer is done paying he wanders back over crouching himself down to eye level with me.

"Not much been going on," I tell him. "Just going to do some yard work today and maybe try and tackle the fence."

"Well, yard work at your place sounds like a full day."

"Are you any less busy now?" I can hear the pathetic tone in my own voice, and I don't even care.

"Yeah, I'm taking the kids on a trip for a few days but back around Wednesday. I have a full week off, so I'll have them, but maybe after they go down one night we could hang out?"

"Yeah, for sure, just call me. I miss your face."

"I miss it too," he jokes. I'm surprised and weirded out he doesn't say I miss you back. It hurts more than I would have expected. I secretly wonder if Greyson's presence is the reason he jokes it off. I watch him as he leaves.

"That was awkward, right?" I ask Greyson.

"Much awkward," he agrees.

The fucking fence has come down for the millionth time. Greyson and I head home and rebuild it with chicken wire, which should allow the wind to blow through without toppling it. *So help me fucking god if that thing comes down one more time . . .*

"Were you at my birthday?" her little voices asks from behind the change room curtain.

"No, I'm so sorry I wasn't. I was out of town," I lie.

"Well, I wish you were there so you could have seen it too," Wes's daughter tells me. She's talking about a kids' movie I asked her about. We're at the community pool because he invited me to come swimming with him and the kids. I fucking hate lying to her. I hate hate hate hate it. I can see so clearly the dream I had on her birthday. I can feel my heart pull to be near to her the way it did that whole actual day.

"Yeah, me too. Maybe one day we can watch it at your house if your dad says that's OK."

The pool makes me nervous and I'm scared to take my eyes off his son for even a second. His daughter is a really strong swimmer and sticks close to Wes. We divide and conquer mainly because the kids want to be in different places, so we really don't get to chat.

His son and I throw a ball back and forth and each time I feign extreme exertion to catch it, he laughs and it lights up my soul. His delighted little squeals and giggles are just the best. He's always on the move, deeper to shallow, one section of the pool to the other, over to the hot tub. Finally, Wes and I end up standing near one another in the pool.

"Did you at least get to enjoy the hot tub for a bit?" he asks. I open my mouth to reply and before I can he follows it up with, "Well, I mean, you have one at home anyway," and he laughs.

This sets me off so hard. Infuriates me. Such a meaningless little comment he would never in a million years give a second thought to. *Fuck you. Actually though. Fuck. You.* It carries a connotation to me that I know is completely unintentional and totally lost on him. He means **nothing** by this. He has no fucking concept of how much it hurts me, pains me, embarrasses me, to have this massive reminder of him taking up half my deck. He has no idea that every morning when I walk out of my bedroom, there it is in the kitchen window, a giant glaring monument to the life I cannot have. I don't even fucking use the thing and if it made financial sense I would have gift-wrapped it and delivered it to his new house on moving day. *He doesn't know.* I tell myself this over and over again. He doesn't know and he will never know, what losing him and the kids has felt like for me.

Months ago, when we had first met, he had longed for someone to always be honest, and truthful, and just say the thing even when it was uncomfortable. He had repeatedly expressed his need for emotion and truth and communication. And so when it got hard I had poured my heart out into a letter for him, foolishly safe in the knowledge that saying the thing was what he **wanted**. That I was doing him the favour of never being blindsided. That me telling him everything even when it was hard was the greatest **gift** I could give to him after what he'd been through. Gift. I actually thought it was a fucking gift. I am such a fucking idiot. I wonder, I truly wonder sometimes, if he remembers the things he told me about what he wanted and needed when we first met. It doesn't matter, as much as he still searches for answers I see now that the questions far predate me.

I say nothing back. I think of Hendrik, I think of his advice to change my expectations. I look at Wes and realize it doesn't matter how badly his comment just hurt me. As quickly as the anger has risen it subsides, and then disappears altogether. I no longer expect him to understand. I don't need him to. This is progress.

I need to make something happen. I want to force a good time. And so I do. I text Fox and Greyson and we all head downtown along with another friend of his. I get blurry.

"We want a drink that has an upside-down beer in it but also tequila," I explain to the waitress.

"We don't have that."

"Well, ask the bartender to make it. I'm sure there has to be something like that he can do."

"What a bitch," Fox tells me as she walks away.

"Yeah, she has the sourest expression I've ever seen and she can't even be bothered to come up the stairs all the way to the table to take our order? Like, why's she hollering at us from five feet away? I'm gonna smoke."

Outside I overhear a guy talking about me; he doesn't realize I'm there.

"So, best I can figure that's Roo and Fox, the guy has to be game-changer boyfriend . . ." *Ouch.* Just hearing the nickname I used to use for Wes on the air burns. "And the girl must be Lucy."

"Well, you're half right," I call to him. "The guy's my buddy and the girl is his friend, but that is in fact Fox in there."

"Oh my god, I didn't see you." The dude is huge; he must be over six feet six. "Can I give you a hug?"

"Sure."

"I haven't been this excited since I met . . ." he cites the name of someone I've never heard of and rambles on.

"It was super nice to meet you," I say as I head back inside.

"Spotted," I tell Fox.

"Fuck . . . been awhile since that's happened, hey?"

"No shit. I hate this place, I don't know why we ever come here, we get bad service and we always end up having to talk to strangers."

"We don't like strangers."

"Nope."

We share not one but several of our tequila beer mix drinks. They come in a huge glass with two straws, and each time the waitress comes to the table she seems to hate me more and more. We order disgusting amounts of deep-fried foods and massively over-indulge.

A cab is hard to get and I'm feeling really sick now, so Fox and I start walking back to her place arm in arm.

"I slept with Wes again . . ." I tell her.

"Of course you did . . ." she laughs. "Any good?"

"Fucking amazing . . . ughhhh . . . like, so good."

"That's because you're not supposed to be doing it." We both laugh.

My cell phone rings and its Greyson, he's managed to catch a cab and is offering to get me home. The whole ride I have to keep the window down with air hitting my face staving off the urge to puke. He and his friend follow me inside to make sure I get into bed safely. Once they've gone downstairs I pull my blanket onto the bathroom floor and puke endlessly.

## August 26

How many times have I told myself over these last two months that it is time to get it together? I think it really is time now. I did a number on myself yesterday, and there's no part of me that feels good about it. It occurs to me that perhaps I've simply switched my pattern from being someone who had developed a daily problem with drinking, to someone who has become a binge drinker. Just because I can go weeks without consuming anything doesn't make it less bad if when I do indulge I attack myself with tequila. I'm disappointed in myself. I had fun with my friends, I think, but I'm not even really sure I did because I don't remember a lot from the evening. I also spent a shit-ton of money. Have I really made any progress at all?

I force myself to go to the gym. I nap all morning after. Greyson and I spend the whole afternoon binge-watching a TV series on his couch downstairs.

Wes calls. "Pulled up next to a Jammer and thought maybe it was you."

"Nope, not me. I'm just binge-watching with Greyson."

"Nice."

"I was gonna see if you wanted to hang out later after the kids go to bed, watch a show or something?"

"Yeah," he says. I'll call you later.

At night I drink coffee trying to wake myself up before Wes calls. I do my makeup and I get changed into a tank top and jeans. I'm just gathering up my purse and keys when he calls and cancels, rescheduling for Monday. I don't have an emotional response to this. I don't know if being hung-over has dulled my capacity for feelings, or if I'm just starting not to care. I wash my face, take my clothes back off, and slip into bed.

## August 27

"I want to have a talk with you about your photography," I tell Hendrik as I'm crawling to a mat on the floor with dumbbells.

"Oh, yeah . . . what about?"

"Well, it's less of a talk and more of just . . . a thing I wanted to say." I'm weirdly nervous only because in the dynamic of our relationship Hendrik is always the wiser, always the one I come to for advice. There's a reason his nickname is "The Shepherd." I have always asked for his opinion and guidance. He has not asked for my input on this particular matter, but I really feel it's something I need to say. Also, since he had the trust to share the photo with me last time, I'm hoping that translates into some leeway to share my thoughts about it with him.

"So, all this stuff you've been telling me about my writing, and to not be afraid and fuck what other people think." He's nodding, and I know he already knows what I'm going to say.

"That's the same with your photography. That picture you showed me, I couldn't stop thinking about it. It was so good, Hendrik, like, crazy good. You gotta put that shit out there for people to see. Everything you've told me applies to you."

"I know," he says. "There's just a few certain people that you wonder what they'll think, or how they'll perceive you or how that might change their perception of you."

"Oh man, I know. I totally know. You think I'm stoked on my dad potentially reading about Wes and I banging?" We both laugh. "But, it just is what it is, and I don't want to have to apologize for who I am anymore. You shouldn't either."

Roxy walks into the gym.

"Roo's just talking to me about the photo," Hendrik says.

She smiles at me and nods with great understanding.

"Trying to tell him it's unreal and people need to see it," I explain.

She flashes him a grin, continuing to nod; this is clearly a conversation they've had many times.

"See," she says. "It's not just your wife who thinks that!"

We lift a lot and talk a ton about our hang-ups with people's perceptions of us.

"The photo was just so good it made me want to beg you to take my picture!"

Chagrin is not a side of Hendrik I've seen often. "Thank you," he bashes. We get each other really riled up about our creations. I leave walking on air, hoping that I've helped encourage him to be the artist I know he is.

At home I receive a call from a program director who wants to hire me out of market for a morning show gig. I am torn. It's a person who I've worked for before that I know, like, and trust. The other players in the team they're building are people I enjoy and admire. I don't, however, want to move to this particular city. I also feel strongly that my mental health is perhaps not at its best, and that being far away from the support system of friends I've built could have dire consequences. Gigs like this don't come around a ton though. Hendrik and I have had many a discussion surrounding the concept of "hedging your bets" and if you're "playing" for now or later. The general idea being how many vices can one have to make life enjoyable without ending it early, and how much should you focus on the present vs. the future. This is a hedge-my-bets dilemma if ever there was one. It's nice to dream as big as the skies and hope that one day something will come of my writing. It's been amazing to try something different, but a girl's got bills. I both need and want to go back to radio one day; I'm just not sure when the time will be right. It feels too soon, but in reality, we are only as in demand as the relevancy of our brand, and each day that I remain off the air I become more obsolete. Leaving at all was risky enough, and delaying my return could stall any further prospects down the line. You only get to turn down a date so many times before he stops asking. I had that opportunity locally, but after a discussion and a promised follow-up nothing has come of it yet. I want to phone Wes because he has a mind for business, negotiations, and career moves. He's always the one whose advice I still want and need. He would know what to do. I don't call.

The last time he was here, James had said he brought me here and now he was leaving me alone. Seamus has suggested multiple times I ditch the house and start over. Greyson abandoned his hometown when he wanted a fresh start. I moved so many times those first fifteen years in radio, I feel "over" it. Not above it, just over it. What if this is the sign that I'm supposed to truly now start over? I'm tempted to call Hendrik for advice, but he's probably with a client. I'd really really love to phone Jer, but after such distance between us lately it doesn't seem like the kind of thing I can throw down out of nowhere. I lose myself in thought, pricing out apartments in the city where the job is. I research hiking in the area. I imagine who I could be if I moved far far away from this city that has brought me so much pain, and who would I be without everyone I love?

At Wes's we eat dinner and I tell him about the job offer. As expected he is full of great advice: "I'd go back to the guys here first."

"That's kind of what I was thinking, shoot buddy an email and explain I've had another offer and see what's doing there."

"I'd even just call, keeps it more casual, less pressure. Keep the whole thing really low key."

"Yeah, I'm hoping I can get something sorted. I just don't want to move."

"Well, maybe it could be a good thing, a big adventure, out of that house, on to something different."

"I know I was just having this conversation with James a while ago when he left about like, why am I here. What am I doing in this city? There is nothing calling me anywhere else but there isn't anything keeping me either, so maybe this is the sign I'm supposed to go?"

"Could be, could be a big adventure."

"You think I should go, don't you?" I ask him.

"I think you should do whatever you think is best for you."

He's so sore from a football game he played recently, he can barely walk as we make our way downstairs to put the finishing touches on the podcast.

"I feel like I'm dragging a dead body around, only the dead body is mine," he jokes, walking with a slumped, hunched, grotesque shuffle for comedic effect. God, he can be funny.

He shows me the final edit he's done on the podcast. The "I love you" he's left in sounds more comfortable and fraught with platitude than the others he's removed. It comes across more as something that was said to make me feel better than the off-the-cusp vulnerable admission included in the portion he removed. I understand his logic for why he's edited it this way, though. He thinks the stuff he took out was too rambly. I also know that what he's left still, to him, feels overly personal and vulnerable. It's a happy medium. At this point I just want to get the damn episode out; it's been weeks since we recorded it, and we've fucked around with editing and debated if its good long enough. It's not that great; it's awkward and choppy and as we both described it previously, a little lacklustre. It is, however, real, and we need to just get the first episode over with so that hopefully we can start producing them on the regular again. I think we're going to shoot for every two weeks instead of once a week. He sets it to load for Friday.

"Ohhh, let's call it season two!" he says excitedly.

"Oh yeah, that'd be wicked, I forgot you could start a new season."

"That way when people come back they'll just be like, 'Ohhhhh the break was because it was a new season.'" I laugh. He changes his voice to be that of a ridiculous idiot character we call Steve who's basically just a giant imbecile. He acts out a scene of Steve sitting down to the new episode. "Babe! Babe, they didn't break up, babe! It was just the start of a new season! Oh wait, no, they broke up."

I answer him back in the fictitious voice of Janine, the annoying girl character we invented to be Steve's girlfriend.

"Oh my gaaaaaawd, babe, I fucking told you they were dooooone."

I can't remember the last time we did Steve and Janine voices at each other. He hobbles his way back up the stairs and we crawl onto the couch to watch some stand-up comedy. He puts his head in my lap and I lightly, and carefully because of his soreness, run my hands up and down his back and through his hair.

"Is that too hard?" I ask, even though I'm touching him with just a fraction of the pressure I normally would.

"No, everything you're doing feels amazing."

We wind up in the bedroom, his turn for a full-body massage. I'm being as careful as I can when I rub my hands over each one of his defined muscles, but I can't stop laughing at the sounds and breaths it elicits from him. Half pain, half pleasure. When I'm done I lay down next to him.

"I should get going," I tell him.

"How bad do you really want to go?" he asks me.

"How bad do you really want me to stay?" I counter. He kisses me in response.

"Sure you're not too sore?" I joke to him.

"We'll find out," he says.

We lie panting against one another.

"You're a fucking beast," I say. "That was incredible."

"Guess I wasn't too sore after all." He smiles at me. *Ughhh fuck him, it's so unfair how good he can make me feel.* He never says too much one way or the other about my performance; however, I figure if I were that bad he wouldn't want it. We shower and lie back in bed for a few minutes.

"Going to be up all night thinking about the job offer?" he asks.

I roll over closer to him.

"Well, you had fucked it out of my mind, but now you've mind-fucked it back in," we laugh.

"Sorry," he says.

"No, it's OK, yeah, I'll definitely be thinking about it."

I catch him checking the time on his phone. "You want me to jet, I'll get going," I say. I re-dress and he follows me to the door, where I kiss him goodbye. On the drive home I wonder if I'm actually doing what Hendrik has suggested. Have I disconnected, or is the emotion just waiting to hit me? I told Wes multiple times when we were together that I was scared that my warmth wouldn't make him more open, instead being with him would make me cold. Has that happened? Am I cold now? I don't think I am. I feel very deeply. I just don't seem to have any deeper left to dig with him.

## August 28

I maybe slept for forty minutes between 4:20 and 5 a.m. I tossed and turned all night thinking about work and my future. To go or to stay, to take the sure thing, or to hold out and have faith that something else will come through and provide the answer or clarity. Wes's brother sent me a playlist for the gym, and I light it up. It puts a fire into my workout I didn't know I could have after such little sleep. I deadlift heavier than I have in a long time and the music and the uncertainty of my life fuels my strength.

"New list?" Wes motions to my phone.

"Yeah, it's the one your brother made. So far only one song I didn't love, the rest were killer."

"Get any sleep?"

"No, fuck no, tiny bit sometime after 4 but other than that I was up all night." We're both packing up and grabbing our stuff. I sit on the bench next to the coat rack while he puts his sweater on.

"Can I ask you a question? Would you not want me to go? Like professional stuff for me aside, just you?"

"I don't understand." He shakes his head.

"I mean like, forget the work stuff for me, just you personally would you not want me to go?"

"Well yeah," he seems like he's trying to answer carefully. "But the future's the future . . . you gotta . . ." he trails off.

"Life?" I ask him.

"Yeah."

And there it is. I feel it really doesn't matter to him if I disappear.

I ask my friends and family on social media why they live where they live and what's keeping them there. Unsurprisingly, most people cite a spouse as their reason for their location, or in some cases a custody agreement. A few say work, cost of living, affordability of housing. No one says their friends and so I wonder if I'm an idiot for not wanting to leave them.

"Are you up?" I ask Greyson via text. "I need to vent about a job thing."

A few minutes later he shuffles up the stairs and I blurt out my dilemma.

"I don't even know anymore why people live where they live! It's not even about the city or the job anymore it's just like, how could I make a decision about where is best to be living when I don't even have a clue anymore what my life is about? What's my end game here? Do people stay places because of friends or is that ridiculous?"

"No no" he tells me. "Sense of community can be hugely important for people. My ex went back to our hometown because of it. You just have to start to think about what lines up with your five-year plan."

"Greyson," I laugh. "I don't have a five-minute plan, let alone five years."

"You should do that thing I sent you. It would really help." He's referring to a link he messaged me a week or so back that's supposed to help you plan your life.

"It was expensive," I say, "like seventy-nine bucks or something?"

"No, you must have looked at the wrong thing. I think it's only like, twenty-something and that's actually a kit for two people."

"Ah OK, yeah, maybe I will." I dread the thought though because I know I'll be met with questions I can't answer.

He has to leave to see a potential client.

"Did I tell you about this person? Corvette lady?" he asks me.

"No?"

"OK, so I went to her house for a meeting, and she wanted to go in through the garage, which I thought, OK, for some reason that must make more sense, but when we went through she walked me right past her Corvette, and I was like, OK, I get it."

"That's so fucked and unnecessary," I laugh.

"Cha" he replies. The Greyson version of agreed.

"I'm not smart enough for this to be a tactic," I joke. "I just wanted to get a sense on if the wheels were still in motion." The local program director I've been in talks with laughs and assures me he is very much still interested in making something happen, he's just been busy but will work on writing a proper offer with a contract and job description that he will get to me. I choose to see this as a sign that staying is the right move, although one can never be certain. I wonder what the offer will be, and if or when I'll wind up back on the air. What would that be like after so long? I was always so sure that radio where was I was supposed to be, and now I have my continued doubts. I used to be so sure. The amount of times over the years when mid-show I stopped and thought to myself, "I can't believe I get paid to do this," is infinite. It's called imposter syndrome, and it's a real thing:

**"A psychological pattern in which an individual doubts their accomplishments and has a persistent internalized fear of being exposed as a fraud."**

Radio has always been so much fun for me, come so naturally, and given me so many successes and accolades that in the back of my mind I always had the hidden fear of getting "caught." Like one day someone was going to come along and say, "Your number's up." To have a career that meant so much to me always made me feel like I had cheated the system. If I could wish anything for the people I love, it would be that they get as much joy and fulfillment from their life's work as I have so far.

I video-chat my dad. He and mom have been travelling a fair amount lately so we haven't had as much luck as usual lining up calls. I explain that I've decided not to take the out of town job and that locally I'll see what pans out. When Greyson returns I give him the rundown too.

"Wow, totally different mindset from this morning hey?"

"Yeah, I really didn't want to move, and if there's any potential around here that can be enough to keep me hanging in. . . something will tell me when the exact time is right to go back."

I text Wes to let him know I'm resolved to stay.

I spend the rest of the night on Greyson's couch downstairs binge-watching the remainder of the series we started this past weekend. Super happy, content and comfy.

## August 29

"Oh my god, it's happening . . ." I whisper excitedly to Wes as I back toward the gym door. "See you later!"

He laughs as I go. There's a trainer at my gym, Suzanne, who for months, OK in all honesty years, I've wanted to make friends with and she's finally invited me for a coffee. I don't make new friends very easily, so this feels monumental.

"So where are you from?" I ask her as I sip my Americano. *Stop asking bad first date questions.*

She's moved around a fair bit and landed here a few years ago. She spent the majority of her career working in the lumber industry.

"It was great money, but I was always just tied to my phone. There were guys who worked there forty years, and nothing wrong with that, I just didn't want to give my whole life to it. Too easy to get trapped."

She has a stunning physique and I'm not surprised to learn she has competed and won several bodybuilding titles.

"It's hard in a town this small, though, can be really hard to make friends."

"Yeah, I hear that, and with you being a trainer people but must get weird. One of my best friends is a trainer and people hold a lot of their own judgments about themselves to him, always watching what he's eating or drinking, people looking in his cart at the grocery store."

"Yeah, or people hide theirs from me," she tells me. "I'll run into someone and I can see they're embarrassed about what they have so they start trying to explain it away. Or if I'm out with people and they have a beer I get the whole, 'I don't normally . . .' speech. They don't seem to understand I really don't care, I'm a person too."

She was married once before. "We just fell out of love, then I met David and we've been together five years now. Not looking to get married again."

"Yeah, me neither," I agree. "Waiting to be proposed to is a young woman's game. Been there, done that."

"If David asked me now, I mean, I'd say yes . . . but I'd be really bummed about it." Her joke sets us both off laughing.

"My, how we change in our thirties, hey?" I shake my head in disbelief. We make plans for a hike this coming weekend. It would appear as though I have officially made a new friend.

"God damn corporal," I say as he walks through the door. Seamus is down in weight since I last saw him two weeks ago.

"You look awesome!"

We hug.

"You can tell?"

"Oh shit yeah, totally."

"Thank you, fat camp," he jokes. He's been seeing a nutritionist.

"So . . ." he asks as we settle under a red sun-umbrella with our drinks. "What's been going on . . . saw on Instagram you were hanging with Wes again?"

I explain how we had a fun night painting the masks and watching a movie.

"Just being that dumb together, that's the shit I can't get from anyone else. That's the important stuff, the silly stuff."

"You could get that from someone else once you've built up the relationship with them. But that won't happen if you're spending all your time with Wes. Just sayin' . . ."

"No, I totally understand, and I'm not spending all my time with him, I swear."

"What about Jer, you haven't talked about him lately?"

"I don't know what's going on with him. He's been crazy busy, texted a bit when I needed a mechanic and stuff but haven't hung out with him in months. I'm sure he's just really busy. He's got lots on his plate, don't want to force someone's time . . ."

"Why? I have to with you all the time." I laugh because he's right—my hermit nature often pushes people out.

"I'll try him again tomorrow," I promise.

"You know what the hardest part of it was?" Hendrik is extending his phone to me. "This. Those three words."

I look at the screen displaying the social media account he has launched for his photography. The description of himself reads "Photographer. Model. Artist."

"Oh my god, it's so funny you should say that. I totally had this weird moment the other day where I was updating stuff and calling myself a writer, and wondering how I have any business doing that." It's crazy how aligned what he and I are trying to accomplish has become lately.

"But," he tells me, "if I had sold the picture I posted to whatever, a magazine or a person, if I had made 500 bucks on it, then somehow I would have felt more justified, even though it would have been the exact same piece. Friends who've known me a long time wouldn't be surprised at all to see me call myself an artist, but people who know me now. . ."

"Probably think you can't be a gym rat and an artist."

"Yeah, exactly."

We talk about what is art, what it means to create.

"When someone makes music and it makes someone feel something, or a painting or writing, that's just so powerful. I always have had this feeling like I'm supposed to be making something," he says.

"I think," I say, "it's not even so much what the person ends up feeling, so much as it is that they feel a certain way that makes them feel understood . . . like . . ."

"They're not alone." He finishes my sentence.

"Exactly, that's all art is, I guess, any kind, some outlet of a feeling that we hope someone else will see and feel connected to so they feel like, 'oh, yeah, I get that.' Even if it's sad or something. Like your photo of you and Roxy, the one in bed, it just felt so intimate, it stirred up this whole 'I want that' type feeling inside of me. Made me miss having that with someone."

"The composition worked, then." He smiles at me.

"Yeah, whatever you did, it made me feel that for sure. That's what I hope writing can do for someone else too, wow this chick's a hot mess, but it's real, right?"

"Right. We've just got to get over the idea that someone else's approval or purchase or assurance of our work is what makes it valid. We don't need someone else to legitimize what we're trying to do."

"Exactly," I agree with him.

Lucy and I have dinner at a nice restaurant in my neighborhood. We contemplated beers, but I'm still very much over drinking for the time-being.

"So how's things with you guys?" I ask of her and her husband. They're still muddling their way through as best they can. Aren't we all.

"School starts soon so it's easy to be distracted. Life gets busy and we both just kind of let it happen. I do OK and then I have days where I'm mad again. What about you? And Wes, how's he been, have you seen him?"

"He's super good." I grin at her.

"Of course." She smiles back, not needing further explanation.

I explain my conversation with Hendrik and the impact it had on me.

"Leave it to him to be able to cut right through all of the bullshit and simplify that for you."

"I know, right?"

"Well, as always, if you're happy, I'm happy."

"I'm bummed you won't be here this weekend. The eleven weeks is up."

"That went fast!" she exclaims.

"Yeah, for you maybe," I laugh.

"So, are you going to be better come Sunday, then?"

I lean in close to her, smiling. "Definitely not."

## August 30

I take a shot in the dark and decide to try Jer.

"Hang tonite?"

"After kiddo's go down? 8ish?"

"Sounds great!" I smile all morning, excited that I'll finally be able to catch up with him.

I look up from my book to the dinging of my phone. Wes.

"Are you home?"

"Yeah for a little bit..what's up?"

"I was going to quickly stop by, traffic so 12 minutes maybe 15."

This seems out of character for him—he's never stopped by on his way home from work.

"Sure I'll be here. Everything ok?"

"Yeah everything is fine. I got you something just wanted to drop it off."

He got me something? What the fuck, what could it be? I'm about to let my mind start guessing, but I decide against it. *No expectations.* The front door opens.

"Hey, what's up?" he asks me.

"Not much, going to Jer's in a bit. What's this, something you're dropping off?"

"It's in the truck."

I follow him out onto the deck and see it right away in his truck bed. A barbecue. I had just been telling him the other day I wanted to find a used one, and his buddy who was moving had this.

"Wow," I say. I am pretty stunned at this gesture. "I love it, thank you so much." I give him a hug.

"You like it?"

"Uh, yeah!"

"It's just a thank you for being there when I was sick and stuff."

I'm literally biting my cheeks to keep from smiling too big. I don't want to make a huge deal out of this because I don't want to weird him out. We unload it from the truck and carry it up to the deck. It looks perfect there and I'm so happy.

"This is seriously unreal," I say again.

"I'm going to go visit Greyson before I head home."

"OK, go get your Greyson on. Thanks so much, Wes." I hug him.

"You're welcome."

He disappears downstairs. I look happily out the window onto the deck at the barbecue and smile.

He's in the garage with the bay door open when I arrive.

"Scared to park too close to my house, or what?"

I look back at the Jammer parked pathetically far back from the door.

"Short-person syndrome, half the time I actually can't see past the end of the hood. Don't tell anyone. Figured better safe than sorry."

I follow Jer inside through the garage.

"Kitchen? Patio table? Outside fireplace?"

"Fireplace," I say. "It's actually cold."

He leans back as he lights it and the flames appear, suddenly dancing then settling.

Jer has been insanely busy with his new role at work and a plethora of other life stuff. As he fills me in on it all, my eyes blur.

"I'm just so happy to see you," I say across the flames. "I was worried I'd done something or that you were mad. I've really really missed you."

He stands suddenly and crosses over to where I'm seated, leaning down to hug me.

"Not mad at you at all. I'm sorry you thought that."

A huge weight comes off my shoulders, and I finally settle more comfortably into my chair.

"It hasn't been two months, has it?" he asks me.

"Yeah, it pretty much has."

We hit everything, taking turns, telling long, drawn-out, intricate stories that bring each other up to speed. It's a beautiful thing to know that there's certain people in this world who you will never lose a rapport with, whose closeness you can pick back up at any second.

I could chill here forever with him and the fire, but his kids will be up early so I excuse myself to head home.

Thinking of the barbeque I open my Google translate and craft a message to Wes in Spanish that means, "Thank you again for the thoughtful gift. It made my day."

"El gusto es mio," comes his reply.

*It's my pleasure.*

## Week Eleven
## August 31

The plumber is super hot and really easy to talk to. He's been here a few times now, so I tend to hang around whenever he shows up. He seems to welcome that. Probably pushing six foot four, ruddy brown hair, a massive beard and a thick Scottish accent with a voice that seems to come from really far back in his throat. His name is Hayden.

I sit at Greyson's table watching as he works away on the inside of one of the access panels for the emergency shut-off valve. He tells me about an upcoming hunting trip, I tell him I hate guns, we laugh a lot and rib one another.

"Do you want to try?" he asks me, holding up a blowtorch and a soldering iron.

"Are you serious?"

"Oh yeah, girl, get in here."

We push the table out of the way making just enough room for me to sneak in right in front of him. This has all the makings of a porno. He's directly behind me and puts the blowtorch in my one hand and the soldering stuff in the other. He's effectively got his arms around me, and the whole thing feels really flirty and sexy.

"So ,you can either hold this button down," He touches a button on the torch and it ignites. "Or, you can use this and it'll stay on." He clicks something, and the flame rushes out.

"Sure, leave it like that," I tell him.

"Angle it up," he tells me, touching my arm to adjust how I'm holding the flame. "That's good, now you gotta let it get hot so just leave that there for a second. Then you're going to take this . . . and just melt a little bit of it right along that line." I try my best to do what he's instructing. "That's good, that's plenty." He shuts the torch off and takes the equipment from my hands. "We'll make a plumber out of you yet, girl," he smiles down and high-fives me.

I have an ear-to-ear grin staring up at him. "Seriously thanks for that, that was so cool!"

"No problem."

"Can I take a picture of it before you finish?" I ask.

"For sure."

I sneak in again to snag a photo.

"Little heavy on the solder but you did great."

He finishes up the job and back on the front porch we settle up.

"Well, it's a small town so I'm sure I'll see you around," he says handing me back my card.

I beam at him.

"Hope so."

"I looked right at him and said 'hope so' back!"

Fox squeals, delighted. "I felt so like, ohhh I'm so flirty and what a naughty thing to say but really it's nothing."

She laughs. "I can't believe he did the arm around thing, that's like full-on Patrick Swayze. He Swayze'd you, Roo."

"I fucking know! I could have died, nothing like that ever happens to me."

"Hey did you ever hear from Banjo guy?" She asks?

"No, he never got in touch."

She's packing all her things for a trip to New York, and I start rambling while she gathers.

"I'm going to miss you," I tell her. "What am I gonna do all long weekend?"

"I'll miss you too. Almost time for our trip." It's just under two weeks until she and I head to California.

"I want that to be now."

I tell her about Wes bringing the barbecue over.

"Trying not to read anything into it, don't want to give myself the wrong idea, but I thought it was so so so sweet."

"Maybe he wants you to get the wrong idea?" she asks.

"Lots of easier ways he could have done that," I laugh.

"Oh bad news." Her face goes serious. "The cat has an owner."

"God damnit!" I yell. An adorable stray we affectionately named Phillip had been hanging around her place, and I was hell-bent on bringing him home with me one of these days.

"Like all men, he was too good to be true," she laughs.

We look at cats and kittens on rescue sites until I head out to actually let her pack.

## September 1

I get a good morning text from Wes that blows`my heart up, followed by some questions about what I'm up to. I have plans with Suzanne from the gym to hike today.

"We're basically best friends now," I tell him. He gives me a rundown of some family stuff he's got going on for the weekend, and then we both get busy. Greyson wanders up to the deck and I tell him all about my hiking plans and Fox's trip to New York. He's oddly quiet this morning.

"You OK?"

"Well . . . my dad's girlfriend died . . ."

"WHAT!" I scream back at him. "What happened?"

"I don't really know yet, my sister called and told me. She'd been unwell for quite a while and stuff, so not 100 percent surprising…"

"Yeah but still, just weird."

"I'm still trying to figure out what reaction I'm having to this." He looks blank.

"Yeah, I've had that happen before when I've lost someone, where it's kind of like . . . under which category do I file this? Where does this go—" I motion to my chest "—in here."

I haven't really seen him like this before, he's just unsettled. I sit near while he calls various family members.

"If you have to get ready for your hike that's OK," he tells me in between calls. "There's just better cell service up here on the deck."

"OK . . . I'll check in when I'm back."

I feel weird leaving him, but there doesn't appear to be anything else I can do.

I'm not nervous when I meet up with her, which is unusual for me with a new friend. It generally takes me a long time to warm up to people. She's quick to tell me stories about her week, and I find her funny and easy to chat with.

"I once asked my boyfriend what we did that first year we moved in together, and he said the reason I didn't remember a ton was because we were always drunk," she says, laughing. I'd been telling her I'm trying to structure my life in a way that's less centered around anything involving alcohol. "Now it's just a glass of wine with a friend or a beer with dinner or something, but not like it used to be."

"Yeah it's just something I wanted to get more of a handle on. Pretty easy for it to feel normal when everyone around you is going hard too," I say.She nods to me in agreement. The whole way up we talk about everything from dogs to divorces to our shared love of weight-lifting. At the peak she takes pictures of me posing next to a Canadian flag.

"You want one?" I ask her.

"Nah, I've got a million of me up here already."

On the way down I explain I'm not great in groups. I think it's something she needs to know so she'll understand why I might decline those types of invites.

"It's OK. I totally get that, the older I get the more inclined I am to do things one on one or just way smaller groups of people."

"Yeah, like, to give you an example my friends and I had this garden goddess flower crown thing earlier this summer, and that was a huge deal for us, and there were just six of us, so, pretty small kinda world I keep."

The whole trip takes close to two hours and is a really great workout.

"Thanks so much for that," I say as she drops me back off at my car. "I had a super good time!"

"Me too, let's do it again soon!"

I check on Greyson at home and he says he doesn't need anything. I start looking for literary agents. If I'm going to get this project of mine to go anywhere, I need to start letting some of my work out into the world. Its nerve-racking, the fear of rejection, especially when I feel I have so little to hold onto right now, but if I don't open myself up to the rejection I'll never chance success either.

I text Hendrik: "Omg I just sent my manuscript to an agent I want to work with!"

"Well fucking hold on tight eh? So proud of you! How hard was it to push send?"

"OMG I must have re written and written and spell checked and read again for a solid two hours before I sent it! I just keep telling myself I'll get a thousand no's before I get a yes and that needs to be ok and expected."

"Finally someone I can respect." His words transform my face into a grin.

"Scary," I reply, "but we gotta start somewhere!"

"And it turns out that's at the bottom..." He proceeds to tell me about a new photo shoot he did last night, and I can't wait to see the images. I promise I'll let him know if I hear anything.

I wake up at 11 p.m. to the dinging of an email:

"Dear Roo . . . thank you so much . . . " my eyes scan ahead. "After reading your letter I'm afraid I just wasn't hooked enough to want to ask you for more." My first rejection letter. I clutch my phone to my chest, not at all sad. This somehow makes my writing seem very real. I think I'm going to print it and frame it. I fall back asleep.

## September 2

I send Hendrik the rejection letter as soon as I wake up: "Gonna be a long game but I'll get there...we will laugh about this letter one day."

"No short game to anything," comes his reply followed by, "I'm looking forward to that."

He sends me some of the new images he's editing, and they're unreal. One he calls "instigator" is Roxy, standing back to the camera, opening her robe toward a woman whose face we can't see. They're on a pool deck, and lounging to their right is a man on a chaise longue wearing a captain's hat smoking a cigar. They have caught his attention, and he's watching the exchange. The whole thing is black and white except for the neon multi-colour of Roxy's robe. It's wicked, just truly awesome.

Greyson sends me a message to let me know he's left town to go be with his family and help with funeral arrangements for his dad's girlfriend. It seems odd he didn't say goodbye.

"We cool? You're not upset with me or anything?"

"No no, you've been amazing, just wanted to hit the road."

"OK," I tell him, "I get that, safe travels."

I haven't seen Wes in a few days, and I'd like to. I don't beat around the bush about it.

"Dear Sir," I text him. "I am wondering when I might be able to see your face? Warmest regards Roo."

"Cool if I go visit your husband?" I text Fox. I know she won't care, but with her being out of the country I feel it respectful to ask before I just show up. She shoots back a message telling me of course. I grab a coffee and head over to their place. I don't even put shoes on, driving the entire way in my slippers.

"So, did you see her on TV?" I ask.Fox is attending a televised tennis match, so he was hoping to catch her.

"No Fox" he says.

"Ah, that's too bad." I think it's pretty cute he was watching trying to catch a glimpse of his wife in the stands.

Now he's watching a TV show about guys who search for lost treasure. "What even is this?" I ask him.

"Just two guys and they go and look for stuff. They never find anything, though."

"Then what's the point of the show? That would be so embarrassing if your entire job was to find stuff and you just couldn't."

"Yeah, and they have investors funding these treasure hunts too, so . . ." he trails off.

"So it's a big fuckaround with everyone's time and money," I say, and we both laugh.

"Bored without Fox?" I ask him.

"Yeah, been a weird weekend, no one at home, dead at work . . . one of the guys had a jumper and I'm just waiting for my turn to come again . . ." His face, though expressionless, I can tell reads sheer dread. Clive works in a location where people often commit suicide.

"Fuck, eh?" I say sympathetically but lacking any better words.

A few months ago, I'd let myself into their house during the day to borrow some dresses from Fox. Clive had been out front by the water. Sensing something was wrong, I'd gone to say hi. "You OK?"

"We had a jumper at work," he told me. The police had intervened and saved the person, but it had been quite traumatic for Clive. He's much older than us, pushing fifty, and he's known for his stoicism. I'd been completely shocked when tears began falling as he'd told me about that day.

"I'm going to hug you now," I'd said awkwardly before leaving.

I think of myself wanting to wander off the pier and shame rushes over me. You forget all the people choices like that impact, not just the ones you love, but the strangers caught up in your decisions. Some guy on a couch somewhere sipping a rum and coke, petting a bulldog. Some dude who's just trying to do his job.

"Dear Madame," comes Wes's reply several hours later. "Very soon, as I finish my maiden voyage across the weekend with the small people of the home island, I will return to you. Sincerely Captain Wes the 1st."

I love when he's silly like this. I write back

"I shall await the day then, I look forward to word of your return."

*Seven days. Seven days. Seven days.* I think it over and over again as I drift off to sleep.

## September 3

"I'm cold," he tells me, snuggling right up. Wes's hair has the familiar smell of a bourbon body wash mingled with smoky scents from the barbecue he's always running.

We intertwine our bodies and talk closely on the couch. He's silly tonight, and it makes me giddy.

"I'm really happy to see you," I beam at him.

"I'm happy to see you too." He smiles back.

"I did something bad yesterday and ate fast food," I admit.

"Didja?" he says playfully. "Didja get yourself a burg?" He kisses my neck over and over again and rubs his beard across my face making me squeal and giggle. God I'm so happy right now in this moment.

"No, I just had some fries, was craving them hardcore."

We kiss lots and stay holding each other, laughing and whispering and joking. We head to the grocery store and load up on treats to eat with our movie. We make a small laughter-filled scene at the self-checkout by entering something wrong and have to get assistance from a store clerk. On the couch watching the movie, we cuddle and laugh and make jokes about the plot. The whole thing dissolves into making out and we decide to watch the rest of the movie another day. We make our way to his bedroom.

"Fuck." I lie breathless on his bed. "It seems unfair that somehow you're getting even better at that." I roll toward him, both of us laughing.

"It's just 'cause you haven't seen me in five days," he says.

"Doubtful," I reply. He follows me to the door and kisses me goodnight. *Six days,* I think on my drive home.

## September 4

*Whoomp, whoomp, whoomp, whoomp, whoomp, thud.* My body rolls over itself again and again, finally coming to a dead stop about ten feet off the path. I'm splayed on my side and scared to move. Slowly, cautiously I roll onto my back staring up the blue sky.

*Am I going to feel pain if I stand up or am I alright?* I right myself slowly into a seated position. *I think I'm OK.* I flip the visor of my helmet up then slide the whole thing off over my head. I bring it down to my arms to look at it. Not cracks no dings no dents. I don't think I've even really hit my head. I make my way to my feet, and I've launched so far away from my mountain bike I actually have to look for it. I find it with a bent rim and a flat back tire. I cry on the walk home and I push my mangled bike, not because I'm hurt, but because I'm so deeply, incredibly lonely.

"Wanna watch the rest of the movie tonite?" I text Wes.

"Ahhh, I can't I've got a meeting with my ex tonite."

"No worries, we can finish Friday when we podcast," I tell him.

The end is starting to feel more like the beginning—time has gone back to moving slowly. It feels like nothing is happening. It feels like the fog is returning. I have this sense that all the epiphanies have happened already, and that somehow I've messed them up. I've missed, or misinterpreted, their meaning. I think of Hendrik.

"I don't think you can—get it wrong, I mean," he said to me recently about this time. It certainly doesn't feel today like I've gotten much right. I force myself to go to the gym, it feels like it does nothing for me. I think of Wes's joke the other night about dragging a body around but the body is his. It seems a weirdly accurate descriptor of me at the moment. Outside myself. Disconnected. I put the body to bed.

## September 5

"Are you actually changing your routine to avoid Chatty Kathy?" Wes asks me. He's just arrived at the gym, and I'm getting ready to leave.

"Pretty much," I tell him. "I can't even handle that guy right now."

We chat a bit more, each wish the other a great day, and then I leave. As I'm getting my coffee in the drive through it occurs to me I'm not only avoiding Chatty Kathy. I might also be subconsciously going earlier . . . to avoid as much time with Wes. I know it to be just the teensiest bit true, although I have absolutely no clue why. I think I'm just embarrassed the eleven weeks is coming to an end and I still feel as strongly about him as I did on day one. It's not that I don't want to see him, but maybe that I don't want him to see that in me? It's not like me to not understand my own behaviour. It's also not like me to not care enough to look deeper at the why of something. I don't. I don't dig deeper, I don't question it, I don't wonder. I remember once telling Greyson that when it comes to my emotions surrounding Wes, "That well runs deep." I think, now, the well is going dry.

"A bit sore, but I didn't actually hurt myself this time," I'm explaining to Hendrik. "So, while I'm not getting better at mountain biking, I clearly am getting better at falling." He turns toward the gym mirror, running his hands over his face and then turning back to me.

"You can't really see it right now because of the stubble but here," he motions to the middle of his lip, "and here," he points to his cheek. "I have huge scars from trying to make a jump on my bike." He tells me a story about being a kid and careening down a hill toward a field trying to shoot a gap.

"The whole time my brother was at the bottom yelling, 'You're not gonna make it! You're not gonna make it." I laugh. It's actually his deceased brother's birthday today, and I like that this story of him has woven its way into our conversation. When I hear that old first-date question of, "If you could meet anyone in the world living or deceased who would it be?" I always think of Hendrik's brother. Jer's cousin. I think of this person I never had the chance to meet, who is so important to people who are so important to me. I've seen photos, I've heard stories, but it's not the same. When you lose someone, I think this is the greatest gift and honour that you could give them. To make their presence so real in your life, that even someone who never had the chance to meet them can feel the effect they had on you. I wonder if the people around me have ever felt this way about Tese.

"The front tire hit, the bike shot forward, I went ten feet up in the air and then right down on my face. My parents kept it together pretty well, but it was bad. My whole lip was cut in half from here to here . . ." he draws a line from directly under his nose to the center bottom of his lip. "Stitches all the way down."

Hendrik is full of big news today. He and Roxy have decided to sell their condo in the city, a decision I know he has not arrived at lightly.

"I've been playing for later, not now. We're not going back there, so what are we holding onto it for." When his brother passed away they had moved back here and while he and Roxy loved their rental they hadn't purchased a place of their own since being back.

"For years I've had this feeling like I haven't been 'home.' We could do that if we do this, get some place that's really ours."

"Wow, that's huge!" I tell him. "That's so exciting, selling the condo. That's big."

"Yeah it's just . . ." he moves his hands downward in a sweeping motion while blowing out an accentuated breath. "Letting go . . ."

Driving back home I think of a young Hendrik on his bike careening toward injury. I think of the naivety it takes to think you're going to shoot the gap unscathed. I think of myself, reckless with my heart, my love, hurtling myself toward Wes. Hendrik and I, each ignoring a voice calling out, "You're not gonna make it! You're not gonna make it!"

## September 6

"Hey!" I hold my hands up to him, stopping him mid-sentence. "That's not fair at all."

Seamus and I have gotten into it. He's claiming if I'm still struggling it's because I haven't done anything different during these eleven weeks. I've made no progress.

"You don't have any right to make that assessment. You have no clue how differently I've done things or how hard I've worked. You think because you see me once a week you get to make those types of judgements?" A woman sitting near us at the coffee shop eyes me—she can tell we are fighting.

"No, sorry, you're right." He backpedals temporarily but then comes at me again.

"Just start over, not some small town either, cut your losses and move to Toronto or Vancouver. Get another job . . ." This is a person who at the peak of my career constantly chided me for being too obsessed with my work.

"I'm gonna go," I snap at him. Today I have no clue why I have a standing coffee date with this person. Today he's hurting my feelings really bad, and it's just too much.

"Try not to slit your wrists at home," he calls after me as I'm walking to the car. *Asshole*. I know it's his dark sense of humor. I know throughout the course of our friendship I have made **much worse**, darker, and more tactless jokes than this to him. I know he just hates seeing me unhappy, I know I know I know. I just cannot do this with him today.

I'm backing the Jammer out of the parking lot when he runs up to the window and motions for me to roll it down.

"I love you, kid," he says to me, reaching through to throw one arm around me and kissing me on top of the head.

"Bye," I say, practically rolling the window back up on his arm. I pull away without even looking at him.

"You won't believe what I just did!" Fox yells into the phone, laughing.

"What? What happened?"

"I was getting into my car, and somehow when I opened the car door, I hit myself in the face with it . . . full on smashed myself in the forehead. I have a huge goose egg now, so I'm at home with an ice pack."

"What? How? With what insane sense of urgency were you flinging the door?" I laugh.

"I don't know," she laughs back. "Like, where could I possibly be off to in such a rush? What am I running late for? Nothing!"

"That's fucking ridiculous and amazing, and you need to send me a picture of your face."

"I will."

The text comes through a few minutes later and she wasn't kidding, she has a giant goose egg across her whole forehead. The message reads, "It's starting to bruise too."

Wes and I are supposed to podcast tomorrow and finish the movie we never got to the end of. Here's the thing, though. I know we aren't going to end up watching the movie, because I know how tired he will be come Friday night. Once we finish the podcast I can almost guarantee he'll just want to crash. It's been such a miserable day, and I haven't shaken the hurt from my conversation with Seamus. I haven't shaken the loneliness that came over me in the woods when I fell off my mountain bike. I've really let Seamus get to me, and I have a dark and unsettled sad that won't fade. I need Lucy.

"I just feel so . . . ughhh, the whole thing really got at me and hurt my feelings super bad."

Lucy hands me a cup of coffee. We sit at her kitchen table.

“Yeah, it’s one thing to say it, but a big part of it is how you say it.”

“Why can’t everyone be as non-judgmental as you, and just let me be how I want to be. Fuck, maybe not even how I want to be but maybe . . . just take me where I’m at.”

She nods. “Yeah, other people don’t get it until they find themselves living moments—” she corrects herself “—lives they never thought they’d be living.”

“That’s it, eh? With us? Just a couple a gals living lives we never thought we’d be living.”

“Yeah, hating people we didn’t think we’d hate, loving people we didn’t think we’d still love.” I can’t read her expression, it’s a look I haven’t really seen before.

“What is it?” I ask cautiously.

“Well. . . I need to talk to you about the book.” I had given her the most up to date version of the manuscript to read.

“Oh God, did you hate it?”

“No No!” she laughs, “Not at all, It’s just . . .”

“What?” I laugh.

“You. . .” she smiles at me. “Have a blind spot when it comes to Wes. . . .don’t get me wrong, I like him, he’s funny, he’s a great dad, but the book is. . .”

I raise an eyebrow to her.

“It’s. . . it was frustrating for me to read because you take all of the responsibility for everything. You have so much guilt about the relationship failing it almost reads like you did something horrible or left something out, which isn’t the case.”

I laugh. “I’ve heard similar.”

"You write about him so nicely."

"That's what love does I guess. . ." I half ask and half tell her this.

"Yeah but that's it though, that's the whole thing that's missing, is that that's how it always was. You seeing the best in him, welcoming him and his kids into your home trying to build a life with them. Loving him flaws and faults and all, always giving him the benefit of the doubt. And in return he just what? Can't overlook any of your perceived shortcomings? Convinces you, you were the problem, like you were some emotional mess that expected too much? You being 'too much' is code for him being not enough. You wanted the things other people in love seem to do easily....that's doesn't make you the crazy person you make yourself out to be. Nowhere in there do you write about the fact that he's just . . ." she pauses because she knows how deeply I love him and how carefully to choose her words.

"He's broken right now."

I nod.

"And the worst part is. . . he's got you convinced you're broken too."

A wrap my fingers tighter around my coffee mug, and reach my head down to my sweater to wipe a tear on my sleeve. I'm not upset with her at all, I'm moved. I leave my head resting there on my arm looking at Lucy.

"I hope you know. . ." she says as she pours more coffee into my mug. "No one who was there for that time, actually there for it, or who's been here after, thinks about it the way you do. Holds you as responsible as you hold yourself."

I stand up to hug her dissolving into tears. The tighter she hugs me the more free I feel. Her words have lifted a burden inside me I hadn't wanted to acknowledge I was carrying.

"And. . ." she pulls back looking me square in the face. "You are not broken. A little chipped maybe, but not broken."

I text Wes: "Would you wanna try and watch the rest of the movie tonite? If you have plans already no worries."

"I gots plans. But we can always podcast then finish the movie tomorrow night ya?"

"Yerp totally," I tell him back.

We exchange a few more messages about The Beast. I need to know his bottom line on price, because I want to take it to a few dealerships and see if anyone will take it off my hands. I notice he doesn't tell me what his plans are, which he normally does. I have a sinking feeling in my stomach about it, then I hate myself for caring. I hate that I wonder, I hate that I hurt, I hate that I'm lonely. I hate that maybe I haven't accomplished anything in this time. The sad is so immense today that it exhausts me.

"I'm having a big cry tonite," I text James. "The 11 weeks is almost up and I made no progress...Seamus came down on me really hard and thinks I should move. I still miss Wes and I'm there for him when he needs me but I'm scared to tell him when I need him like I did today. Fox is crashing early after her trip to New York, Lucy is leaving for Seattle, Greyson is still away….no you anymore. My world just feels really small today."

"I'm sorry," comes his reply. "I'm sure Seamus meant well. As someone who has talked to you along that way I'd say you've made progress. A change would be good but it doesn't have to mean moving. When do you leave for Cali? Focus on that."

"The 15th," I tell him. "Sorry for text bombing you with sadness."

"It's the new photo bomb. . ." he writes back.

About twenty minutes later he calls. "Doin' any better?" He asks.

"Well, I went to the bulk section at the store and bought some treats, so basically going to eat my feelings tonight."

"Been there, done that," he tells me. We catch up on how his new job is going and how he likes the coast. His voice softens the sadness around me. When we hang up the house seems even quieter. I turn the volume up extra loud to cut through the silence. I tearfully toss and turn all night on the couch.

## September 7

I knock my phone off the coffee table checking the time. 5:05 a.m. I should get up and go to the gym. I should take the dogs for a walk. I should make coffee. I pull the blanket back over my head, punch a few of the couch cushions to try and make it more comfortable, and go back to sleep.

At 7:12 my phone dings. A text from Hendrik. He's had a scheduling error and wants to know if I can train later in the day instead of at 10 a.m. Unfortunately, I can't because I have an appointment to have the value of The Beast assessed. I tell him no worries and we'll reschedule for next week. I close my eyes again. Yes, the ending is feeling so much like beginning. Why can't I get going? What is actually wrong?

At 8:16 my phone dings again, waking me up.

It's Wes. "No gym this morning?"

"Yeah...not daying very well..just couldn't."

"Why not daying? If it makes you feel any better I dropped my phone from my truck and cracked it in two places."

This information does nothing to make me feel better. "Honestly couldn't tell ya...I dunno I'm just not. Ughhhh that sucks."

I pull the blankets back over my head for the millionth time, refusing to leave my nest on the couch.

By 11 a.m. I need to force myself to get moving. All of me feels heavy. I wander thrift stores and buy fall sweaters. I grab coffee. I move about aimlessly without purpose. Nothing seems real today. I struggle to make conversation at the salon where Meesh's junior stylist washes and styles my hair for practice. I get lowball offers for The Beast from the dealerships I meet with.

*What a huge fucking waste of money.* I stand in the driveway staring at the truck. *I fucking love this stupid thing.*

"I think . . ." I'm telling Wes about my mountain-biking bail. "How much the whole thing upset me is just a testament to how profoundly lonely I am. Everything with Seamus too . . . I'm just like, low."

"What about the book?" he asks. "You seem down on it."

"No, I mean the work stands on its own, I just don't think I got what I wanted out of the eleven weeks. You did it better than me," I tell him.

"Oh I would not say I'm doing better at life than you," he disagrees.

"No, I didn't mean life . . . I meant the breakup."

"Oh," he says. He seems cautious now. He's nervous of saying the wrong thing. I can tell he's thinking things but not saying them.

"What?" I ask. "Just say it."

"No, it's just . . . I think you focused on it so much, so it was a big deal for you. I'm just like do do do do do," he hums, " . . . through life. So I'm fine." *He's fine*. I say it back to myself.

"Once you go back to radio you won't think about it so much."

I think of holding him when he was sick and sad and crying. I think of the number of times over the last few months I've reassured him he will be OK. I think of how often I've told him "You're doing better than you think," "You've got this," "Great things are going to happen for you." I wish he could see how much I need these things too. He's already told me he's too tired to watch a movie after the podcast, I totally called it. We finish the show and right away I tell him, "I'll get out of your hair."

I sleep on the couch again, alternating crying with tossing and turning. For the first time ever, I am sick over the thought of Wes ever reading this. I used to think if he ever chose to read it, it would give insight into my heart and my mind, and what he meant to me. Now I see only one possible outcome for me: humiliation. Hundreds of pages devoted to processing the loss of someone who is just "do do do". . . humming his way through life. "Fine." Right now, I am ashamed to feel what I feel.

## September 8

Her little boy has gotten so big!

“God, he looks just like you,” I say to my cousin.

Julie smiles proudly.

“Weird, right? For genes that are so weak and pathetic and pale, they sure seem dominant in the appearance department.”

Her husband is participating in a cycling race, so she’s come through town and it means we get the chance to hang out for a few hours while he rides.

“So . . .” she looks at me when he heads to the starting line and we’re finally alone. “What the fuck, dude?”

I shrug. “Everything got fucked up to the point where I wouldn’t even know how to start telling you how I got here. Also, it’s embarrassing so . . .”

“Ummmm . . .” she laughs this off. “Consider who you’re talking to!”

I forget that at one point she sold all her belongings, quit her job, and then found out the dude she was supposed to relocate for had been unfaithful and no longer wanted her to come. Homeless and in possession of nothing, she had been about the same age I am now when she had to start over.

“Fuck, that’s right,” I say back. Things come tumbling out and I tell her as quickly as I can how sideways I let things get. She grabs my shoulder and holds onto my arm while I tell her.

“It never ever ever seems like it at the time, but it is going to get better.”

“I know,” I nod.

I think of her, broken, broken-hearted, completely having given up hope. She never wanted kids. Then she met her husband, and I’ve never seen two people who laugh so much together. Everything is a joke with them and it's adorable to watch. I look at her son, the life-altering soul she loves more than anything in this world. I think of the years and years and years she didn't want children. He is a walking living breathing adorable two-year-old example of the transformative power of love.

Wes calls at night and tells me all about a brutal day he's had.

"What are you doing?" he asks.

"Nothing, just laying on the couch."

"When's your eleven weeks up?"

"Tonight . . . like, technically at midnight, tomorrow, the ninth, however ya wanna say it. Not the exciting ending I had hoped for, but it is what it is. Guess that's real life . . ." Fox and I originally had big plans, but she's been exhausted since coming back from New York and things just never seemed to get lined up.

"I'm sorry it didn't end up being more of a thing. You could come over and I could bang you . . ." We both laugh.

"Well, I wouldn't say no to that offer, what's the saying? 'Out with a bang?' Should I come over?"

He's quiet for an absurdly long time.

"Well, I'm pretty tired, but . . ." his silence drags on.

"OK," I say testily, "well, if you have to think about it that long, then it's a no. I don't need a pity fuck."

Hard reverse on his part.

"No no no no no . . . that's . . . Roo, that's not what I meant." I can tell by his tone he is genuinely sincere. "I was just trying to think of what we could do. I can't stay up super late, so I wasn't sure if you'd want to hang out for just an hour, but come over and we can finish a movie or something."

We settle onto the couch of his basement and watch an episode of "The Purge."

We get super into it, swatting at one another and crying out at the gross or scary parts.

"That was so good," he says at the end.

"I know, right? I can't wait for the next one!"

I head home around 11 and lie on the couch staring up at the ceiling. Part of me had always wondered if on this evening I'd be listless waiting for midnight to come. Wide-eyed and eagerly awaiting September ninth. I'm not and I don't. I shut all the lights off and go to sleep.

## Final Day Of The Eleven Weeks

## September 9

5 a.m., and I'm wide awake. I slowly watch the sunrise from my front porch, thankful for the beautiful day it's forming. It looks like it's going to be really nice. I spend way longer than normal doing my hair and makeup, selecting an outfit, and picking jewelry. I choose a gold bustier I haven't been able to fit into since before I met Wes and a black pencil skirt.

"Here, this should work," Fox says, handing me a black leather jacket when she arrives.

She has a leather jacket on as well and looks amazing. *This is happening. I'm done.*

"Coffee? Orange juice?" The waitress asks us.

"Mimosas," we say in unison.

"Oh, we can't serve until 11 a.m."

"What time is it?" Fox asks her.

"8 a.m.," the waitress says, the judgment in her tone obvious.

"OK, just coffee and water, then," Fox answers. She turns to me. "Guess we're just having breakfast," she rolls her eyes sarcastically.

We both rip through our meals, uproariously laughing the whole time and catching irritated glances from the other patrons.

"Let's go to the liquor store on our way home and we'll make our own mimosas," I tell her.

We actually have to Google how early they'll be open.

"If ever there was an indicator you need to rethink your life choices, it's when you find yourself googling what time the closest liquor store opens," she jokes.

"No shit, the guy inside is going to think we're complete wastes of life. Starting way too early."

"No way," she tells me, "he's going to think we've been going all night."

Inside we're both asked to present two pieces of ID.

"Made my day," I tell the cashier as I slide the cards over to him.

We blast music on the way home and sing at the top of our lungs, car-dancing like crazy.

"You wrote a fucking book!" she shouts at me over the music.

"I knooooow!" I scream back at her happily.

We make mimosas and sit on the porch.

"Ya know . . ." I lean back against the porch rail with my drink. "I think one of my big takeaways is going to be how fucked everyone is. Not in a mean way or anything, but just . . . nobody really super happy."

"Remember when we first met?" she asks me. "Now just think of how differently both of us think . . . about everything. We were so . . . traditional and logical and hopeful." We crack up. "Now," she says, "my level of judgement is so much lower, it's just like weird how much your opinions on stuff can change."

"Yeah, mine too. I spend half my life wondering now if there's some weird way in which you, me, and Lucy can live platonically and function as a unit."

"That weirdly appeals to me too," she laughs.

"You know what sucks?" I lower my glass and lean back, turning my face up to the sun.

"I know I keep saying this over and fucking over, so I'm sorry . . . but . . . my best friend, Fox! I just really really . . . I just wanted to do life with him. And no matter how much time passes, I don't think that's going to change."

"Probably not," she tells me, patting my leg.

We call a designated driving service to confirm Fox will have a way of getting her car home, both laughing when they inform us they "don't normally operate until the PM."

We go to a pub and do another round of mimosas.

"Jer!" I stand up yelling. "Hey, Jer!"

He's coming out of the corner store next to the pub.

"Wow." He walks up eyeing the sight that is us. "That's a whole lotta leather!" he grins leaning down to hug me. "What are you guys doing?"

"We're celebrating!" I tell him. "It's been eleven weeks!"

"You look thirsty," Fox tells him. "Have a beer with us!"

"I can't. I got the kids in the car." We chat for a bit before he heads out.

"Wow, how crazy is it that he was here," Fox says. "We just need Wes to show up and then that's the end of your book."

No sooner does she say it than he calls.

"Hey, we were just talking about you."

"My ears must have been burning," he says.

"Yeah all good things. Super good, I promise."

"I feel like you saying it was good things means it probably wasn't."

"No it was. I swear." He offers to drive us anywhere we need.

"I think we're OK, but thanks."

"That was sweet of him," I tell Fox when I'm off the call. "I weirdly wanted to say something big to him today, but I don't even know what that would be. Maybe I should just be honest and tell him like, how much I want him hasn't changed."

"Do it!" she encourages.

I write the text. "Thanks for calling I appreciate it so much...77 days / 11 weeks and how bad I want you hadn't changed a bit…" I hit send.

We catch a cab back to my house.

"He hasn't written back. I probably super weirded him out." I laugh.

"Fuck whatever, fuck that," Fox says. "You're the one person who's always honest, so if that's weird it's weird, but it's not a you problem."

"I feel like I'd be really complimented by that text . . . but then again getting it wrong when it comes to Wes is sorta my specialty, so . . ." we laugh.

My phone dings: Wes's reply.

"Might not be good for the book, eh?"

"Well fuck," I say laughing. "I don't know what sort of response I was expecting, so . . ."

The designated driver service arrives to take Fox home. I crawl into bed and fall asleep.

I wake up to the sound of drumming coming from downstairs. *Greyson is finally home!* I shoot him a message telling him to come upstairs when he's done drumming.

"You!" I throw my arms around him when he appears. "I missed you so much. I'm really glad you're back!" We sit on the couch and I hug him tightly while he tells me all about his past week and his dad's girlfriend's funeral.

"Have you eaten yet?" I ask.

"No, you?"

"Nope, let's go get food."

He drives us to a pub and laughs when I order three beverages: a beer, water, and a coffee.

I eat sickening amounts of food. Hummus and veggies and a full burger.

"It actually hurts when I breathe," I tell him.

"All food, no room for lungs," he laughs.

I tell him about my conversation with Wes the other day. "It was the first time ever that I realized I'm terrified for him to read what I've written. I'm . . . embarrassed."

"I don't think you have anything to be embarrassed about."

"I told him I didn't think I'd gotten what I wanted out of the time . . ."

"What didn't you get that you were expecting to?"

"I thought I'd love him less," I admit.

"Yeah, guess there are just certain people you'll always love."

We talk about the hot tub and how I'm hoping it'll go soon. I tell him all about the lowball offers on The Beast. He tells me more about his time away and his family and how his dad is doing.

"I actually can't finish this," I say, motioning to my beer. "Which in and of itself is a form of progress because I drank today and didn't binge drink, like make myself sick or whatever. No puking," I laugh.

"Let me get this," he says about the bill. "You bought last time, and it's a big day for you."

I thank him, and we head home.

We sit on the couch petting all three dogs, who fight each other for our attention.

"Well, I guess I should go to bed, long day of driving and I have to work tomorrow."

"OK," I say, following him to the top of the stairs. "Thanks again for dinner, I'm really glad you're home."

"Me too." We hug again before he undoes the baby gate that blocks my dogs from his suite. He fumbles to do the cord that holds it in place back up, then with an exaggerated giving up gesture he laughs and says, "You can get that . . ." disappearing around the downstairs corner yelling an extended "byeeeeeeee."

I'm laughing as I shout back, "Goodnight!"

I crawl into bed. This is the end, and this is reality. In the Hollywood version of my life some new person would have bumped into me as I left the pub, and we would have exchanged a glance that gave the audience hope for me yet. Or maybe Wes would have shown up, professed that he still loves me and fuck it it's a mess, but let's try and make this thing work. It all would have been wrapped up with some beautiful semblance of closure and optimism. I would feel better. Seamus and I would have made up. Lucy would have had an epiphany about how to proceed next. There would have been resolution for myself and for the people I love. There is none, we're all still as lost as we were eleven weeks ago. The end is just me and two dogs cuddled up close watching a ceiling fan spin. And that's OK.

## Eleven Weeks And One Day

## September 10

What have I learned at the end of eleven weeks?

I have learned it's never black and white. We're always able to see how we think someone should respond when we aren't the ones feeling the emotional intricacies of a situation. Things, people, feelings . . . they are so layered and deep and complicated, and you don't get to judge someone for going back to the thing that causes them pain. A person, alcohol, drugs, food, whatever it is, we have all gone back to the thing that hurt us. We are all a little bit broken. Find the people whose presence gives you peace and ease and calm and laughter and enjoyment, and cut out **everyone** else. These people who bring the calm to us, who make a dark world seem brighter by being themselves, they will help you grow. They will foster intelligent conversations and thoughts that change you. They will be there for your best and your worst. They will save you.

I have learned that perception is truth. Allowing myself to own my version of what Wes meant to me, was my greatest turning point in healing.

I learned that there is huge power in touch. At several points throughout the eleven weeks, I had people either grip me by, or hold onto, my shoulder. Something about this gesture was incredibly impactful each time and profoundly moving. When I felt I had nothing to cling to, the very act of someone clinging to me, holding onto me, it was so so big. Do this to people, it will help them.

I have learned there is only so much you can learn from something. I have held my feelings and this experience up to the light. I have looked at it under the microscope. I have examined and exhausted every possible thing that could be processed, and now it's time to stop. I have thought constantly about asking Wes to give us another chance, to rebuild, to go slow, to start again, but I've finally accepted it isn't what he will ever want. So I stay silent and enjoy the time as it is, for what it is, even when I don't know what the fuck it means. There is an inevitable expiration date on how long he and I can carry on like this. I will want more before he can give it. It will end again. It doesn't matter anymore. Going forward, if I ever am so lucky to fall in love, or be loved again, I won't have to rehash this. I have made my peace with what has happened and what I've lost. There is no more processing left to do. At some point a well that runs deep can run dry, and once a well has run dry, isn't it just a hole? I have glared into the empty hole for seventy-seven days, and there is simply nothing left to see. It is time to raise my eyes and look ahead.

I have learned I never have before, and never will again, love **anyone** the way I love Wes. . . and that's a good thing.

I have learned you can't smash a microwave with your fist.

# Acknowledgements

Thank you Mom and Dad, for everything, always. I don't make it easy on you, and there are no words or expressions of gratitude big enough. Sorry for putting you in the position where you now have an answer to the question "was it harder to read about your daughter's sex life, or her suicidal ideations?"

To each one of my friends in this book, thank you for trusting me to include just tiny little facets of the wonderful, deep, amazing characters you are.

Lucy, you are the exemplification of the kindest and most wonderful parts of what life has to offer. I want to be you when I grow up.

Fox, you get the worst of me, and always always always give your best. You got a shit deal and I truly don't deserve you. I apologize publicly for the many shortcomings of mine you somehow always manage to overlook. I could say I'll be better for you, but more likely than not I will be a burden to you until the day I die.

James, you show me day in and day out that there is life after heartbreak. We can get unmarried as many times as ya want but you'll never be rid of me. Thank you for everything you have done, and continue to do for me. Seeing you happy in the world brings me more joy than you could ever possibly understand.

Greyson, thank you for always helping me try to slay the dragon of challenge, walk the path of moral virtue, and attempt to balance the fine line between chaos and order.

Jer, Hendrik and Roxy, sweet "family" of mine, I love you all so much. You are all the superheroes in the story of my life.

Little Hat and Pookie, thank you for being the first two beta readers / editors and for your careful work and excellent insights.

Scott George, thanks 'Terry.' It's been a pleasure dude.

Jamie, thank you for always being there to help me with the monsters, I seriously don't know how I would manage two unruly rescues without your help. We will always love and remember Kingston.

Brooks Becker, editor extraordinaire and person who I have now basically latched onto and refuse to leave alone. . . I could NOT have done this without you. You took a rambly, ridiculous mess and helped me make it into a story I believe worth telling. Your careful eye and patience turned my bullshit into a book. You are so gifted at what you do. I'm perfecting my tap dance skills to come be glamorous with you in the near future . . .

And Wes. . . If you ever find yourself wondering "Does she miss me and the kids? Does she think of us? Does she still love me?" Yes. Every day. Always.

Made in the USA
San Bernardino, CA
10 January 2019